The Sporting Goods Industry

The Sporting Goods Industry

History, Practices and Products

RICHARD A. LIPSEY

with a foreword by Thomas B. Doyle

McFarland & Company, Inc., Publishers

Jefferson, North Carolina, and London

Library of Congress Cataloguing-in-Publication Data

Lipsey, Richard A.
The sporting goods industry : history, practices and products /
Richard A. Lipsey ; with a foreword by Thomas B. Doyle.
p.   cm.
Includes bibliographical references and index.

ISBN-13: 978-0-7864-2718-5
(softcover : 50# alkaline paper) ∞

1. Sporting goods industry — United States.
2. Sporting goods industry — United States — History.   I. Title.
HD9992.U52L56   2006   338.4'768870973 — dc22   2006014797

British Library cataloguing data are available

Cover photograph ©2006 PhotoSpin

Manufactured in the United States of America

*McFarland & Company, Inc., Publishers
Box 611, Jefferson, North Carolina 28640
www.mcfarlandpub.com*

Acknowledgments

My heartfelt appreciation and thanks go to a long list of individuals, all of whom contributed greatly to the development of this book. To Professor James Santomier of Sacred Heart University who encouraged me to create an online course, which served as the basis for the book; Tom Doyle, NSGA Vice President of Information and Research who constantly provided his support and commitment not only for the book but also throughout my entire career in sporting goods; Bob Carr, the iconoclastic editor of *SGB's Inside Sporting Goods*, whose depth of knowledge and understanding of the sporting goods industry and vision for its future has never been and probably never will be equaled; and Steve Phoutrides, Director of Marketing Research at Nike, a client and friend for many years, who has never faltered as a supporter and advocate of my ideas from the time we first met.

And more — my grateful appreciation to the editors of *Sporting Goods Business* magazine, especially Judy Leand, for their insight covering the industry so thoroughly and for their splendid cooperation; Dan Kasen, information whiz at NSGA for always knowing the answer to every question I've ever asked; Rusty Saunders for his heretofore untapped editing skill and for championing the cause of education in the industry; to Joyce, for putting up with my late-blooming authorship and all the rough spots that go with it; and last but not least thanks to my wonderful family — Charlie, Patti, Claudia, Little Rick, Carrie and Rick — who are always there for me and who bring me great joy.

Richard A. Lipsey

Contents

Foreword
by Thomas B. Doyle

The sporting goods industry, once perceived as a simple and uncomplicated market-place, is now exceedingly complex.

Richard A. Lipsey, drawing on more than 35 years of experience in dealing with all major industry segments, has written the first book that allows you to look at the industry "players" and see how the growing complexities of the industry demand their interaction with one another. I emphasize the word "interact" because a change in one industry segment invariably has an impact on every other segment. When you know or at least can make an intelligent guess about those interactions, you can function more successfully in the sporting goods industry.

Here's an example.

Sporting Goods Chain A acquires Sporting Goods Chain B. Manufacturer C is the primary supplier of basketballs to Sporting Goods Chain A, but Manufacturer D supplies basketballs to Sporting Goods Chain B. Both manufacturers, C and D, know that Sporting Goods Chain A, because of its larger size, is in a stronger negotiating position when buying basketballs. Manufacturer C theoretically has a potential opportunity to sell to both chains because of their relationship with Chain A, the buyer. However, Manufacturer D also now has an opportunity to develop a new proposal for Manufacturer A, risking C's current relationship with A. If Manufacturer C loses Sporting Goods Chain A or if Manufacturer D loses Sporting Goods Chain B as accounts, this will have a major impact on annual sales of the losing company. How do I negotiate? Price? Advertising allowances? Unique promotions? Special make-up or packaging? As a manufacturer, I turn to the advertising agency that is my marketing arm. However, their experience is primarily in print media. Is it time to change to an agency with more experience in dealing with the retail community?

Another dimension to the acquisition — Sporting Goods Chain A and Sporting Goods Chain B are headquartered in different sections of the country. Sales Agency F that covers Sporting Goods Chain B will lose its major account. Will it be able to survive and will it be willing to sell my products to smaller accounts? Because of its increased volume, Sporting Goods Chain A may no longer be willing to deal with Sales Agency G. It may wish to deal directly with the manufacturer and remove the sales agency's commission from the cost of goods. As Sporting Goods Chain A integrates Sporting Goods Chain B into its operations, it no longer needs two agencies. If I have been the agency to Sporting Goods Chain B, what approaches can I take to salvage the potential loss?

Another example.

A mid-sized manufacturer of team sports products is developing a growth strategy for the next three years. Participation in the sports and product sales in their categories have been flat or declining.

A careful examination of available data indicates youth female participation remains strong in team sports, but also indicates a significant decline in participation among junior high and high school boys. At the same time, participation in extreme sports has been growing.

What options can be pursued?

If the company continues to focus on its current market, it can grow only through increased market share. In a stable or declining market, brand share can be increased through price reductions or innovative new products. If a price reduction route is chosen, is the company able to reduce costs sufficiently to maintain margins? If a product innovation route is chosen, does the company have the resources (financial, technical, marketing) to bring the product to market?

On the strength of their brand, the company might seek growth by expanding into non-team categories or into team-related soft goods. However, the company must consider whether or not such product offerings will be accepted in the channels of distribution it serves and how such an expansion might impact its core business.

Although the company's brand may be strong, the company may feel it lacks the expertise to move outside its current market. Licensing its brand name for non-team categories or team-related soft goods then becomes a possibility.

These examples indicate how a single change can force interactions across multiple segments of the sporting goods industry. In this book, Richard A. Lipsey provides the materials you need to better anticipate and understand those interactions. It is the first time so much material has been gathered in one place. As industry changes continue, use this book as a starting point to better understand and effectively deal with them.

Thomas B. Doyle is vice president of information and research for the National Sporting Goods Association

Preface

With a long history behind it, the sporting goods industry has come of age. It was steeped in tradition and confidentiality from the mid-1800s until the early 1980s. During that period, no one except insiders knew anything about the industry. Only widely recognized brand names such as Wilson, Spalding, Rawlings, and Titleist were known in the public sphere.

Over the past 25 years, public ownership and the geometrically expanding footwear and apparel product offerings have resulted in an exploding marketplace. Sales of sports apparel and footwear products are as large as, if not larger than, sales of equipment. Fewer than 20 years ago, only one company's sales exceeded $1 billion. Today, over 20 companies have sales exceeding $1 billion.

Explosive growth has created the need for many more and better-prepared employees. A major purpose of this book is to provide a better understanding of the industry by drawing together a widely dispersed multitude of industry sources.

This book provides a knowledge base relating to the industry's unique policies, programs and practices. Ideally, students considering a career in the industry will find that it shortens their learning and training period, enhancing their opportunity to be immediately productive. Career changes and industry entrepreneurs will also find valuable lessons in its pages. The book covers all major aspects of the industry, with separate chapters dealing with historical background, industry structure and size, vendors, distribution, sports medicine and product liability, marketing, advertising, sales trends, and e-commerce. Nearly all industry-related topics, macro and micro, fall under at least one of these subject areas. In each chapter, an overview is followed by intensive discussion. Each chapter ends with a directory of relevant websites and several exercises designed to help readers focus on key points developed throughout the chapter.

The discussion section in each chapter explains how the featured topic is structured within the industry, how it works, how it has evolved to the point where it exists today, and where it might be in the future. Attention is given to reasons why industry practices are unique to sporting goods. Many chapters contain pertinent statistical data, drawn from leading industry sources. The Sports Business Research Network, an online database of historical information from leading industry organizations such as the National Sporting Goods Association (NSGA) and trade publishers such as VNU and *SportBusiness International*, was used extensively in preparing material for this book.

A directory of leading sporting goods vendors and retailers and a bibliography of industry publications and organizations round out the book's content. The book does not provide detailed coverage of individual company activities, except to present illustrations of the topics discussed. It provides valuable background information for new business entrepreneurs, although it does not provide specific information as to how to start a sporting goods company. This information is readily available from organizations supporting various trade segments within the industry, and they are listed in the book's bibliography.

1

Historical, Cultural, and Technological Perspectives on the Industry

OVERVIEW

"If you have a body, you're an athlete."
Bill Bowerman, Nike Cofounder (with Phil Knight), 1974

This chapter has two dimensions: (1) an orientation to the industry online and in printed resources, and (2) an overview of historical, cultural, and technological perspectives on the sporting goods industry, chronicling the evolution of all facets of sports promotion and marketing, sports participation, and sporting goods equipment. As part of the recommended exercises for this chapter, you'll want to visit websites of leading sporting goods companies, many of which contain their enlightening histories.

One major driving force within the industry is a dynamic relationship between culture and technology, both of which have continuously impacted the shape and structure of the industry from its earliest development right up to the present. Changes in technology include innovations in materials as well as innovations in product design and function.

At the end of this chapter, you should be able to:

- Identify significant historical, cultural, and technological factors contributing to the rise of sports in the United States.
- Understand the synergistic relationship between culture and technology and its effect on the development of the sporting goods industry.
- Understand the nature of outside factors that influence the industry, but over which the industry has no control.
- Identify issues, topics, and ideas that you may have related to the recommended reading assignments.

DISCUSSION

Organized sports in the United States grew in the decades prior to the Civil War because of stimuli from three groups:

1. the American social aristocracy
2. the metropolitan "rabble" or rowdies; and
3. immigrants

The English brought with them not only their sporting heritage, but also handmade sporting goods and fishing and hunting equipment, cricket, soccer, and lawn bowling, while the Germans brought gymnastics and the Scotch brought golf and track and field. In addition, the following contributions from the industrial revolution contributed directly and indirectly to the development of modern sport: the steam engine, specifically the steamboat and the railroad; the telegraph and penny press; the sewing machine; electric lights; and the camera. Although religious prejudices against sport remained very strong in rural areas, recreation was a key element in church activities.

For the most part, prior to the Civil War, only the social aristocracy could afford the expensive special equipment of prewar sporting goods dealers. There were a number of significant social trends in the United States that contributed to a high degree of sports consciousness at that time. They included:

- the outdoor heritage of frontier society
- the English interest in sporting life
- colonial and aristocracy support of the "turf" (horse racing)
- a growing secular spirit in the country
- urbanization
- extension of leisure time allied with economic prosperity and a rising standard of living
- increasing concern for health
- the recognition by educational authorities of the value of exercise and a more open attitude toward athletics

It is important to realize that the development of sport in the United States was as much a product of industrialization as it was an antidote to it (Betts, 1974).

Between 1865 and 1900 an athletic impulse swept the United States and baseball won the popular support of men and women of all social classes. The growth of a national interest in sport was, in fact, increasingly more dependent on the spectacular treatment that it received from the daily press. By the 1890s the sports sections of daily papers across the country were changing and expanding rapidly. The expansion of sports news was directly related to the telegraph, which made possible the instantaneous reporting of sports results.

Albert Spalding turned to manufacturing sporting goods shortly after the formation of the National League. Spalding opened his "baseball and sporting-goods emporium" in 1876 in Chicago. Spalding "consciously sought to capitalize on his reputation as a famous ballplayer and baseball magnate, both to capture and to extend an expanding market for athletic equipment among middle-class Americans" (Levine, 1986). A.G. Spalding and Brothers successfully dominated a sporting goods industry it helped shape. Spalding capitalized on and often created opportunities for publicity and profit, including a contract to supply the National League with baseballs for all league games in exchange for the exclusive designation as the maker of the league's official ball.

Early on, Spalding recognized the benefits of vertical integration, that is, owning fac-

---

Ashland Manufacturing Company was founded in 1913 to develop innovative ways of using the slaughterhouse buy-products of the meatpacking firm Schwarzchild and Sulzberger. In 1914, Thomas E. Wilson was named president and the company broke off on its own to specialize in sporting goods.

tories that make merchandise as well as owning the retail stores that sell them. Today, this violates antitrust law, but in the late 1800s and early 1900s these laws didn't exist. In 1879, the Spalding and Wilkins Manufacturing Company was opened in Hastings, Michigan. The factory manufactured baseball bats, croquet implements, ice skates, and fishing gear. By 1896, A.G. Spalding and Brothers were reported to have developed a national network of specialized sporting goods manufacturers. Spalding manufactured bicycles, golf equipment, tennis racquets, dumbbells, Indian clubs, bicycle shoes, stocking caps, football shoes, football pants, jackets, and hunting goods and clothes.

By 1892, the American Sports Publishing Company, owned by A.G. Spalding and Brothers, became a separate enterprise. In addition to extensive publishing, Spalding also developed a national retail and wholesale marketing system to move its goods. Spalding continually sought new approaches to attract the general public and other businessmen to its brand.

By 1886, with the Library of American Sports in place, the promotion of Spalding products had nearly become a business in itself. Spalding's involvement in the 1900 and 1904 Olympic games provided even more exposure. He aggressively manufactured and marketed bicycles but, by 1899, Spalding was feeling the effects of increasing competition from smaller manufacturers, so he founded the American Bicycle Company, which was a giant trust comprising 48 companies and valued at $22 million. The success of A.G. Spalding and Brothers was based on modern concepts of industrial organization, with an emphasis on innovation and diversification (Levine, 1986).

In 1906 the Sporting Goods Manufacturers Association (SGMA) and the National Collegiate Athletic Association (NCAA) were founded. The attempt to make football safer for participants resulted in modifications to football equipment. The National Sporting Goods Association (NSGA) was founded by a small group of sporting goods dealers in 1929. Consumer spending on sporting goods in the United States declined until immediately after the Korean War, when domestic prosperity returned and intercollegiate athletics developed into a commercial enterprise. In the 1970s there was increased recognition of product liability and injuries associated with sports equipment. This led to the founding of the World Federation of the Sporting Goods Industry (WFSGI). This organization helped to make coaches and sports administrators more concerned about risk management. In the 1980s and 1990s several significant sporting goods manufacturing companies emerged including Nike and Reebok. These companies, along with other footwear and apparel suppliers, were so successful that, by adding apparel and footwear as major product categories, the industry today has more than tripled in size since the early 1970s. As apparel and footwear became fashionable items to wear, the industry's visibility increased geometrically. Also enhancing the industry's visibility was the move toward public ownership which began in the early 1980s and has continued unabated since then.

Defining the Sporting Goods Industry

The sporting goods industry includes a wide range of sports and recreation activities. While most people tend to think of the industry in relatively narrow terms related to their own experiences, in reality, the industry includes six basic types of activities, shown below with a list of examples:

> A.G. Spalding opened his first sporting goods store in Chicago in 1876. He went on to dominate the industry for the next 50 years.

1. extreme sports (inline skating, skateboarding, snowboarding, surfing/surfboarding, wakeboarding)
2. fitness (all types, including martial arts)
3. individual sports (badminton, bowling, boxing, golf, gymnastics, skiing, tennis, wrestling)
4. indoor games (billiards, darts, table tennis)
5. outdoor recreation sports (archery, backpacking, bicycling, boating, camping, canoeing/kayaking, climbing, fishing, hiking, hunting/shooting, ice skating, water sports)
6. competitive team sports (baseball, basketball, field hockey, football, ice hockey, lacrosse, roller hockey, soccer, softball, swimming/diving, track and field, volleyball)

These activities attract consumers of all ages and all income groups, and the industry produces an enormous range of specialized equipment, apparel and footwear for all these activities. Marketing and distribution strategies vary widely between the types of products produced and the sports and activities for which these products are made. One need only to visit a sporting goods store, such as Dick's or The Sports Authority, to appreciate the enormity of product choices within the industry.

There is a tendency on the part of team sports athletes and sports fans to consider team sports the primary segment of the sporting goods industry. On the contrary, whether it be participation rankings, equipment sales, or apparel and footwear sales, figures do not bear this out. Only with respect to visibility is this the case. There are millions of fans whose only exposure to sporting goods is through their favorite team. However, a significant percentage of these fans neither participate in team sports when they become adults nor do they purchase equipment, with the exception of licensed apparel.

Dynamics Peculiar to the Sporting Goods Industry

Very few, if any, other consumer products are affected by so many different factors that significantly influence the success of the business but are things over which the industry has little or no control.

In order to deal with these factors, with extremely rare exceptions, company officials, particularly senior management leaders, are most often individuals with lots of sporting goods industry experience, most having worked in some capacity in the industry for the better part of their career.

Five factors which can affect sales of sporting goods but over which the industry has very little control are changing fashion trends; changing cultural trends; political, social and pricing pressures of overseas production; seasonal and weather factors; and the behavior of athletes. These trends exert the most influence on the apparel and footwear segments of the industry. Combined, these categories represent approximately 50 percent of all expenditures for sporting goods equipment, apparel and footwear.

Changing Fashion Trends

An excellent example of changing fashion trends—what's trendy to wear—occurs in

In 1974, cowhide replaced horsehide as the cover for major-league baseballs. Horsehide had been used for over 100 years.

the licensed products industry, in which apparel and footwear products bear the names of teams or athletes. During the mid-1990s, licensed products were very much in fashion and industry sales boomed. One result of this was an overexpansion of producers, which came to an abrupt halt in the late 1990s when fashion tastes shifted away from licensed athletic apparel to other types of casual apparel and footwear. Several leading companies either went out of business (Starter Sportswear is one example), while others such as Nutmeg Mills were absorbed by larger companies in the industry, such as Russell Athletic. After a period of decline and consolidation, however, consumer interest in licensed sports products revived and licensed products are once again becoming a major factor in fashion trends.

Changing Cultural Trends

Among the most fundamental cultural changes—shifting patterns of popularity of specific sports and sports-related activities—that have occurred over the past ten years are:

- the emergence of a teenage and young adult market for extreme sports
- adult demand for fitness activities and products
- exploding interest in outdoor activities, particularly hiking, backpacking, overnight camping and paintball
- the growth of organized youth sports, at the expense of recreational participation

Over the past 20 years, teenage and young adult participation in traditional sports such as football, baseball, basketball, golf and tennis has stagnated in growth, whereas extreme sports such as inline skating, skateboarding, wakeboarding, snowboarding have surged in popularity.

Giving impetus to the growth of extreme sports is support from television and more recently, the Internet. While ratings have recently declined for professional sports such as basketball, broadcast coverage and ratings have significantly grown for extreme sports such as the "X" games on ESPN. Broadcasters have long coveted the ability to reach the youth market, and extreme sports events represent prime opportunities for them.

Because extreme sports and team sports appeal to the same teenage market segment, it would appear on the surface that the surging extreme sports market negatively impacted participation in team sports. However, a more careful analysis largely negates this theory. Of the two most popular extreme sports, snowboarding is a winter sport (therefore not affecting most team sports which occur in the fall, spring, or summer), and skateboarding is primarily a recreational sport, appealing to a somewhat different psyche than that for team sports.

Participation trends in the fitness activities of adults have increased significantly over the past ten years. Significant growth in activities such as calisthenics, weight lifting and training, exercise walking and fitness club membership have combined to create an industry of over $4 billion in just sales of equipment, making fitness the largest single sporting goods category after boating and cycling.

Over the past ten years, participation has also grown significantly in outdoor camping, hiking and backpacking. More than likely, the dramatic growth of these outdoor activities resulted among individuals with limited athletic skills, who are unable to participate in competitive games, but who seek physical ways to express and enjoy themselves outdoors. However, while the outdoor trend may not have been a major factor in the decline of traditional sports, it has strongly influenced the types of products sold in sporting goods outlets.

Recent industry statistics for team sports, comparing changes in total youth participation vs. participation in interscholastic (high school) participation over the past ten years, reflect different patterns. Total youth team sports participation is declining, compared with growth trends for most interscholastic teams, suggesting that recreational (non-organized) participation is declining steeply enough to offset the gains registered for interscholastic participation. This cultural phenomenon has inspired the industry to support programs to increase recreational participation.

Overseas Production

Within the sporting goods industry, it has become a fact of life since the mid-1970s that nearly all production of athletic apparel and footwear, and a significant amount of production of sporting goods equipment, is done in foreign countries, primarily in the Far East — Taiwan, China, South Korea and Japan, and India representing the primary sources. The result is an industry susceptible to the political and economic developments in these countries over which it has no control but which can impact consumer attitudes in the U.S. market. One aspect of this issue are the social and labor pressures in the United States concerning wage levels, child labor and gender. American companies must deal with these issues in their foreign factories, requiring them to be more sensitive than ever to the dynamics of social responsibilities, quite apart from focusing more narrowly on manufacturing and production technology and efficiency.

Seasonal and Weather Factors

Certain segments of the sporting goods industry are much more susceptible to weather than others. Skiing, snowboarding, golf, tennis, soccer and baseball, for example, require appropriate conditions such as snow, dry weather, or warm weather. Slight changes in the number of days available for participation will have a significant impact on overall sales and participation levels. Marketing programs are precisely developed to start at a certain point, and for most sports, a significant amount of equipment purchasing is done at or right after the beginning of the season for the sport. Even a modest delay in the start of a season can result in sales declines on a year-to-year comparison, particularly for products whose consumption is specifically related to the number of "playable" days during a season, such as golf or tennis balls or even apparel.

An experience that best illustrates this point happened in 1970 to a recent graduate (known to the author) of a leading university business school program. Although he had a metropolitan background, the recent graduate chose to start a business in the outdoor recreation market. He bought a piece of land on Lake Sebago, a beautiful place in Maine, and set up a camp for recreational vehicles and campers, which were emerging at that time as a growing market. He invested heavily in marketing, and during the summer, we often spoke of his success, because his campground was nearly filled every week during the season.

The season was the problem. A piece of information missing from his research was that the camping season in Maine is typically ten weeks long because of weather limitations. He needed a twelve week season to break even. As a result, he lost most of his investment. Although we haven't been in touch in recent years, I'm sure he's a better man today for the lesson he learned early on, which apparently wasn't part of his high-priced business education.

The Behavior of Athletes

Athlete behavior has been a two-edged sword in the industry from the time athletes were first used to endorse products, beginning in the late 1800s. Problems occur in various forms, including violations of the law by athletes, a lack of emotional appeal of athletes even if their athletic performance is excellent, and long-term or permanent injuries to athletes who have been signed to endorse a product.

It's important to recognize that most endorsement programs in the industry have been successful and ongoing. Recent athletes such as Michael Jordan and Tiger Woods, and historical ones such as Ben Hogan, Walter Hagen, Jack Kramer, Sam Snead, and Ted Williams are and have been enormously successful as product endorsers. As we'll see throughout this book, athlete endorsement is the primary promotional medium used to sell most sporting goods products, whether it be in advertising, through personal appearances, or by the athlete using a sponsor's product while competing.

An extreme example of a negative experience was a situation in the early 1990s in which Reebok signed a superb college basketball player from Maryland, Len Bias. About the time of the signing, Bias passed away from what was suspected to be a drug overdose. A more recent situation in the news involves to Kobe Bryant, a star player for the Los Angeles Lakers, who was accused of raping a woman at a rehabilitation center in Colorado.

Finally, quoting from a recent article in the leading trade publication, *Inside Sporting Goods*, "It appears that Grant Hill will sit out next season to rehabilitate his surgically repaired left ankle. Maybe Fila should have a line of Grant Hill casuals." To appreciate the scope of this development, imagine if you were hired to be the product manager for Fila basketball shoes bearing Grant Hill's name!

Using Technological Developments from Other Industries

Sporting goods vendors, particularly those producing equipment, do relatively little to develop new materials for use in the production of their products. However, they are constantly seeking ways to adapt new technologies and new materials from other sources to produce more effective and higher quality sporting goods products. Examples include using titanium to produce golf and tennis equipment, using new apparel technologies for better absorption of perspiration (Under Armour), and using resistance machine technology for fitness equipment. Successful sporting goods companies are able to combine acute awareness of athlete needs with awareness of the latest developments in technology that might have applications to their products.

Apparel and Footwear Create Explosive Industry Growth

From its earliest beginnings until the early 1970s, the industry was primarily defined by sporting goods equipment. Apparel was largely limited to uniforms and some casual wear for athletes and coaches. Basketball and cleated shoes dominated a limited footwear market, even for other sports such as tennis. Licensing sales were very limited; professional and collegiate league offices, which now dominate licensing programs, were negligibly involved in licensing, which at that time was managed locally by each team. The fitness market was very small — existing mostly in a limited number of retail fitness clubs; the home market was negligible. Adidas, a German company, dominated the world market for footwear and apparel. Leading sporting goods equipment companies were Wilson, Spalding, Rawlings, Titleist, Dunlop, MacGregor, Worth, K2, Coleman and Head. Many of these companies — notably Wilson, Spalding, Rawlings, Titleist and MacGregor — had been dominating the industry for over 60 years.

But the industry changed dramatically in the early 1970s. Nike began marketing athletic footwear, competing head-on with Adidas, and the industry never looked back. While the equipment market has grown steadily since then, athletic apparel and footwear sales now comprise nearly 50 percent of all sales.

In May 2004, *Sporting Goods Business* magazine published an extensive article entitled, "Adding It Up: A By-the-Numbers Look at How the Sporting Goods Industry Continues to Evolve." This article is reprinted in its entirety below, because it represents an outstanding discussion of the industry, with a focus on trends that are most likely to influence future developments and structure.

Adding It Up: A By-the-Numbers Look at How the Sporting Goods Industry Continues to Evolve
(*Sporting Goods Business*, 2004)

To truly understand the "big picture" of sporting goods participation, sales, and product trends, it is necessary to peel back a few layers, to dig a little deeper to see what makes each sport and its retail segment tick. Only then can the state of the sporting goods market over the past five years be understood.

On the surface, the industry seems to have grown nicely since the late 1990s, although a slump at the turn of the century makes that overall growth number less than impressive. While the industry as a whole has had a few noticeable peaks and valleys, the true story resides in the shifting roles of individual segments:

Apparel: This category logged the most significant decline in market share within the overall sporting goods industry. According to the NSGA, the segment accounted for 27 percent of sporting goods sales in 1997, 24 percent in 1999, and only 22 percent in 2003.

Footwear: This segment, which also lost share within the general sporting goods category, fell from slightly more than one-third of category sales in 1997 to just over 30 percent in 2003.

Equipment: As a result of the declining fortunes of footwear and apparel, sporting goods retailers increasingly turned to the equipment category, which grew from 43 percent of sales in 1997 to more than 47 percent in 2003. In fact, hard goods currently account for almost half of all sporting goods sales.

Both the apparel and the footwear segments lost market share not necessarily because of decreased unit sales, but for one simple reason: price. This is most apparent in apparel, where an increase in units sold was offset by an even stronger pattern of declining average prices, directly attributable to the growth in private label and store brands, over-retailing, and consumer caution. The same pattern holds true in footwear.

The good news is that Americans are still playing sports, and participation numbers continue to at least mirror general population growth. Research from the SGMAI indicates that 35 percent of Americans ages 6 and older participate in some physical activity on a frequent basis—that's almost 90 million people out there walking, throwing a ball or lifting weights. Moreover, almost 70 percent of Americans report participating in sports at least occasionally.

While the overall participation numbers have remained relatively stagnant over the past five years, there have been some significant changes—both good and bad—in individual activities.

Team Sports: The bad news is that there has been a very noticeable decline in total participation numbers in traditional sports such as baseball, softball and volleyball, and no growth in basketball. The good news is that the number of serious participants playing frequently on organized teams has increased dramatically. Pickup games are out, organized sports are in.

Outdoor: As in team sports, the number of fishers, hikers and hunters has remained flat—only tent camping has seen a sales increase in the past five years—but the business remains strong thanks to a reliable core of frequent participants. Industry marketing efforts are centered on attracting a new generation of participants.

Fitness: Health club memberships have risen in past years despite a weak economy. SGMAI numbers also indicate that sales of home exercise equipment rose in 2003, as well. Here, though, the number of frequent participants has remained as flat as their stomachs, suggesting a lot of trying-and-buying but not nearly as much buying-and-using among less-than-dedicated exercisers.

Action Sports: This category, which includes board sports, continues to grow, with "older" snowboarders providing an unexpected lift up the sales mountain.

The bottom line on these participation numbers is evident: although the number of frequent sports participants has increased, there has been no growth in the percentage of frequent participants. It was, as indicated, 35 percent in 1998 and it remains 35 percent in 2003. In short, the industry's growth has mirrored population growth.

On the bright side, the greatest growth in the overall sports market is in recreational (read: non-competitive) sports. Americans love recreational walking (85 million participants overall, 40 million frequent participants); swimming (92 million total, 15 million frequent); and biking (53 million total, 15 million frequent). Apparently, these enthusiasts just don't like keeping score.

Herewith, *SGB* presents an in-depth look at footwear, apparel and equipment category market share; category rankings of top manufacturers according to 2003 U.S. wholesale sales; sports participation numbers; and average retail selling prices in key product categories.

• THE TOTAL MARKET

Equipment has grown steadily as a percentage of overall sporting goods sales in the past five years, while apparel and footwear both lost ground. The cause is as much due to increased equipment sales as it is to lower relative price points of both apparel and footwear.

Total Sporting Goods Retail Sales in 2004
Equipment: 51.7%   Footwear: 27.4%   Apparel: 20.8%
(Author's Note: This table is updated from the original article, which reflected 2003 data.)

Total Sporting Goods Retail Sales in 2000
Equipment: 52.6%   Footwear: 25.6%   Apparel: 21.7%
(Author's Note: This table is updated from the original article, which reflected 1999 data.)

Total Sporting Goods Retail Sales in 1997
Equipment: 42.8%   Footwear: 33.3%   Apparel: 27%
Source: NSGA.

• FOOTWEAR

Although "brown" shoes generally refer to the rugged outdoor category, and "casual" shoes are a mix of non-technical outdoor, comfort and casual/athletic footwear, it is apparent that the casual segment (which at times overlaps with the brown shoe market) has won out in terms of market share in the past five years.

While casual shoes have managed to maintain their price points, performance athletic footwear (also known as "white" shoes) dropped in price per pair. This price deflation, coupled with slower sales as performance gave way to increased consumer interest in casual/fashion footwear (and, to a lesser extent, consumer interest in brown shoes), cost the performance category in terms of market share.

2003
Fashion/Casual: 23.3%   Outdoor/Brown: 7.9%   Performance: 69%

1999
Fashion/Casual: 18.8%   Outdoor/Brown: 8.2%   Performance: 72.3%

2003 Sales of Athletic Footwear to Men, Women and Children
Children: 18%   Women: 27%   Men: 55%
Source: SGMA.

In footwear, the casual segment showed consistent, long-term market share growth. In equipment, outdoor products were the big winners. And while men bought more sports apparel overall, women paid more per unit purchased.

• EQUIPMENT
The growth in outdoor products—both in increased usage and in greater availability—has made this category the big percentage winner, along with exercise/fitness equipment. The big drop comes in golf. Team sports remain basically flat in terms of percentage of sales.

2004

Outdoor:	29.7%	Exercise/Fitness: 21.9%	Team:	15.2%
Golf:	13.7%	Snowsports:	6.5%	Action Sports:	2.5%
Tennis:	1.6%	Other:	8.9%		

Other: Archery, Backyard Sports, Billiards, Optics, Racquetball, Table Tennis. (Author's Note: This table is updated from the original article, which reflected 2003 data.)

1999

Outdoor: 32.2%	Golf:	17.6%	Exercise/Fitness: 16.5%
Team: 16.4%	Snowsports:	4.4%	Action Sports:	2.5%
Tennis: 1.7%	Other:	8.8%		

1997

Outdoor: 23.2%	Golf:	19.6%	Exercise/Fitness: 15.5%
Team: 15.3%	Snowsports:	4.1%	Action Sports:	3.2%
Tennis: 1.6%	Other:	17.3%		

Source: NSGA.

• APPAREL
These charts clearly indicate that while men actually buy more sports apparel, women pay significantly more per unit purchased.
Interestingly, the research also reveals that in regard to "active sports apparel" (apparel purchased with the intention of being used for an athletic activity), men bought 44.7 percent, women 40.1 percent and children only 15.2 percent.
When it comes down to the actual buying, women rule. They purchased 60.4 percent of all sports apparel, compared to men (30 percent), and children (less than 10 percent).
These charts track three primary categories: men versus women versus children.
Total Sports Apparel Sales (percentage by dollars)
A comparison of apparel sales from 2003 to 1999.

2003
Children: 19.2%   Men: 36.3%   Women: 44.5%

1999
Children: 23%   Men: 38.5%   Women: 38.5%
   Here is a comparison of dollar sales in each category to unit sales, which differ
greatly. The numbers are for 2002.

Total Sports Apparel Sales (percentage by dollars)
2002
Children: 19.2%   Men: 36.3%   Women: 44.5%

Total Sports Apparel Sales (percentage by units sold)
2002
Children: 27.5%   Men: 37%   Women: 35.6%
Source: SGMA.

- POINT-OF-SALE ANALYSIS
   It's difficult to grow dollar volume in an industry that's beset by price deflation.
But that is precisely the challenge facing sporting goods retailers and manufacturers
in key categories covered by SportScanINFO.
   According to point-of-sale data captured by SportScanINFO, the average selling
price of items in five key merchandise categories has declined over the past three
years. All athletic footwear—and two of the segment's largest categories, running
shoes and basketball shoes—has shown a steady decline, as have treadmills and
tents.
   The categories that have shown increases are insoles, bats, basketballs, braces,
nutritional bars and sleeping bags. These gainer categories have all experienced a fair
degree of innovation. For example, Spalding's Infusion technology has boosted the
basketball category, and several bat makers have introduced new technologies that
boosted the average selling price in that category by 15 percent. Product innovation
and improved marketing have also fueled the insole and nutritional bar categories.
   Average Retail Selling Price in Full-Line Sporting Goods Chains

Category/2002/2003/2004 (YTD)
Athletic Footwear/$48.71/$46.43/$47.50
*Running Shoes/$58.87/$57.79/$57.90
*Basketball Shoes/$54.76/$51.42/$52.61
Insoles/$16.21/$16.92/$18.17
Treadmills/$553.02/$569.26/$508.47
Baseball/Softball Bats/$54.54/$54.38/$62.96
Basketballs/$19.88/$19.47/$20.19
Braces/$24.11/$26.84/$28.76
Nutritional Bars/$1.16/$1.21/$1.29
Sleeping Bags/$28.35/$28.75/$29.63
Tents/$79.54/$75.33/$58.56
Source: SportScanINFO.
Athletic footwear.

- SPORTS PARTICIPATION (1999–2004)
   Although camping and hiking numbers and rankings increased in the past five years,
despite their popularity Americans are not drastically increasing their participation.
   There is a core of dedicated outdoor enthusiasts, but real growth has been slowed
by time constraints and lack of easily reachable outdoor recreation areas.
   Use of exercise equipment has increased in the past five years, as evidenced by the
sales growth seen in home exercise equipment. Exercise classes, however (labeled as
"aerobics"), have seen decreased participation. In fact, SGMAI numbers indicate that
the number of people who exercise at least twice a week has actually declined in the
past decade from 23.2 percent to only 19.8 percent.

Team sports participation barely shows up on these charts, with only basketball registering near the bottom of the top dozen sports. Yet other figures indicate that although the numbers are flat, "frequent" participation numbers are up considerably.

Obviously, Americans like to walk.

Sports Participation 1999 (in mil. of part.)

Exercise Walking:	80.8	Exercise Equipment:	45.2	Basketball:	29.6
Swimming:	57.9	Bicycling:	43.4	Hiking:	28.1
Camping:	50.1	Bowling:	41.6	Golf:	27.0
Fishing:	46.7	Billiards/Pool:	32.1	Aerobics:	26.2

Sports Participation 2004 (in mil. of part.) (Author's Note: This table is updated from the original article, which reflected 2003 data.)

Exercise Walking:	84.7	Bowling:	43.8	Aerobics:	29.5
Camping:	55.3	Bicycling:	40.3	Hiking:	28.3
Swimming:	53.4	Fishing:	38.2	Basketball:	27.8
Exercise with Equipment:	52.2	Billiards/Pool:	34.2	Golf:	24.5

Sources: National Sporting Goods Association, Sporting Goods Manufacturers Association International, Outdoor Industry Association, as well as industry estimates.

- HOW THE VENDORS FARED

Here is a summary of the financial gains and losses of key sporting goods footwear, apparel and equipment manufacturers. The figures reported here are U.S. wholesale sales in $ millions and come from the companies themselves as well as from industry sources. (Author's Note: More recent data appears in chapter 8 dealing with financial aspects of the industry.)

Branded Apparel
Company/'03 Sales/'02 Sales/Comment
1. Nike/$1,398/$1,269/USOC deal should provide Olympic-size spark.
2. Sara Lee Corp./$1,088/$1,098/Figures represent U.S. sportswear (including Champion and JogBra) within intimates and underwear segment for fiscal year ending June 29.
3. Russell Corp./$1,085/$1,076/Brands include Russell Athletic, Moving Comfort, Jerzees and Bike. Wal-Mart represented 21 percent of biz in '03.
4. VF Corp./$737/$667/Outdoor sales (including The North Face apparel) rose 14 percent and licensed apparel was up 17 percent last year.
5. Reebok Intl./$561/$461/Will soon have a trio of exclusive licensed apparel pacts after purchase of The Hockey Co. is complete.
6. Columbia Sportswear/$519/$495/Sportswear was a gainer last year.

Athletic Footwear
Company/'03 Sales/'02 Sales/Comment
1. Nike*/$3,005/$3,052/Q2 futures suggest that "Happy Days are Here Again."
2. Reebok/$1,036/$932/Is aiming to maintain accelerated market share in 2004.
3. New Balance/$910/$910/Focusing on distribution, $70 to $100 retail price points in the running category.
4. Adidas/$750/$810/Retooling under "Impossible is Nothing" mantra; Sees flat to slightly positive North American revenue growth in '04.
5. K-Swiss/$369/$245/After a strong year, added color pops to classic fare.
*Nike total is for the 12 months ended Nov. 30.

Outdoor/Rugged Footwear
Company/'03 Sales/'02 Sales/Comment
1. Timberland/$676/$645/Has redefined its outdoor performance classifications for Fall '04.

2. Wolverine/$300/$284/The footwear group consists of Wolverine, Bates, Harley-Davidson, Hy-Test and Stanley Brands. These niche brands combine to bring in big top line numbers.

3. Merrell/$160/$140/Has successfully expanded its multi-sport, casual offerings. Recent Sebago acquisition should help open up the marine footwear market.

4. Columbia/$78/$57/The footwear division just celebrated its 10th anniversary. Total includes Sorel.

5. Genfoot/Kamik/$60/$60/Company relies on price/value equation; is expanding women's and kids' lines.

6. Teva/$54/$46/Parent Deckers is broadening the brand's reach by expanding offerings, licensing.

7. Rocky/$48/$42/Figure includes rugged footwear only; company is strong in the hunting market.

8. LaCrosse/$40/$40/Rubber boot categories remain a bright spot.

9. Danner/$29/$26/The company's fortunes have shown steady improvement since its acquisition by LaCrosse in 1994. Ninety percent of Danner's styles incorporate Gore-Tex.

Lifestyle/Casual Footwear
Rank/Company/'03 Sales/'02 Sales/Comment

1. Skechers/$563/$682/Has new Mark Ecko and Rhino Red brands under license.

2. Vans/$411.4/$330.2/Appealing product, along with marketing and event sponsorships, have built Vans into an alternative sport market leader. (Sales figure for '03 represents trailing 12 months.)

3. Clarks/$325/$311/The company is the worldwide leader in the comfort footwear category in terms of revenue.

4. Rockport/$319/$345/Rockport is launching its I. Travel men's line this Fall. The collection, which boasts new footbeds and logos, is aimed at better department stores and independents.

5. GBMI/$260/$142/Includes Diesel, Nautica, XOXO, Mecca, Dry-ShoD and Pony sales. Pony will have a complete year in 2004; GBMI also plans to open four Pony stores to sell shoes and accessories.

6. Ecco /$145/$110/The company is making a statement with women's fashion golf shoes.

Equipment
Rank/Company/'03 Sales/'02 Sales/Comment

1. Icon Health*/$975/$850/Founders Watterson, Stevenson to embark on church mission; will complete China plant this year.

2. Brunswick Corp./$854/$819/Includes Life Fitness, billiards/bowling segment; is building Cardio fitness plant in Eastern Europe.

3. Acushnet Cos./$800/$746/Still the kingpin of golf. Brands include Titleist and Cobra Golf.

4. Adidas-Salomon/$700/$548/Taylor-Made-Adidas Golf and Salomon included in total.

5. Amer Sports/$635.2/$642.9/Although figures are for North America, 91 percent of that market's net sales came from the U.S. Brands include Wilson Racquet Sports, Golf and Team Sports; Atomic; Suunto; and Precor.

6. K2 Inc./$569/$437/Will it leapfrog to top of the chart in '04 with a blockbuster deal? Acquisitions accounted for $114 million of increase.

Icon total is for the 12 months ended Nov. 30.

RELATED WEBSITES

American Sportfishing Association (ASA): www.asafishing.org
Canadian Sporting Goods Association (CSGA): www.csga.ca
National Bicycle Dealers Association (NBDA): http://nbda.com/site/intro.cfm
National Golf Foundation (NGF): www.ngf.org
National Marine Manufacturers Association (NMMA): www.nmma.org
National Shooting Sports Foundation (NSSF): www.nssf.org
National Sporting Goods Association (NSGA): www.nsga.org
SnowSports Industries America (SIA): www.thesnowtrade.org
Sporting Goods Agents Association (SGAA): www.r-sports.com/SGAA
Sporting Goods Business (magazine): www.sportinggoodsbusiness.com
Sporting Goods Dealer (magazine): www.sgdealer.com
Sporting Goods Manufacturers Association International (SGMA): www.sgma.com
Surf Industry Manufacturers Association (SIMA): www.sima.com
Tennis Industry Association: www.tennisindustry.org
World Federation of the Sporting Goods Industry (WFSGI): www.wfsgi.org

EXERCISES

1. Visit at least four of the websites listed above. Study these websites and note in one or two paragraphs how each company or organization functions. If you are ever working either in the industry or with an organization that serves the industry, you'll undoubtedly need to use or at least be aware of the services they provide.

2. Go to www.nike.com, www.adidas.com and www.newbalance.com. Search for and read the "Company History" for each of these companies. (Nike's history is in the "Heritage" section for "About Nike." New Balance's is in the "About Us" section.

Adidas' is accessible by clicking on "Performance," and then clicking on "about us." What additional insights do these sites add to your understanding of the history of the sporting goods industry? Again, in one or two paragraphs briefly summarize your findings.

3. Go to www.nsga.org and www.wfsgi.org and explore both sites. On the NSGA site, click on "Guest" and review the site in order to understand their objectives and programs. On the WFSGI site, read "History" and "Latest News." Based on information you learned from visiting these sites, summarize your perceptions and understanding of the sporting goods industry in two to three paragraphs. From your perspective, what are the most significant issues facing the industry in the next two to five years?

2

Structure and Size of the Industry in the United States

OVERVIEW

Skateboarding was the fastest growing sport between 1998 and 2002.
(NSGA)

This chapter deals with how the market for sporting goods equipment, apparel and footwear is served in the United States and in foreign countries. The sporting goods market is composed of two major market segments; (1) individual consumers and, (2) professional and amateur sports leagues and teams. Other smaller but important segments include corporations; commercial institutions such as health clubs, public and private sports clubs, YMCA/YWCAs, etc.; and premium buyers (users of sporting goods as incentives for the promotion and sale of other products). The industry has organized itself to meet the unique needs of each market segment it serves, remaining flexible in the face of changing market size and composition.

At the end of this chapter, you should be able to:

- Evaluate the size and total market trends of industry sales.
- Evaluate the importance from a sales standpoint of three distinct product categories—footwear, equipment and apparel.
- Identify the different types of buyers of sports equipment, apparel and footwear.
- Recognize the significance of the wide disparity of demographic characteristics depending on which products are purchased.
- Identify the process by which sporting goods products are created, produced, distributed and sold.
- Discuss the potential implications of e-commerce (selling products over the Internet) on the industry.
- Identify the overall size of the industry in terms of the numbers of vendors, retailers and buyers.

DISCUSSION

The structure of the industry is predicated on the specialty product differentiation aspects of the sporting goods equipment, apparel and footwear market. Consumer demand ranges widely with respect to price and a desire for high-performance products, depending on interest and skill levels among sports participants. Over the past 30 years, an exploding market combined with the increasing material and production technologies has greatly influenced the capabilities of vendors to satisfy their customers and the changing retailing environment. The exploding market, along with increasing product knowledge on the part of sports participants, has allowed discounters, mass merchants and "big-box" sporting goods specialists to all gain substantial market share. Industry growth is fueled by new products, by broadening the appeal of existing activities (such as the growth of soccer over the past 30 years) and by the creation and introduction of new sports activities (such as extreme sports).

The importance of new products in spurring industry growth cannot be overstated. When a revolutionary new product is introduced, it must perform a function that has not been performed before or perform a function significantly better than existing products in order to be successful. Rapid growth follows the introduction of a revolutionary new product because these new products speed up the normal replacement cycle. For example, if 10 percent of all golfers replace their golf clubs every year, the introduction of a major innovation, such as large-headed golf clubs, will stimulate a faster replacement rate, perhaps to as much as 15 percent, for a period of time. In addition, revolutionary new products often have a higher price than existing products, resulting in an even greater sales increase.

Conversely, the absence of any new products is often characterized by stagnant or even declining sales in a sporting goods market segment. For example, ten years after the introduction of the oversize golf club head, total sales of golf clubs are actually below those of the period when the oversize head was introduced.

From a career standpoint, 75–80 percent of the industry workforce is engaged in retailing or other forms of distribution, with 20–25 percent engaged in producing products or contracting for their production. There are several distinct types of retailers who sell sporting goods products, ranging from stores that only sell sporting goods to mass merchants and department stores that sell a wide range of different types of products.

The word "manufacturer" has come to be used interchangeably with the word "vendor," because most sporting goods products are actually manufactured overseas by contractors under license to American companies such as Nike, Wilson, etc. Thus, the word "vendor" has come to represent companies who either produce products in their own factories or hire independent contract producers to produce products bearing their name. Throughout this book we will use the word "vendor" to represent manufacturers.

Market Size

Sporting goods products are divided into three major segments: equipment (including sports medicine), footwear, and apparel.

When defining market size, one needs to consider what to include. Best estimates of market size range from $84 billion for products purchased primarily for sports to $110 billion if purchases for casual (non-sports) activities are included.

Table 1 reflects estimated consumer expenditures for sporting goods comparing 1998 and 2004, ranked according to consumer expenditures in 2004. While expenditures grew 21 percent over this period, if recreational vehicles are excluded from the figure (since they are not typically considered sporting goods), growth is a more modest 16.9 percent, or less than 3 percent annually, which is roughly comparable to the rate of inflation. Apparel numbers represent what consumers said they spent for apparel to be used in participation. Footwear numbers include all athletic footwear regardless of whether they were purchased for participation or for casual wear (estimates range from 50 to 75 percent of all athletic footwear sold for casual (non-sports) wear).

TABLE 1: CONSUMER EXPENDITURES FOR SPORTING
GOODS BY MAJOR CATEGORY, 2004 VS. 1998

Product Category	Consumer Exp. (in mil. of $)		
	1998	2004	% Change
Equipment	19,222.6	22,934.3	+19.3
Apparel (purchased for sports)	12,844.4	11,200.8	-12.8
Footwear	13,019.6	14,751.8	+13.3
Recreational Transport (incl. recreational vehicles)	24,743.2	35,797.4	+44.7
TOTAL	69,829.8	84,684.3	+21.3

Source: NSGA

TABLE 2: CONSUMER EXPENDITURES FOR LEADING
CONSUMER SPORTS EQUIPMENT AND RECREATIONAL
TRANSPORT CATEGORIES, 2004 (EXCLUDES RECREATIONAL VEHICLES)

Product Category	Cons. Exp. in 2004 (mil.)
Pleasure Boats/Motors/Accessories	$16,054.1
Outdoor (Firearms/Hunting, Fishing, Camping)	6,416.2
Exercise Equipment	5,011.8
Bicycles and Supplies	4,897.7
Team Sports *	3,400.0
Golf Equipment	3,148.1
Ski/Snowboard Equipment & Accessories	1,490.2
Optical Equipment (Sunglasses, Binoculars)	858.8
Billiards & Indoor Games	627.2

Includes athletic goods team sales + consumer purchases of team sports products measured by NSGA.
Source: NSGA.

The decline of apparel purchases does not necessarily reflect a decline in purchasing. Sales of apparel companies have generally grown during the same period. This decline is interpreted as a growing tendency for athletically-inclined consumers to purchase athletic apparel that they also wear for casual purposes, and that they consider the purchase as much, if not more, for casual wear than for athletic wear.

Table 2 reflects the leading consumer expenditure categories for sporting goods equipment in calendar year 2004, ranked according to consumer expenditures in 2004. Outdoor categories (boating, fishing, camping, etc.) represent the largest categories in terms of sales in the industry, followed by exercise equipment, bicycles, team sports and golf equipment in that order.

Expanding on the data in Table 2, Table 3 reflects consumer expenditures for all sporting goods equipment categories (excluding bicycles), ranked according to consumer expenditures in 2004. Of the three major components of the outdoor market in Table 2, firearms/hunting equipment is the largest, followed by fishing and camping in that order. Another interesting trend: dramatic increases in snowboard sales, compared with significant declines in alpine and cross-country ski sales. This is an example of how important it is for sporting goods companies to be alert to changing consumer preferences and act accordingly, lest their business be lost forever. Today, nearly every ski company produces snowboarding equipment.

Table 4 reflects consumer expenditures for sports apparel (apparel purchased primarily for sports), ranked according to consumer expenditures in 2004. Clearly apparel for outdoor activities such as camping, hunting and fishing dominate the "purchased primarily for sport" apparel market. One major and obvious reason for this is the wide variety

TABLE 3: CONSUMER EXPENDITURES FOR SPORTING
GOODS EQUIPMENT BY CATEGORY, 2004 VS. 1998

Product Category	Consumer Exp. (in mil. of $)		
	1998	2004	% Change
Exercise	3,233.4	5,011.8	+55.0
Golf	3,657.7	3,148.1	-11.0
Firearms & Hunting	2,200.1	2,870.2	+30.5
Athletic Goods Team Sales	2,338.0	2,517.2	+7.7
Fishing Tackle	1,902.7	2,014.8	+5.9
Camping	1,204.0	1,531.2	+27.2
Optics	710.3	858.8	+20.9
Billiards & Indoor Games	347.2	627.2	+80.6
Skiing Accessories	671.1 *	722.1	+7.6
Wheel Sports & Pogo Sticks	508.9	580.1	+14.0
Skiing (Alpine)	717.7	457.5	-36.3
Tennis	317.6	361.7	+13.9
Skin Diving & Scuba Gear	345.3	351.3	+1.7
Baseball & Softball	304.1	346.0	+12.5
Archery	261.3	331.6	+26.9
Basketball	298.7	310.7	+4.0
Snowboards	163.8	269.9	+64.8
Bowling	156.7	181.6	+15.9
Hockey & Ice Skates	153.0	142.0	-7.2
Football	81.5	83.4	+2.3
Soccer Balls	61.1	64.2	+5.1
Water Skis	53.6	48.9	-8.8
Skiing (Cross-Country)	66.2	40.7	-38.5
Volleyballs & Badminton Sets	31.0	33.7	+8.7
Racquetball	46.5	29.6	-36.3
Table Tennis	38.0	n/a	n/a
Total Athletic & Sport Equipment	19,222.6	22,934.3	+19.3

* Year 1999
Source: NSGA.

of products needed to withstand all types of weather conditions for outdoor recreation participants. Apparel purchased for sports such as golf and tennis are much more likely to be worn for both casual wear and sports participation; thus the figures below will significantly understate the total market for apparel designed for golf and tennis.

An interesting trend reflected in Table 4 is that apparel sales declined in total and for many categories. Since participation in these sports was either stable or increased, this would indicate that the trend is toward more purchases of sports apparel for casual wear compared with purchases to wear for participation. This change in dynamics is important for sports apparel designers to consider when planning future apparel product lines.

Table 5 reflects consumer expenditures for athletic footwear, ranked according to consumer expenditures in 2004. Had this same survey been available 30 years ago, basketball and tennis shoes would have been the dominant categories—running, cross training, aerobic, fitness and sandals hardly existed at that time. Fitness-oriented footwear, primarily for running and fitness, are among the fastest-growing categories. Other major footwear categories—sport sandals, hunting boots and skateboarding shoes—have also experienced above-average growth.

Table 6 reflects consumer expenditures for recreational transport. Products such as boats and recreational vehicles have historically been perceived as separate from the strict sporting goods industry definition. However, they are included in Table 6, because they

TABLE 4: CONSUMER EXPENDITURES FOR SPORTS APPAREL
(PURCH. FOR SPORTS) BY CATEGORY, 2004 VS. 1998
(EXCLUDES TEAM PURCHASES)

Product Category	Consumer Exp. (in mil. of $)		
	1998	2004	% Change
Camping	2,095.8	2,538.8	+21.1
Golf	2,106.1	1,577.2	-25.1
Swimming	1,745.4	1,429.6	-18.1
Hunting	1,179.3	1,365.7	+15.8
Fishing	1,027.4	954.3	-7.1
Skiing (Alpine)	854.1	n/a	n/a
Bicycling	868.1	757.6	-12.7
Aerobic Exercising	921.4	717.4	-22.1
Running/Jogging	829.5	640.2	-22.8
Bowling	714.8	477.9	-33.1
Soccer	400.7 *	415.5	+3.7
Tennis	244.7	181.6	-25.8
Martial Arts	257.9	145.0	-43.8
Total Apparel Market	12,844.4	11,200.8	-12.8

Year 2000
Source: NSGA.

TABLE 5: CONSUMER EXPENDITURES FOR ATHLETIC FOOTWEAR BY
CATEGORY, 2004 VS. 1998 (EXCLUDES TEAM PURCHASES)

Product Category	Consumer Exp. (in mil. of $)		
	1998	2004	% Change
Walking Shoes	3,191.6	3,496.2	+9.5
Gym Shoes/Sneakers	2,009.6	2,220.5	+10.5
Running/Jogging Shoes	1,469.4	1,989.4	+35.4
Cross Training Shoes	1,401.7	1,326.6	-5.4
Basketball Shoes	999.5	876.7	-12.3
Hiking Shoes/Boots	929.9	814.2	-12.4
Fashion Sneakers	572.9 (b)	683.1	+19.2
Sport Sandals	408.1	543.9	+33.3
Tennis Shoes	514.6	508.1	-1.3
Fitness Shoes	317.2	391.6	+23.5
Aerobic Shoes	334.0	236.9	-29.1
Footwear — Golf Shoes	220.3	230.4	+4.6
Baseball/Softball Shoes	253.8	203.2	-19.9
Hunting Boots	181.9	257.2	+41.4
Skateboarding Shoes	119.3	233.6	+95.8
Soccer Shoes	182.5	189.4	+3.8
Boat/Deck Shoes	201.6	180.0	-10.7
Football Shoes	93.0	104.9	+12.8
Cheerleading Shoes	48.0	43.4	-9.6
Cycling Shoes	51.9 *	42.5	-18.1
Bowling Shoes	39.9	42.4	+6.3
Volleyball Shoes	43.6	39.0	-10.6
Track Shoes	26.1	37.4	+43.3
Water Sport Shoes	34.0	35.0	+2.9
Trail Running Shoes	24.0†	26.1	+8.8
Total Athletic & Sport Shoes	13,019.6	14,751.8	+13.3

Year 1999
†Year 2001
Source: NSGA.

TABLE 6: CONSUMER EXPENDITURES FOR RECREATIONAL
TRANSPORT BY CATEGORY, 2004 VS. 1998

	1998	2004	% Change
Rec Transp — Pleasure Boats, Motors & Accessories	10,539.3	16,054.1	+52.3
Rec Transp — Recreational Vehicles	8,363.9	14,018.2	+67.6
Rec Transp — Bicycles & Supplies	4,957.2	4,897.7	-1.2
Rec Transp — Snowmobiles	882.8	827.4	-6.3
Total Recreational Transport	24,743.2	35,797.4	+44.7

Source: NSGA.

are essential ingredients for individuals involved in outdoor recreation, which is perceived to fall within the sporting goods industry definition.

The Team Sports Market

As indicated in Table 2, total 2004 sales of team sports equipment (baseball, basketball, football, ice hockey, lacrosse, soccer, softball, volleyball), including sales to teams as well as individual consumers equaled $3.4 billion, excluding non-uniform apparel and athletic footwear. Sales to teams represent over 70 percent of this market, whereas 30 percent of sales are made to consumers who purchase products in order to participate. Thus, while team sports enjoy enormous visibility because the huge professional and college fan base, and are considered by many to be the "sporting goods market," sales of team sports products actually represent only about 5 percent of all expenditures for sporting goods, exceeded by outdoor, fitness, outdoor recreation and boats, and nearly exceeded by golf equipment.

For individuals seeking careers in sporting goods retailing, particularly with large full-line sporting goods retailers, these figures take on great significance. Clearly, fitness and outdoor recreation are major categories with respect to sales volume, in contrast to sales of traditional team sports equipment and wheel sports (skateboarding, inline skating, etc.). Knowledge, appreciation of and attention to these figures are all essential if one is to enjoy a successful career in the industry.

Sports Participation

Another way to measure the scope and structure of the industry is to examine sports participation trends. Tables 7–13 reflect a cultural shift from traditional team sports participation to outdoor activities, extreme sports and fitness participation. Team sports, however, will never disappear from the sporting goods scene, with millions of Americans still participating and hundreds of millions of team sports fans, emotionally involved (often beyond the bounds of sanity!), with their favorite professional and college teams.

Tables 7–13 reflect participation trends by major type of activity, a meaningful way to reflect the industry's dynamics. Categories reported separately include outdoor (Table 7), fitness (Table 8), team (Table 9), extreme (Table 10), winter (Table 11), water (Table 12) and other sports (Table 13). Participation trends tend to correlate with sales figures reported earlier in this chapter — growth trends are strongest for outdoor recreation and fitness-oriented activities.

TABLE 7: SPORTS PARTICIPATION IN OUTDOOR RECREATION ACTIVITIES (EXCLUDES WATER, WINTER SPORTS), 2004 VS. 1998 (NUMBER OF INDIVIDUALS PARTICIPATING AT LEAST ONCE DURING THE YEAR)

Activity	1998	2004	% Change
Camping (Vac/Overnight)	46,470,000	55,265,000	+18.9
Bicycle Riding	43,535,000	40,317,000	-7.4
Hiking	27,190,000	28,342,000	+4.2
Target Shooting with Firearms	12,755,000	19,154,000	+50.1
Hunting with Firearms	17,285,000	17,711,000	+2.5
Backpack/Wilderness Camping	14,622,000	17,280,000	+18.2
Mountain Biking/Off-Road	8,610,000	8,019,000	-6.9
Hunting with Bow & Arrow	5,591,000	5,818,000	+4.1
Target Shooting-Airgun	4,094,000*	5,095,000	+24.5
Kayaking/Rafting	3,210,000	4,721,000†	+47.1
Muzzleloading	3,057,000	3,810,000	+24.6

* Year 2002
†Year 2003
Source: NSGA.

TABLE 8: SPORTS PARTICIPATION IN FITNESS ACTIVITIES, 2004 VS. 1998 (NUMBER OF INDIVIDUALS PARTICIPATING AT LEAST ONCE DURING THE YEAR)

Activity	Number of Participants		% Change
	1998	2004	
Exercise Walking	77,645,000	84,718,000	+9.1
Exercise with Equipment	46,145,000	52,168,000	+13.1
Work out at Club	26,544,000	31,805,000	+19.8
Aerobic Exercising	25,764,000	29,458,000	+14.3
Weightlifting	24,558,000*	26,237,000	+6.8
Running/Jogging	22,525,000	24,665,000	+9.5
T'ai Chi/Yoga	7,058,000†	5,573,000‡‡	-21.0
Pilates	4,900,000**	5,400,000	+10.2
Martial Arts	4,560,000	4,657,000	+2.1

* Year 2001
† Year 2000
‡ Year 2002
** Year 2003
Source: NSGA.

TABLE 9: SPORTS PARTICIPATION IN TEAM SPORTS, 2004 VS. 1998 (NUMBER OF INDIVIDUALS PARTICIPATING AT LEAST ONCE DURING THE YEAR)

Activity	Number of Participants		% Change
	1998	2004	
Basketball	29,417,000	27,847,000	-5.3
Baseball	15,856,000	15,850,000	-0.04
Soccer	13,167,000	13,287,000	+0.9
Softball	15,595,000	12,501,000	-19.8
Volleyball	14,788,000	10,790,000	-27.0
Football (Touch)	9,643,000	9,569,000	-0.8
Football (Tackle)	7,448,000	8,195,000	+10.0
Cheerleading	3,100,000	4,100,000	+32.3
Ice Hockey	2,131,000	2,423,000	+13.7
Roller Hockey	3,093,000	2,235,000*	-27.7

* Year 2001
Source: NSGA

TABLE 10: SPORTS PARTICIPATION IN
EXTREME SPORTS, 2004 VS. 1998
(NUMBER OF INDIVIDUALS PARTICIPATING
AT LEAST ONCE DURING THE YEAR)

Activity	Number of Participants		% Change
	1998	2004	
Inline Skating	27,033,000	18,845,000	-30.3
Scooter Riding	11,621,000[†]	12,915,000	+11.1
Skateboarding	5,782,000	10,338,000	+78.8
Snowboarding	3,635,000	6,572,000	+81.1
Wakeboarding	n/a	2,288,000*	n/a
Surfboarding	1,282,000	1,030,000*	-19.7
Windsurfing	644,000	449,000*	-30.3

*Year 2001
†Year 2000
Source: NSGA.

TABLE 11: SPORTS PARTICIPATION IN
WINTER SPORTS, 2004 VS. 1998
(NUMBER OF INDIVIDUALS PARTICIPATING
AT LEAST ONCE DURING THE YEAR)

Activity	Number of Participants		% Change
	1998	2004	
Snowboarding	3,635,000	6,572,000	+81.1
Skiing (Alpine)	7,680,000	5,903,000	-23.1
Skiing (Cross-Country)	2,643,000	2,352,000	-11.0
Snowshoeing	857,000*	1,014,000[†]	+18.3

*Year 1999
†Year 2000
Source: NSGA.

TABLE 12: SPORTS PARTICIPATION IN
WATER SPORTS, 2004 VS. 1998
(NUMBER OF INDIVIDUALS PARTICIPATING
AT LEAST ONCE DURING THE YEAR)

Activity	Number of Participants		% Change
	1998	2004	
Swimming	58,249,000	53,449,000	-8.2
Freshwater Fishing	38,640,000	36,265,000	-6.1
Boating, Motor/Power	25,715,000	22,773,000	-11.4
Saltwater Fishing	11,037,000	10,283,000	-6.8
Canoeing	7,093,000	7,479,000	+5.4
Water Skiing	7,215,000	4,730,000	-34.5
Kayaking/Rafting	3,210,000	4,721,000[†]	+47.1
Sailing	3,589,000	2,583,000	-28.0
Wakeboarding	n/a	2,288,000*	n/a
Scuba (Open Water)	2,558,000	2,134,000*	-16.6
Surfboarding	1,282,000	1,030,000*	-19.7
Windsurfing	644,000	449,000*	-30.3

* Year 2001
†Year 2003
Source: NSGA.

TABLE 13: SPORTS PARTICIPATION IN
OTHER SPORTS, 2004 VS. 1998
(NUMBER OF INDIVIDUALS PARTICIPATING
AT LEAST ONCE DURING THE YEAR)

Activity	Number of Participants		% Change
	1998	*2004*	
Bowling	40,063,000	43,832,000	+9.4
Billiards/Pool	32,289,000	34,228,000	+6.0
Golf	27,496,000	24,479,000	-11.0
Tennis	11,227,000	9,619,000	-14.3
Racquetball	3,979,000	3,385,000*	-14.9
Kick Boxing	2,300,000	2,785,000	+21.1

* 2002
Source: NSGA.

Vendors

There are over 3,000 vendors of sporting goods products, ranging in size from giants such as Nike and Adidas to very small companies who manufacture a particular product, such as an archery bow for hunting or a special type of fishing lure. Most smaller vendors in the industry specialize in one or two product categories or in one or two sports. Many further refine their efforts to sell only certain products for a specific sport or product category.

Technology has always been a major factor influencing industry structure. Several revolutionary products have been introduced to the industry by individuals from other fields, particularly people with extensive knowledge of materials. Among the best examples are Howard Head (metal skis) and Karsten Solheim (Ping Putters).

Another factor influencing industry structure is that many vendors often function as assemblers. For example, the production of golf clubs is really an assembly operation — vendors buy clubheads from one source, shafts from another, grips from a third source, and then refine and assemble these components into finished clubs, using their own unique techniques.

Distribution

Of all consumer products offered, sporting goods products have the most diverse distribution channels. Over 35,000 retailers (storefronts) sell sporting goods products.

Products such as food, toiletries, drugs, toys, automobiles, and appliances tend to be sold in, at the most, three major trade classes. In the sporting goods industry, however, there are at least six, and often as many as ten, major retailer types that sell a particular sporting goods product. In sporting goods, you have an industry with thousands of vendors, most of them specialists in a sport or in a product category, selling their products to consumers through a multitude of different types of retailers. Another unique aspect of the sporting goods industry is that many products are used both for sports and for casual wear. Products like athletic jackets, ski jackets, winter outerwear, polo-type shirts, shorts, warm-up suits, sweatsuits, fleecewear tops and bottoms, T-shirts, hats and caps, thermal undergarments and footwear have become commonplace casual wear for millions of consumers. While these products were "spawned" in the athletic market and produced by companies considered athletic companies, e.g., Russell, Champion, Bike Athletic and others, marketing practices are quite different depending on whether the company is trying to appeal to the athletic or casual wear market.

Over the past 30 years, structure within the sporting goods industry has been strongly influenced by the dramatic growth of sales of athletic footwear and apparel. Companies such as Nike, Reebok, Adidas, Russell, New Balance, and more recently fashion designers such as Tommy Hilfiger, Polo, and Nautica, produce athletic apparel products such as shoes, jackets, T-shirts, caps, fleecewear, shirts and shorts that are designed for athletic wear but are being worn more and more for casual wear. And professional leagues such as the NBA, NFL, NHL and MLB improved their marketing; licensed products have become major factors in the apparel market.

As far back as the early days of the industry and up through the 1960s, equipment sales dominated the industry. Today, footwear and apparel represent more than 50 percent of industry sales. Footwear and apparel products are sold not only through traditional athletic stores but also through department stores and discounters, and these types of retailers have expanded their offerings in the sporting goods market to include equipment as well. This major shift has caused all vendors in all categories to restructure their operations with a much greater focus on marketing and sales strategies, and the recognition that the health of the sporting goods industry is much more dependent on fashion trends than it ever was in the past.

E-commerce represents a relatively small but growing presence within the industry, currently representing approximately 5 percent of all consumer purchases. Originally, online sporting goods sales were dominated by online-only retailers, but as of late, this trend has reversed itself. Today, the great majority of online sales of sporting goods products are made by traditional storefront retailers who have an online site. One interesting aspect of this has been the emergence of GSI Commerce, a firm which produces websites for several leading competitive sporting goods retailers. Retailers receive royalties from GSI. These royalties are significantly less than revenues retailers would receive by owning their own sites, but retailers are spared all costs related to site production and development. These costs can be substantial for many reasons, not the least of which is the enormous number of different products sold by sporting goods retailers that must be offered on their site to attract potential consumers.

It's Entrepreneurship All the Way

The sporting goods industry is a veritable fountain of entrepreneurship. It's a very easy business to enter — it doesn't require a lot of money to get started — and you don't need sprawling factories or enormous center-city retail space right away. Phil Knight started Nike from the trunk of his car in the early 1970s, and he built the largest sporting company ever to exist.

What is needed is an idea for a product or retail format that is better than anything else like it in the market, plus a real commitment to turn vision into reality, a few dollars, staying power and a creative way to bring the idea to market. The sporting goods indus-

---

Among the top 25 athletic apparel retailers in 2003, 37 percent of athletic apparel business was done by six general discounters and department stores such as Wal-Mart, Sears, etc.

try is a haven for entrepreneurs, and almost every company in the industry, large and small, has the mark of entrepreneurship in its foundation.

Most sporting goods companies were founded by individuals with one of two characteristics. Either they actively participated in the sport for which they developed their idea and recognized the need for a product, or they brought scientific or technical expertise to bear on a sporting goods product. Regardless of background or experience, however, they all had in common the ability to transform their idea into a product that met the needs of sports participants, at a retail price the consumer was willing to pay for their creation.

The aura of entrepreneurship still pervades the industry, and quite likely it always will. Given the unique factors which dictate how sporting goods products are produced and marketed, operating by committee rarely gets one very far in the industry. The dynamics of the industry often require quick action, and many operating processes and procedures considered normal in other industries simply won't succeed in sporting goods.

It's relatively easy to enter the market with a new product. Most products are produced in overseas factories which have high levels of manufacturing skills, easily adaptable to products similar to what they already produce. Thus, new products face the threat of having competitors respond to their introduction with similar products of their own. Given these circumstances, entrepreneurship continues to be needed but in a different form. The original entrepreneurial approach was needed to get started — ongoing entrepreneurial tendencies are needed for survival in a highly competitive, easy-to-enter industry.

This is not to say that sporting goods companies, large and small, avoid generally acceptable business practices. Quite the contrary. They need to be sharper at these practices than companies in other industries, because they normally can't afford to hire expensive consultants to guide them through the maize of modern-day business practices and requirements.

Serving the Individual Consumer Market

- Broadly defined, individual consumer market segments include:
- winter sports (skiing, snowboarding)
- water sports (swimming, skin diving)
- outdoor recreation (archery, boating, camping, fishing, hunting)
- fitness (exercising with equipment, running, walking)
- extreme sports (skateboarding, inline skating, wakeboarding)
- competitive individual sports (golf, tennis, squash)

Consumers purchase products through retail stores (and their websites), online-only retailers (Amazon, eBay, NFL, etc.) and catalog sellers. The combined consumer market represents approximately 90 percent of actual dollar sales of the industry.

Diagram 1 on the following page summarizes these various methods of distribution.

Market Demographics

Overall, sporting goods products have universal demographic appeal. Every segment of our population participates in some activity requiring sporting goods products — whether it is segmented by age, region, income level, gender or family circumstance.

Diagram 1: Methods of Product Distribution

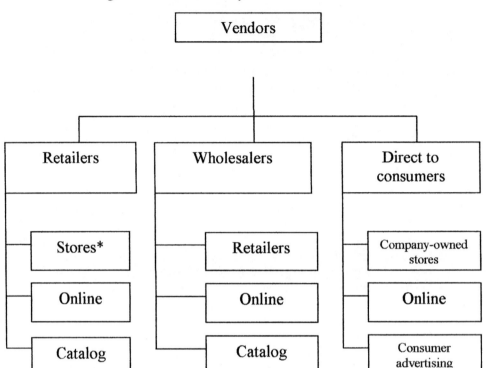

* Stores include full-line sporting goods stores, sports specialty stores/pro shops, athletic footwear stores, department stores, discount stores, warehouse clubs, and footwear/apparel specialty retailers.

For example, a substantial percentage of all sales of team sports products occur in the youth (ages 7–17) market, as are sales of extreme sports products. Sales of winter sports and water sports products occur primarily in the teenage and young adult markets, and in the geographic areas where one can participate. Fitness equipment sales occur in all age segments, but primarily in the over-35 and baby-boomer market segments. Fitness is the only category where for many products, women represent over 50 percent of all sales. Sales of outdoor recreation products occur across all segments, and family circumstances play a major role in the types of equipment purchased.

Seasonality

The sporting goods industry is highly seasonal. Consumers purchase most equipment during the season when people are participating in the sport, particularly at or near the beginning of the season. The primary exceptions are certain types of footwear and apparel, which are not so much tied to a particular sport as to a particular lifestyle.

As would be expected, there are significant variations to this pattern depending on the seasonal factors relating to the product.

Serving the Team Sales Market

Most professional, collegiate and high school sports teams purchase their equipment, footwear and uniforms through what is called a "team dealer." As a rule, team dealers spe-

TABLE 14: PERCENT OF SALES BY MONTH FOR
SPORTING GOODS STORES AND BICYCLE SHOPS, 2000

Month	Percent of Sales	Month	Percent of Sales
January	6.2	July	8.8
February	6.5	August	9.0
March	8.0	September	8.0
April	7.8	October	6.9
May	8.6	November	7.8
June	9.1	December	13.3

Sources: NSGA, U.S. Census.

cialize in selling to organized sports programs, high school and college teams, rarely offering products for sale to individual consumers.

Team dealers provide certain services unique to the needs of sports teams. One such service relates to the need for specialized sewing equipment needed to apply player names, team names and numbers to the uniforms. Team dealers often work with vendors in order to provide products with unique features desired by teams and leagues.

(sb) "Everywhere you turn in 2005, team dealers are reporting a resurgence in their football business and a gradual leveling off of the once high-growth soccer market." *Sporting Goods Dealer*, January 2005. (sb)

While actual sales to sports teams represent a relatively small percentage of total industry dollars, as discussed above, team purchases influence sales in the much larger consumer market by way of implied endorsement. When team participants and spectators purchase products for their own, individual use, they are often favorably inclined toward products and brands they are accustomed to using when they compete on organized teams.

Industry Organizations

The three largest multisport organizations are the National Sporting Goods Association (NSGA), which primarily serves the interests of sporting goods retailers and team dealers; the Sporting Goods Manufacturers Association (SGMA), primarily serving the needs of sporting goods vendors; and the World Federation of the Sporting Goods Industry (WFSGI). All three organizations have extensive research and information services, which are available to any individual or organization interested in the industry.

The National Sporting Goods Association (NSGA), founded in 1927, offers three different types of memberships: retailer/dealer wholesaler, supplier (vendor) and sales agent, and industry associate (includes advertising, consulting, design/development, finances/investments, marketing, publications, public relations, and research firms and sports agencies). With the NSGA there are several subgroups representing the interests of specific categories such as the Team Division, the Special Fitness Retailer Division, and the Ski Retailers Association. The NSGA also sponsors the leading educational industry program, the annual Management Conference and Team Dealer Summit. This program is geared to leading retail and vendor executives from all product categories and provides in-depth insight into current developments, future trends and issues facing the industry.

The Sporting Goods Manufacturers Association (SGMA), founded in 1906 sponsors research, organizes trade shows (the Super Show), lobbies on the industry's behalf in Congress and serves as a catalyst to stimulate market growth. As the SGMA has evolved, so has their mission: "To increase participation in sports and foster industry growth and vitality," which involves serving as liaison between vendors and amateur sports. Within the SGMA are several subgroups representing the interests of specific categories, such as the Athletic Footwear Association, Baseball & Softball Council, Billiard & Bowling Institute, Fitness Products Council, Outdoor Products Council, the Racquet Sports Committee, Soccer Industry Council of America, Sports Apparel Products Council, and the Volleyball Council.

The World Federation of the Sporting Goods Industry (WFSGI), headquartered in Switzerland, has a worldwide membership base. Among its objectives are

> (1) to play a strategic role in support and in the promotion of the sporting goods industry. It provides the forum in which countries of Europe, Asia, North and South America and Oceania forge the tools of their cooperation to promote increase free and air trade and improve the well-being of mankind through the practice of sports; (2) various industry support programs from promoting free and fair trade to contributing to increase sport participation throughout the world, and (3) to provide the platform for the harmonization of standards, provides intergovernmental cooperation with regards to the International Organizations interested or affected by sports, expand the cooperation on the protection of intellectual property rights, improve human rights issues related to working conditions in the world.

Other sporting goods trade associations deal with a particular sport or sports activity. Examples include SnowSports Industries America (SIA), which focuses on skiing and snowboarding; the National Shooting Sports Foundation, whose members include vendors of firearms and ammunition; the National Marine Manufacturers Association, serving the boating industry; the American Sportfishing Association, serving fishing tackle manufacturers; the Outdoor Recreation Council of America, serving outdoor equipment vendors; the Sporting Goods Agents Association, serving independent sales representatives; and the National Bicycle Dealers Association, serving retailers of bicycle equipment and supplies.

An interesting and enlightening discussion of the relative roles in the industry played by vendors, retailers and independent sales agencies who represent vendors comes from the Sporting Goods Agents Association (SGAA). They state that vendors and their sales agency's responsibilities to retailers are threefold:

1. Exposing dealers to products and programs on a timely basis.
2. Preparing purchase orders completely and accurately. These orders should contain information necessary for vendors to ship exactly what dealers ordered, at the same time providing dates, customer information, shipping instructions, billing terms, quantities, prices, sizes, colors, styles, etc.
3. Delivering merchandise to stores in the requested quantities and time frames requested.

The SGAA continues,

> Increasingly, though, factories and sales agents recognize that they must go beyond the basics. They must be marketing and merchandising partners with retailers. Many of these responsibilities fall to agents. Typically, their job is just beginning when a retailer's purchase order is received. They must, in effect, treat the dealer's business as if it were their own.
> Having information is the key to maximizing results during the most important point of interaction between agents and retailers-the sales call-which is discussed later. Before and after merchandise is delivered to a dealer, the agent must work with the store's buyer or merchandise manager to figure out the best ways to display, advertise and sell

it. This includes training the store's sale personnel about merchandise features and how to best present them to customers.

The SGAA defines a dealer's responsibilities to vendors and agents as follows:

> The most important thing dealers can do for factories and agents is to give their product lines a fair hearing. This means accepting and keeping appointments, then affording the sales agent the time to properly present lines and programs. Late cancellations can devastate an agent's tightly scheduled day.
>
> It also means remaining open-minded, especially with new lines or products with which they are unfamiliar. A common trait of successful retailers is their willingness to take risks and try something new, either in the way of products or merchandise presentation. Smart retailers know they don't have all the answers and listen closely to the agent, who can help their business greatly because of their travels and dealings with other retailers and vendors.

Trade Shows and Conferences

The sporting goods industry has a long tradition of trade shows. A trade show is simply an event where sporting goods product vendors present their products to retailers attending the show. Sporting goods trade shows historically have been a vital link connecting products with retailers, largely because of the thousands of vendors and retailers in the industry. However, in recent years, with industry consolidation growing rapidly, trade shows have evolved into something quite different from their historic multisport composition.

The major change has been a shift from "horizontal" trade shows, that is, shows featuring a wide range of products, to "vertical" trade shows, which feature a specific product category or group of categories. With far fewer retailers to contact, and more advance buying done by major retailers working directly with vendors, the horizontal trade show has all but lost its significance. Until recently, there were three major U.S. horizontal shows—the Super Show (SGMA) and World Sports Expo (NSGA) in the summer and the NSGA Expo in the fall. Neither of the NSGA shows exists today, and the Super Show, which still operates, has shrunk greatly in size and significance, with an uncertain future.

Interestingly enough, the dominant sporting goods trade show in Europe, the International Trade Fair for Sports Equipment and Fashion (ISPO), is a horizontal show. It is held twice a year in Munich, Germany, and continues to survive and thrive, primarily because it has upgraded and updated its approach to vertical marketing—in effect, acting like a series of vertical trade shows with a fashion orientation.

In the U.S. market, vertical trade shows have become dominant. Not only is it easier for buyers to focus on the category, but vertical shows attract individuals and companies serving vendors, bringing people and information together with a focus on a specific sport or product category. The result is a show that is a much more productive experience.

The list below contains many of the leading trade shows currently operating in the industry.

- ASR (Action Sports) Show
- DEMA (Diving Equipment & Marketing)
- Health & Fitness Business Show
- ICAST/The Sportfishing Show
- Interbike (bicycling)
- Let's Play Hockey International Expo
- PGA Merchandise Show (golf)
- Shot Show (firearms, hunting)
- SnowSports Industries America (SIA) Show
- Surf Expo

In addition to these vertical sporting goods shows, many vendors and retailers will attend national apparel (MAGIC) and footwear (World Shoe Association) trade shows. Exhibitors at these shows offer all types of footwear and apparel, including athletic and non-athletic products.

Other trade shows are sponsored throughout the year by various buying groups (retailers and team dealers) and independent sales representative organizations for their members.

A major program related to industry education is the NSGA's annual Management Conference and Team Dealer Summit. The leading educational conference in the industry, it is attended by senior retail and vendor executives from all major segments of the industry, and features topical speakers and educational seminars. In addition to this conference, various publications and associations also sponsor seminars and conferences throughout the year, focusing on subjects of topical interest, such as licensing and new technology.

RELATED WEBSITES

American Sportfishing Association (ASA): www.asafishing.org
Canadian Sporting Goods Association (CSGA): www.csga.ca
National Bicycle Dealers Association (NBDA): http://nbda.com
National Golf Foundation: www.ngf.org
National Marine Manufacturers Association (NMMA): www.nmma.org
National Shooting Sports Foundation (NSSF): www.nssf.org
National Sporting Goods Association (NSGA): www.nsga.org
SnowSports Industries America (SIA): www.thesnowtrade.org
Sporting Goods Agents Association (SGAA): www.r-sports.com/SGAA
Sporting Goods Business (magazine): http://www.sportinggoodsbusiness.com/
Sporting Goods Dealer (magazine): www.sgdealer.com
Sporting Goods Manufacturers Association International (SGMA): www.sgma.com
Surf Industry Manufacturers Association (SIMA): www.sima.com
Tennis Industry Association: www.tennisindustry.org
World Federation of the Sporting Goods Industry (WFSGI): www.wfsgi.org

EXERCISES

1. Go to www.nsga.org, www.nssf.org and www.sgma.com. These organizations deal with the broad spectrum of vendors and retailers in the sporting goods industry. Study them and make a list of the kinds of services they offer. Determine how the organizations are similar and how they are different.

2. Visit a retail sporting goods store in order to put a face on the information provided in this book. When you do, observe how merchandise is presented and how the sales floor is handled.

3. Using the participation tables (7–13), write an analysis of the overall trends. Concentrate on trends within each of the tables. Focus on the kinds of sports that have grown since 1998 vs. the sports that have not grown or have declined over the past six years, and discuss some reasons you think affected the growth (or decline) of these sports.

4. Is equipment, apparel or footwear the largest segment of the market? What factor

or factors did you use to decide — was it dollar sales, your estimate of how many people made purchases? Why did you make this choice?

5. What are the six major consumer market segments within the overall industry? Is the consumer sporting goods market primarily concentrated among teenagers and young adults, or does it appeal to an "across-the-board" market?

3

Sporting Goods Vendors: Products, Market Size, Organizational Structure, and Market Segmentation

OVERVIEW

In early 2004, after 129 years, Spalding, the company many consider to be the modern sporting goods industry's founder, ceased to exist as a separate entity.

This chapter deals with sporting goods vendors (as we indicated in a previous chapter, "vendor" is the word we now use for manufacturers). These companies provide the products and services for the industry.

Sporting goods vendors operate in an environment often affected by outside influences over which the industry has no control. These outside influences play an important role. Some of these issues are consolidation, recreational facility management, and constraints of public ownership with a focus on profits, often resulting in reduced research investment compared with historical private ownership. Other issues, such as sourcing practices and the wide variety of vendor types e.g., footwear, apparel, and equipment, each with different production and marketing schedules, are less fundamental but nevertheless important when studying the industry. In most cases, sporting goods companies are physically structured similarly to other consumer product vendors who import all or most of their products, with brand/product management, sales and marketing management, field services and financial management.

At the end of this chapter, you should be able to:

- Determine the leading companies in the sporting goods industry.
- Understand why the industry is served by literally thousands of vendors.
- Identify the mission and purpose of a vendor.
- Identify the organizational structure of sporting goods vendors.
- Analyze common problems facing vendors in the industry.
- Analyze the different types of jobs held by sporting goods vendor employees.

DISCUSSION

Perhaps the most dramatic testimony to the uniqueness of the sporting goods industry is reflected by failed forays into the industry by consumer product companies in non-sports categories such as food and toiletries. During the 1970s, leading consumer products companies such as Pepsico (Wilson), Colgate (Bike, Bancroft, Ram), and Questor (Spalding) came and went, leaving with burned fingers and financial statements. More recently, the Italian apparel firm Benetton (Prince, Nordica, Rollerblade) had the same experience. While packaging and store display are important to the sale of sporting goods products, performance orientation and athletic imagery and understanding are far more important — they are absolutely vital to success. Until athletic footwear and apparel companies began to establish strong brands beginning in the 1970s, the industry was dominated by a few vendors— Wilson (golf, tennis, team), Spalding (golf, team), Rawlings (team), MacGregor (golf, team), Easton (baseball), Titleist (golf), Penn (tennis), Head (skiing), Rossignol (skiing), Salomon (bindings), Shakespeare (fishing), Remington and Winchester (firearms), Roadmaster and Huffy (bicycles), Coleman (camping), Hillerich & Bradsby (baseball), and CCM (ice hockey). While some of these companies still have substantial industry stakes, hundreds of other vendors have entered the marketplace, all participating in the enormous market expansion over the past 30 years. Coincidental with this expansion has been a strong move to overseas production, a changing retailer marketplace, and an enormous growth in sports coverage by broadcast and now Internet media resulting in a dynamically growing and shifting consumer demand for sports equipment, apparel and footwear.

There are over 3,000 companies who produce and sell some type of sports equipment, apparel or footwear. Over 80 percent of all companies are vertical; that is, they produce products for only one sport or one type of product for a sport, and their sales tend to be relatively small (less than $30,000,000). The Table 1 reflects sales of the majority of leading sporting goods companies in the equipment, apparel and footwear segments.

Other large sporting goods companies are listed below. Their sales figures are not available because they are privately owned or part of a conglomerate that does not publish separate data for these companies.

- Amerex Group
- Browning Arms Company
- Champion Products, Inc.
- Coleman Company
- Colt Holding Corporation
- Daiwa Sports
- Dunlop Sports
- Easton Sports
- Evinrude Outboard Motors (Bombardier)
- Marlin Firearms
- Mizuno Sports
- Outboard Marine (Bombardier)
- Prince Sports/Ektelon
- Winchester Rifles & Shotguns

How Sporting Goods Companies Are Organized

Vendors experienced what can be called a revolution between 1990 and 2000, in the form of consolidation, startling growth for some new companies (Under Armour, Callaway), the emergence of factory-owned retail stores (Nike, Reebok), and the emergence of online retailing of sporting goods (eBay). Many of the old ways of doing business are no longer viable.

By mid-2005, there were 12 major sporting goods conglomerates operating in the United States—conglomerates in the sense that they own several major brands. They are listed as a part of Table 1 below.

TABLE 1: LEADING SPORTING GOODS
COMPANIES WORLDWIDE SALES
(LATEST AVAILABLE DATA. SALES IN MIL.
UNLESS OTHERWISE INDICATED)

Company (FY)	FY Sales
Nike ('04)	12,300
Adidas-Salomon-TaylorMade ('04)	6,478 (euro)
Brunswick Corp. ('04) *	5,430
Reebok ('04)	3,785
Puma ('04)	1,530 (euro)
Timberland ('04)	1,501
Russell Corp. ('04)	1,298
Quiksilver ('04)	1,267
Fortune Brands (Golf Div.) ('04)	1,212
K2 Corp. ('04)	1,201
Columbia Sportswear ('04)	1,095
Wolverine World Wide, Inc. ('04)	992
Icon Health & Fitness ('03)	975
Skechers ('04)	920
New Balance ('03)	910 (est)
Callaway Golf ('04)	814
Oakley ('04)	586
Stride Rite (all products) ('04)	558
Wilson (Sub of Amer Group) ('04)	543
Nautilus Group ('04)	524
Head ('04)	479
Remington Arms ('04)	393
Johnson Outdoors ('04)	355
K-Swiss ('02)	290
Decker's ('04)	215
GIII Apparel ('04)	214
Ashworth ('04)	173
Sturm Ruger ('04)	146
Rocky Shoes & Boots ('04)	132
Cutter & Buck ('04)	128
Lacrosse Footwear ('04)	106
Cybex ('04)	103
Everlast ('04)	55
Aldila ('04)	53
Sport-Haley '04)	21

Sources: SGB's Inside Sporting Goods, Sporting Goods Business.

- Adidas (Headquartered in France: Adidas, CCM, Jofa, Koho, Reebok, Sport Maska, TaylorMade, The Hockey Company, Valley Apparel)
- Amer Group (Headquartered in Finland: Atomic, Precor, Salomon, Wilson)
- Brunswick Corporation (Brunswick Bowling and Billiards, Life Fitness, Mercury Marine, several boating companies)
- Fortune Brands (Cobra, FootJoy, Titleist)
- Icon Fitness (Gold's Gym, HealthRider, Icon, Image, NordicTrack, Pro Form, Reebok Fitness, Weider, Weslo)
- Johnson Outdoors (Eureka, Minn Kota, Ocean Kayak, ScubaPro)
- K2 Corp. (K2, Marker, Marmot, Rawlings, Ride, Shakespeare, Volkl, Worth)

- Nautilus Group (Bowflex, Nautilus, Schwinn Fitness, Stairmaster)
- Nike (Bauer, Converse, Hurley, Nike, Shaq, Starter)
- Quiksilver (Quiksilver, Rossignol)
- Russell Corp. (American Athletic, Bike, Nutmeg, Russell, Spalding)
- VF Corp. (Eastpak, Izod, Jansport, Kipling, Napapijri, Nautica, The North Face, Van's)

Five of these companies (Brunswick, Fortune Brands, Icon, Johnson and VF) own companies with similar product lines and/or serving similar market segments. Five companies (Adidas, Amer Group, K2, Nike and Russell) own companies in at least two distinctly different market segments and distinctly different product lines.

Consolidation has escalated in recent years. In 2005 alone, two major mergers occurred — Amer's acquisition of Salomon from Adidas and Adidas' acquisition of Reebok.

Within the sporting goods industry, it is often difficult for a single company to enjoy synergistic benefits from owning several brands. That's because either the brands offer products in different sports, or there is significant variation between demographic market segments served by the different brands, resulting in the need to focus on different channels of distribution and different media strategies.

The following article explains some of the basic business strategies underlying this recent trend towards mergers and acquisitions within the industry.

Salomon Sale to Amer Sports Extends Consolidation Trend
(SGB's Inside Sporting Goods, Vol. 16, no. 16, May 6, 2005)

The ski industry used to be run by a large number of independent companies, often owned by independent people with a long history in the sport. In the US, many companies were founded by veterans of the 10th Mountain Brigade. They created the US ski business after World War II. But things have changed in recent years.

More and more companies need a global presence to grow their brands. They also need economies of scale to offset economic conditions and currency fluctuations. Production in the US and Europe has become expensive for companies without the most modern production facilities.

K2 has been developing a ski/outdoor portfolio of some of the world's top wintersports brands (K2, Völkl, Marker, Ride, Liquid, Morrow and 5150). It also expanded its presence in the outdoor apparel sector via Ex-Officio and Marmot Mountain. KTO has taken huge steps in amassing revenues through acquisitions. Its CEO Richard Heckmann has been loudest about the importance of size and synergies in the current trade.

Recently, there was another merger in wintersports. Quiksilver surprised many by buying Rossignol. The trade and investors will have to wait until this synergies that have been promised will take place. The acquisition of Salomon from Adidas-Salomon by Amer Sports is just another example of consolidation driven by the new industry dynamics.

Three major sporting goods categories are dominated by one or two major vendors: Icon and Nautilus in fitness, Wilson and Prince in tennis racquets and Coleman in camping.

As Dick Cann, owner of Marlow Sports, Forestville, MD, sees it, the team sporting goods business is no di›erent than any other industry when it comes to consolidation. "The good will get better and grow," he says. "The ones that aren't good will get bought out by others or go out of business." *Sporting Goods Dealer,* November/December 2003.

Synergies are expected by Amer to reap savings of EUR 40 million by the end of FY08.

Adidas-Salomon CEO Herbert Hainer correctly said the acquisition of Salomon by Amer Sports would benefit both parties. The wintergoods/cycling/outdoor company did not fit all that well with its former parent, which has been forced to spend millions to recoup its Adidas footwear/apparel position in the US market. It tried hard to improve Salomon's bottom line by expanding its offerings to 12 months of the year. It gave special attention to the women's outdoor apparel market.

There were many more opportunities for growth and share appreciation in the Adidas brand and its soaring TaylorMade-Adidas Golf, which has been charging into the vacuum left by Callaway Golf and its conservative product introduction schedule.

In FY04, Salomon sales fell 0.8% to EUR 653 million. The gross profit fell to EUR 259 million (-2.8%). But the operating profit was a mere EUR 9 million vs. EUR 73.6 million. In 1Q05, Salomon sales continued to fall, down 8.5% in euros to EUR 112 million. The operating profit plunged 50.5% from a EUR million loss in '04 to another loss, EUR 25 million. It had to be clear to the AG's management in Herzo that much more money would be needed to bring Salomon back to its past glory.

Amer saw three reasons for the poor performance. First of all, there were the currency issues relating to the dollar and the yen.

Salomon's production was tied highly to the euro. The market conditions in Japan were no help. Salomon had a higher cost of ski production than Amer's Atomic. Salomon had earlier announced its intention to move much production to Rumania from France. Finally, there were unprofitable product lines.

There were rumors for months that the brand was on the block. The mark still had plenty of equity, but as Hainer put it, it was better situated where there could be economies of scale and synergies. This was critical to Adidas' search for a partner, he said.

At a Helsinki press conference, Amer CEO Roger Talermo spoke like Heckmann's echo, citing the consolidation of accounts as a major reason for the acquisition. He has seen six major customers combine into three in recent years. Suppliers are also consolidating, and the company did not want to be outside this trend.

Amer has to be very worried about the KTO onslaught; however the Salomon acquisition gives Amer very strong leverage. It makes the company the world leader in wintersports, with revenues of about EUR 600 million. It also brings more balanced global distribution. Salomon is much stronger as a company in Europe, while Atomic gets most of its sales from North America. The combined company would have had pro forma '04 revenues of EUR 1,688.9 million, with a gross profit of EUR 694.5 million and EBIT of 109.5 million. The result of the combination will make Amer the largest sports equipment manufacturer in the world, which Talermo said was the company's vision for some time.

The new company had, on a pro forma basis, 45% of its FY04 sales from North America, 10% from Asia Pacific and 45% from EMEA, a more balanced mix for Amer. Salomon would have been 39% of sales on a pro forma basis (not broken down into categories); golf 9%; racquet sports 12%; team sports 11%; wintersports (excluding Salomon) 12%; sports instruments 5%; and fitness 12%.

Amer will acquire a portfolio of hard and soft good brands along with Salomon. There could be a problem with the soft goods side in that Amer has no expertise in it. Wilson offers footwear but it's a small player. Talermo said the company had not wanted to get into apparel on its own, as it didn't have the expertise. Presumably, the acquisition will bring the talent needed to manage an apparel/footwear business.

But if Amer can improve Salomon's offerings, it would give K2 a very serious challenge. K2 owns some of the world's top selling wintersports marks. One ski exec told ISG last year, he was unimpressed with Salomon as an acquisition because its product leadership had fallen so much under Adidas ownership. It would cost him too much money in the short term to revive the mark.

It looks more and more as a battle between KTO and Amer for the leading position in general equipment sales. They go head-to-head with each other in the team sports sector. KTO owns Rawlings (Worth) while Amer has Wilson. Heckmann wants no part of the tennis business, which is too unprofitable for his taste. Although one of the first shareholders of Callaway, Heckmann has shown no interest in golf.

It's in wintersports that Amer gains a leg up. While it owns the Volant, Atomic and Dynamic ski brands, the acquisition brings more top brands and product categories. It seems our vendors are heading to a world where a limited number of companies own the majority of the world's marks.

Personnel/Job Functions

Sporting goods vendors have the following personnel/job functions:

- product design and development
- financial management
- web design, development and management
- field promotion specialists
- marketing/advertising/public relations/communications
- operations management
- manufacturing/sourcing
- sales
- customer service (in-house)

Companies selling products for multiple sports are usually structured with separate groups managing all aspects of product design, development and sales and marketing for each sport. Finance, personnel and customer service are most often centralized.

Complicating the vendor's ability to serve the marketplace is the need to service a

TABLE 2: ESTIMATED NUMBER OF
SPORTING GOODS VENDORS, BY CATEGORY
(DOES NOT INCLUDE SPECIALTY FIRMS WITH
SALES VOLUME LESS THAN $2–$3 MIL.
COMPANIES HAVE BEEN COUNTED MORE
THAN ONCE IF THEY OFFER MULTIPLE PRODUCT LINES)

Category	Number of Vendors
Apparel (All Types)	500
Golf	225
Fitness/Exercise	180
Camping (Outdoor)	175
Water Sports	135
Footwear	125
Baseball	110
Uniforms	85
Skiing	80
Snowboarding	80
Soccer	65
Hunting/Shooting	60
Optical Products	60
Fishing	54
Football	50
Ice Hockey	50
Basketball	40
Tennis	35
Volleyball	25
Field Hockey	10
Lacrosse	10

Sources: NSGA, SBRnet.

variety of different types of retail accounts. Pro shops or retail specialty stores may require more "hands-on" communication from vendors because purchasing is done by each outlet. Chain retail customers require different services—soliciting orders from the chain headquarters but servicing the merchandising and display needs of individual stores within a chain by vendor field sales personnel.

Overall Industry Vendor Structure

As discussed above, companies such as Wilson, Nike, Callaway, K2, and Icon Fitness offer a wide range of products in the market. As a rule, they divide assignments within the company according to product line. In most larger companies, similar sports e.g., racquet sports (tennis, racquetball, squash), are grouped under a director, with managers specializing in each sport reporting to the group director. If the product line is large enough, promotion specialists could be a part of this same group.

In some cases, vendors will license other companies to produce and sell products for which they are not set up to produce or import themselves. This practice has been prevalent almost from the industry's inception in the late 1800s. It might be interesting to know that up until the 1950s, Penn made all the tennis balls produced in the United States—under the Penn, Spalding and Wilson names.

Footwear and apparel products are offered by all several different types of companies:

- Companies offering only sports-oriented footwear and/or apparel. Among the better-known sports-oriented vendors of sports footwear and apparel are Reebok, New Balance, Saucony, K-Swiss, Puma, Fila, FUBU, Vans, Champion Sports, and Danskin.
- Companies selling sporting goods equipment as well as footwear and apparel. A good example is Russell Athletic, heretofore an apparel-only company, having recently acquired Spalding team sports products. In addition, equipment companies will often license apparel and footwear vendors to produce products using their name — such as Spalding T-shirts, Rawlings hats, etc. Other examples include Nike, Adidas and Wilson.
- Companies specializing in the general (non-sports) footwear and/or apparel markets but which have offerings in sports. Products are produced under the company's own name (such as Polo) or under the name of a sporting goods company. Among the best-known general apparel or footwear vendors offering sports products are Nautica, Polo, Ralph Lauren, Easy Spirit, Skechers, and Tommy Hilfiger.

The great majority of sporting goods vendors sell their products to retail customers by engaging the services of independent sales representatives. This approach has been with the industry since its early stages. Sporting goods is an industry with thousands of suppliers, most of whom are specialists in one or two product categories. In order to survive and prosper, retailers are obliged to offer their customers a wide choice of products which are produced by a very large number of manufacturers, but retailers simply don't have the time to meet with sales representatives from every one of their suppliers; thus the emergence of the independent sales representative. These organizations represent several vendors, usually no more than one in a single product category. They operate regionally, normally covering four to five states for the lines they represent.

Sourcing

Sourcing is a prime function within a company, involving locating suppliers in foreign countries, negotiating contracts, overseeing production and quality control, and shipping and warehousing. Sourcing management is usually done at the highest levels within a company because of its vital role in overall operations. In some cases, overseas factories produce merchandise for more than one vendor; thus the sourcer's role requires a great deal of skill and diplomacy, in addition to product and manufacturing expertise.

For example, at Wilson, sourcing is managed at the highest level for the product being sourced i.e., the director of product design and development, in conjunction with engineering design people on his or her staff.

Industry experts estimate that over 80 percent of all products are imported from other countries. Products that are not sourced overseas generally include such items as wooden baseball bats, athletic tape, basketball backboards, and food/liquid containers.

Here is a summary of the sourcing patterns for major segments of the market:

- Activewear: Nearly all activewear apparel is produced overseas.
- Baseball: Batting gloves, mitts and balls are largely produced overseas.
- Bicycles: Most bicycles are produced overseas, particularly those at higher price points.
- Boats: Most boats are produced in the United States.
- Firearms and ammunition: Ammunition is mostly made in the United States. Guns are produced both in the United States and in foreign markets.
- Fishing tackle: Nearly all fishing tackle is sourced from other companies, except for lures, for which a substantial portion is manufactured in the United States.
- Fitness equipment: Most products such as elliptical machines, home gyms, rowing machines, stationary bikes and treadmills are produced overseas; weights and weight benches are largely manufactured in the United States.
- Footwear: Nearly all footwear is produced overseas.
- Golf: The great majority of parts for golf clubs (shafts and heads) are sourced from other countries, although some heads and shafts are made in the United States.
- Inflated balls: Most inflated balls, particularly rubber balls, are produced overseas. Leather balls are produced both overseas and, to some extent, in the United States.
- Ski equipment: Most skis, boots and bindings are produced overseas.
- Sports medicine products: Most sports medicine products are manufactured in the United States.
- Swimwear: Nearly all swimwear is produced overseas.
- Tennis: Nearly all racquets are produced overseas; whereas most balls are produced in the United States.
- Uniforms: Uniforms for professional, college and high school teams are produced in the United States as well as overseas, although numbers and letters are most often applied in the United States.

Branding

In July 2005, *Sporting Goods Business* magazine reported on results of a major research project which they sponsored to identify the significance of branding in the industry. According to *SGB*, the sporting goods industry is one of America's last bastions of power brands.

Brand Perceptions
(Sporting Goods Business, July 2005)

Twenty years ago this month, *Rolling Stone* magazine launched an award-winning advertising campaign, the goal of which was to debunk conventional wisdom and show potential advertisers the power of their audience.

The campaign had a simple theme: "Perception vs. Reality." On one side of the page, the ad featured stereotyped images of the readers marketers thought were subscribing to the magazine. There were long-haired hippies waving peace signs while standing in front of a beat-up Volkswagen van. The ad carried a bold, one-word caption: "Perception." On the opposite page was a photo of well-dressed, well-scrubbed preppies standing in front of a European luxury car. This full-page image also carried one word: "Reality."

The message, of course, was that although you may believe one thing to be true about a magazine's audience, the truth is often quite different. The same perception versus reality test can be applied to the sports brands in the market today.

What brands do consumers know and what do they really think of them? Those were the questions we sought to answer four years ago when we launched the SGBrand Study, which initially measured consumer recognition of top brands and athletes. Over the past four years, SGB has refined the study to focus on consumer recognition and perception of top sports brands and retailers. Part I of the study, which covers the brands, appears on the following pages. Part II, which covers consumers' experiences in stores and their opinions of those stores, will run this fall.

Herewith are the key findings in this year's study.

The SGB 50: The most widely recognized sports brands by American consumers 10 to 65 years old.

RANKING/COMPANY NAME/PERCENTAGE

1. Reebok/96.5%	19. Fila/74.6%	34. The North Face /60.1%
2. Adidas/96.4%	20. K-Swiss/73.4%	35. Body Glove/58.5%
3. Nike/96.1%	21. Nautilus/72%	36. Avia/56.7%
4. Spalding/90.9%	22. Coleman/71.8%	37. Jantzen/56.1%
5. Puma/90.4%	23. Russell Athletic/71.7%	38. Etonic/55.2%
6. Converse/90.3%	24. Oakley/70.5%	39. Saucony/55.1%
7. Speedo/89.1%	25. Louisville Slugger/69.5%	40. Vans/54.2%
8. Wilson/88%	26. Birkenstock/68.9%	41. Starter/53.6%
9. New Balance/86.2%	27. Everlast/68.4%	42. Rollerblade/53.2%
10. LA Gear/85.6%	28. Ocean Pacific/67%	43. Head/52.2%
11. Swiss Army/82.4%	29. JanSport/66.4%	44. Quiksilver/51.2%
12. Schwinn/82.3%	30. Columbia Sportswear /66.2%	45. Pony/50%
13. Timberland/81.7%	31. Dunlop/65.4%	46. Riddell/49.4%
14. Rawlings/80.8%	32. Danskin/63.5%	47. Callaway/48.8%
15. Champion/80.5%	33. Asics/61.7%	48. Umbro/47%
16. Skechers/78%		49. K2/45.8%
17. Huffy/77.5%		50. Teva/44.7%
18. Gold's Gym/75.3%		

- BRAND POWER RATING

Respondents were asked to rate their perceptions of the quality of the products offered by top brands.

Respondents were instructed to base their perceptions on personal experience or anything that they may have heard about the quality of the products. Since many of the brands offer a variety of specific products (footwear, apparel, etc.) respondents were also directed to base their answers on their OVERALL perceptions of the quality associated with the products offered by the brands.

A five point scale was used, where a "5" meant extremely high quality and a "1" meant extremely poor quality.

The Brand Power Rating incorporates two dimensions: awareness and perceptions of quality. The BPR is derived using a simple mathematical calculation: awareness level multiplied by the mean quality rating. Therefore, a perfect BPR would be 500.

The following chart displays the Brand Power rating for some of the most well-known and relevant brands.

Brand/Awareness Level/Mean Quality Rating/Brand Power Rating

Nike/96.1%/4.1/394
Adidas/96.4%/3.8/366
Reebok/96.5%/3.6/347
New Balance/86.2%/3.9/336
Swiss Army/82.4%/4/330
Timberland/81.7%/4/327
Spalding/90.9%/3.4/309
Wilson/88%/3.5/308
Puma/90.4%/3.4/307
Converse/90.3%/3.2/289
Rawlings/80.8%/3.5/283

Champion/80.5%/3.5/282
Nautilus/72%/3.7/266
The North Face/61%/4.2/256
Skechers/78%/3.2/250
Russell/71.7%/3.4/244
Everlast/68.4%/3.4/233
LA Gear/85.6%/2.7/231
Ocean Pacific/67%/3.2/214
Dunlop/65.4%/3.2/209
Under Armour/41.4%/4/166

The Million Dollar Questions

Which three brands are for people your age?
16–24/25–34/35–44/45–54/55–65
Nike 74.7%/Nike 73.8%/Nike 73.9%/Nike 62.4%/Nike 54.6%
Adidas 60.2%/Adidas 38.8%/Adidas 37.7%/Adidas 28%/Adidas 22.3%
Reebok 19.3%/Reebok 27.6%/Reebok 35.8%/Reebok 26%/Reebok 21.5%
New Balance 13.3%/New Balance 18.2%/New Balance 15.6%/New Balance 22.8%/New Balance 15.4%
Puma 10.8%/The North Face 5.6%/Wilson 6.6%/Wilson 9.6%/Wilson 11.5%
Under Armour 6%/Asics 5.1%/Champion 6.6%/Champion 4.8%/Titleist 10%
The North Face 6%/Puma 4.7%/The North Face 4.3%/The North Face 4%/Callaway 7.7%
The North Face 6%/Puma 4.7%/The North Face 4.3%/The North Face 4%/Callaway 7.7%

Which three brands are for serious athletes?

Nike/56.3%	Under Armour/6.3%	Saucony/3.4%
Adidas/27.7%	Asics/4.7%	Mizuno/3.2%
Reebok/16.4%	The North Face/4.3%	
New Balance/11%	Wilson/3.7%	

Which three brands provide value for the money?

Nike/38.7%	Wilson/8.2%	wear/5%
Adidas/25.2%	Champion/6.3%	Asics/3.7%
Reebok/21.5%	Converse/5.2%	Puma/2.9%
New Balance/18.7%	Columbia Sports-	

Which three brands are worth spending money on?

Nike/46.6%	Patagonia/4.5%	Callaway/2.9%
Adidas/20.6%	Asics/4.1%	Columbia Sportswear
Reebok/13.4%	Wilson/3.4%	/2.6%
New Balance/12.1%	Puma/3.1%	

Marmot, Titleist, Under Armour, Mountain Hardwear, Saucony, Mizuno and Ping all scored higher than 2%.

Which three brands are cutting-edge?

Nike/58.4%   Asics/4.1%   Puma/2.8%
Adidas/22.4%   Under Armour/3.9%   Arc'Teryx/2.7%
Reebok/14.2%   Patagonia/3.4%
New Balance/10.1%   Mizuno/2.8%

Which three brands are old and outdated?

Converse/25.9%   Nike/11.5%   Wilson/6.5%
Reebok/23.2%   Puma/9.5%   Champion/4.7%
Adidas/15.9%   Keds/8.6%   K-Swiss/4%

Which three brands were, but are no longer, cool?

Reebok/25.2%   Puma/8.7%   Fila/3.4%
Converse/23.2%   Keds/6.1%   Champion/3.3%
Nike/17.5%   Wilson/4.4%
Adidas/16.6%   New Balance/4.1%

Respondent Profile

Male: 52.3%   Female: 47.7%   Mean Age: 41.2
Mean Annual Spending on Sports & Recreation: $721
Median HHI: $62,500

(Editor's Note: Because the study was conducted over the Internet, the sample skews older, whiter and more affluent than the U.S. population.)

How the study was conducted

The SGB Brand Awareness study was conducted by Leisure Trends, Inc. of Boulder, CO, in April 2005 among a nationwide sample of Americans between the ages of 16 and 65. Potential respondents were sourced from lists of Americans who had self-classified themselves as having an interest in sports and recreational activities. The study was conducted via the Internet. Potential respondents were e-mailed an invitation that linked them to a self-administered Web-based questionnaire. All respondents were informed that the completion of the study would enter them into a random prize drawing that included cash awards.

In total, 1,031 individuals between ages 16 and 65 participated in the study. Total results from this study can be projected to the U.S. population of Internet users with a margin of error of +/- 3 percent.

Major Issues Facing Vendors

Some of the major issues facing sporting goods vendors include product liability, human rights overseas, e-commerce, and athlete endorsements.

Product Liability

Perhaps the most dramatic reflection of product liability problems is that the number of football helmet vendors is now three, compared with over 50 companies offering helmets as recently as 20 years ago.

Human Rights Overseas

The great majority of sports footwear and apparel vendors contract for production directly from overseas producers. The issue of human rights has become a major consideration for all sports athletic and apparel vendors, particularly with college students who have participated in the formation of organizations to pressure sports apparel companies to adopt standards related to the wide disparity of labor practices in many far-east companies compared with U.S. labor and salary standards. This problem is more visible in the sporting goods industry because of the emotional ties that often exist between sporting goods companies such as Nike or Reebok and their customers.

E-commerce

E-commerce has been a particular problem for vendors to manage for a variety of reasons. Most vendors don't sell products on their own sites in deference to their retail customers, who obviously frown on such tactics. Another problem facing vendors—how to create and maintain a website in keeping with the quality and high performance levels of their products, while at the same time doing so within the framework of limited funds allocated to web development and maintenance.

Athlete Endorsements

Athlete endorsement expenditures are often significant for sporting goods companies. The ability to predict the success of an athlete's endorsement on product sales and to choose athletes who can most benefit the brand is as much an art as it is a science. Judging how much, with whom and when to spend on athlete endorsement can be critical to the ultimate success of most large sporting goods companies.

RELATED WEBSITES

ADIDAS: www.adidas.com
American Sportfishing Association (ASA): www.asafishing.org
Burton: www.burton.com
Coleman: www.coleman.com/coleman/home.asp
Icon Health & Fitness: www.iconfitness.com
K2 Corp: www.k2sports.com
National Golf Foundation (NGF): www.ngf.org
National Marine Manufacturers Association (NMMA): www.nmma-intl.org
National Shooting Sports Foundation (NSSF): www.nssf.org
National Sporting Goods Association (NSGA): www.nsga.org
Nike: www.nikebiz.com
Outdoor Recreation Council of America (ORCA): www.ORCA.org
Rawlings Sporting Goods Company: www.rawlings.com
Reebok: www.rbk.com
Remington Arms: www.remington.com
Russell Athletic: www.russellathletic.com
Salomon Sports: www.salomonsports.com
SBRnet: www.sbrnet.com
SnowSports Industries America (SIA): www.thesnowtrade.org
Sporting Goods Agents Association (SGAA): www.r-sports.com/SGAA
Sporting Goods Manufacturers Association (SGMA): www.sgma.com
Wilson Sporting Goods Company: www.wilsonsports.com

EXERCISES

1. Choose three companies (larger ones, such as Adidas, Burton Snowboards, Callaway, Coleman, Icon Fitness, K2 Corp., New Balance, Nike, Rawlings, Reebok, Reming-

ton Arms, Russell, Salomon, Titleist, or Wilson) and review their websites. Analyze each site and compare them with respect to the following criteria:

- What you believe they are trying to accomplish
- How well they present their products
- How informative they are about the company
- Ease of navigation
- Ability to find what you might be looking for when visiting the site

2. For two of the three companies you chose for Exercise 1, compare the two companies for each of the following questions:

a. What products do they sell?

b. Do they offer products for sale on the web, or do they try to drive prospects to their retail stores, or both?

c. How well do you think they present their products? If you are familiar with the company from your past experience, is their presentation on the web consistent with your image of the company? Why or why not?

d. How easy (or difficult) is it for you to navigate their site?

e. What was the most meaningful/exciting thing you learned at each of these sites? Briefly explain why.

f. In your opinion, what is one thing each of these two companies can do to improve their site?

3. Of the vendors who manufacture sporting goods, which product category has the most number of vendors? The smallest number of vendors?

4

Channels of Distribution: Consumer Retail, Consumer Online, Team Dealers, and Distributors

OVERVIEW

Approximately 50 percent of sporting goods equipment sales are done in stores other than full-line and specialty sporting goods stores.

NSGA

This chapter deals with how sporting goods products are distributed from the producer to the ultimate consumer. There are really three different types of consumers (approximately 90 percent of all industry sales): individuals, teams or institutions; and corporations. The consumer market is defined as individual purchases for the buyer's own use or as a gift. Within the consumer market, there are considerable variations in the relative importance of different retail outlets, depending on a number of variables that will be explored in-depth later in this chapter. Economic considerations and overall retailing trends have exerted a major impact on retailing within the industry, in the form of retailing company consolidations, rapid growth in the size of typical full-line sporting goods retailers and the growing trend toward public ownership of retailing firms. Other trends impacting the consumer segment of the industry include an expanding role of department and discount stores in the sports apparel market, and the growing ability of traditional full-line sporting goods stores to sell high-performance products, which historically has been the province of sports retailing specialists.

Full-line sporting goods stores have experienced a dramatic change over the last 30 years, from basically locally-owned stores to the national and retail chains of today that dominate the full-line sporting goods retail landscape. Not only have chains become the dominant factor, but store size has also increased dramatically. It's not unusual to find full-line sporting goods stores of at least 50,000 square feet — with many even larger than that — compared historically with stores in the 10,000–15,000 square foot range. Larger stores have several advantages, not the least of which is to enable full-line sporting goods retailers to give the appearance of lower prices as they compete with mass merchants such as Wal-Mart and Target, who have aggressively increased their involvement in sporting goods, particularly since athletic apparel and footwear have become so important within the overall marketplace for sporting goods.

Interestingly enough, while it might seem that larger full-line retailers would inhibit

49

growth of specialty stores, the opposite has actually happened. Specialty stores, which cater to experienced, performance-oriented customers have actually grown in importance, and specialty store chains are now a major factor in this retailing category. With the enormous growth of the industry over the past 30 years and the increasing importance of technology-driven products, it is the personal expertise uniquely delivered by sporting goods specialty retailers that has become more important than ever.

The team market includes schools and amateur and professional leagues. The commercial markets include private clubs, fitness clubs, and corporations. Team dealers continue to dominate sales of equipment and apparel to sports teams and leagues. Sales to commercial markets are made primarily by vendors or wholesalers.

At the end of this chapter, you should be able to:

- Evaluate the different types of retailers that sell sporting goods to consumers.
- Identify how the type of product influences the choice of retailers.
- Identify how the market to be reached influences the choice of retailers.
- Identify the organizational structure of sporting goods retailers.
- Understand the recent consolidation trends in the industry.
- Analyze common problems facing retailers and wholesalers in the sporting goods industry.
- Analyze the different types of jobs held by sporting goods company employees.
- Identify the names and types of associations serving retailers.
- Understand the role of team dealers in the industry.

DISCUSSION

Factors Influencing Consumer Retailing Preferences

Consumers face a wide range of retailing choices when purchasing sporting goods products. Three major factors significantly influence where they ultimately shop:
1. demographics/lifestyle of the consumer (age, income, gender, etc.)
2. participant market segmentation (skilled vs. unskilled, new vs. experienced, and frequent vs. occasional participation)
3. purpose of purchase (casual use vs. participation use)

Demographics

One fascinating aspect of sporting goods purchasing behavior is that interest in a sport often transcends age differences. For example, no matter what your age, if you're a low-handicap golfer you'll most likely find a way to raise enough money to purchase high-performance clubs, no matter what your personal income happens to be. However, income often plays a major role in where consumers make their purchases. Using golf as an example, higher-income golfers tend to play at private clubs, and at least some of them purchase their clubs at their club pro shop because they are regularly exposed to the products in these shops. Higher-income hunters and fishermen will be more likely to purchase products from specialty hunting/fishing retailers, as opposed to discount stores and full-line sporting goods stores.

Gender is an important factor for many sporting goods products. Women are accustomed to shopping at department and discount retailers, and are generally more inclined to purchase footwear and apparel, as well as equipment at these outlets. However, traditional sporting goods retailers are making a concerted effort to attract more women to their stores. To the extent that these efforts succeed, the role of gender will become less important in determining where sporting goods products are sold.

Participant Segmentation

As indicated above, the most obvious participant differentiation occurs in three areas—experience, skill level, and the frequency of participation. These factors play a major role in determining how much money the participant is willing to spend and in the characteristics and features of the product they ultimately purchase. As a general rule, the skilled and/or deeply involved participants prefer to purchase from sports specialty shops focused on the sports of interest to them, providing of course that the specialty shop offers sufficiently wide brand and product feature selection.

Historically, the difference between traditional sporting goods stores and sports specialists was clearly defined. Specialists featured top-of-the-line products, whereas full-line sporting goods stores generally featured lower- and mid-priced products. In recent years, the pressure on major full-line retailers to increase sales resulted in pressure on vendors to make all their products available for sale to them, even higher-priced merchandise. Specialists retaliated by offering improved services, including specialized advice, instructional programs, and allowing consumers to "demo" products. However this ultimately resolves itself, the consumer will be the ultimate winner.

Purpose of Purchase

Knowing how consumers use the products they purchase is particularly important for sporting goods footwear and apparel. Industry studies have consistently shown that over half of most athletic footwear and apparel is purchased for casual wear, and that over half of the people who participate in most sports activities only occasionally or rarely purchase athletic footwear and apparel for casual wear. Clearly, this impacts how much the consumer is willing to spend for these products, what types of products they purchase and where they make their purchase. For example, cleated footwear is sold exclusively to participants, but tennis shoes appeal to a wide casual market. Individuals who purchase such products as tennis shoes or golf-type shirts for casual wear are less likely to buy top-of-the-line products, and they are more willing to make their purchases at department or discount stores.

Sporting Goods Retail Market Segmentation

Over 90 percent of consumer sales are made in approximately 42,000 retail stores. The remaining 7 percent of sales are made by mail order and online-only retailers.

Full-line sporting goods, sports specialty and discount stores sell all three main categories of products—equipment, apparel and footwear. Department stores primarily sell apparel, footwear, and fitness equipment. Other types of outlets sell products appropriate for their non-sports offerings—family shoe stores sell some athletic footwear, women's apparel outlets and chains sell some athletic wear, etc.

Illustrating the dramatic growth of large sporting goods chains, Table 2 reflects dollar sales (in millions) of the top ten full-line sporting goods retail chains. Sales of the top 15 chains more than doubled between 1997 and 2004.

TABLE 1: NUMBER OF OUTLETS SELLING SPORTING GOODS

Type of Outlet Goods	# Retailers Selling Sporting
Full-line Sporting Goods Stores	7,000*
Sports Specialists/Pro Shops	
(Golf, Skateboard, Ski, Tennis, Surfing, Fitness, etc.)	18,000*
Athletic Footwear Stores	5,000
Department Stores	3,000
Discount Stores	4,000
Other (Family Footwear, Warehouse Clubs,	
General Specialty, Factory Outlets, etc.)	5,000
Total	42,000

* These numbers are storefront, that is, the number of store locations. Many of these locations may be owned by a single chain.
  Sources: NSGA, Sporting Goods Business, U.S. Census.

TABLE 2: ANNUAL SALES OF LEADING SPORTING
GOODS AND ATHLETIC FOOTWEAR CHAINS
(RANKED BY 2004 SALES)

Retail Chain	Dominant Products	$ Sales (bil.) rounded to nearest bil.		
		1997	2004	% Change
Foot Locker	Footwear	$3.9	$5.4	+38.5%
The Sports Authority‡	Full Line	1.5	2.4	+60.0%
Dick's**	Full Line	0.6	2.1†	+250.0%
Cabela's	Fish/Hunt/Camp/Boat	0.6	1.6	+167.7%
Bass Pro Shops	Fish/Hunt/Camp/Boat	0.3	1.6 (est.)*	+433.3%
Finish Line	Footwear	0.4	1.2	+300.0%
Pacific Sunwear	Sun/Fun	0.2	1.2	+500.0%
Academy Sports	Full Line	0.4	1.1 (est.)*	+175.0%
REI	Hike/Camp/Climb	0.5	0.8 (est.)*	+60.0%
Modell's	Full Line	0.3	0.5	+66.6%
Hibbett Sporting Goods	Full Line	0.1	0.4	+300.0%
Total		8.8	18.3	+108.0%

*Year 2003
†Includes Galyan's for last six months of 2004.
‡Includes The Sports Authority, Gart, Sportmart, Oshman's.
**Includes Dick's and Galyan's.
Sources: SGB's Inside Sporting Goods, Sporting Goods Business, financial reports.

Sales growth for these leading retailers (+108 percent between 1997 and 2004) is significantly greater than total industry growth during the six-year period between 1998 and 2004 (+8.5 percent). Every chain in Table 2 experienced significantly above-average growth compared with the total industry, thus reflecting, among other things, the enormous consolidation that occurred among the largest sporting goods retailers.

An interesting aspect of these trends is the wide variety of retailing product strate-

---

Wal-Mart is the largest sporting goods retailer in the U.S. market, with sales of $8.5 billion in 2003, nearly twice as much as Foot Locker, the number two retailer.

In 2004, Dick's Sporting Goods purchased Galyan's Trading Company. Sales of Dick's and Galyan's combined exceeded $2.2 in 2003, rivaling sales of The Sports Authority (the result of a merger between The Sports Authority and Gart Sports in 2003) for the largest full-line sporting goods chain in the U.S. market.

gies that prevail—full-line sporting goods coverage (Dick's, The Sports Authority, Academy, Modell's, Hibbett), the sun/fun market (Pacific Sunwear), the camping/hiking/climbing market (REI), and the hunting/fishing/boating/camping market (Bass Pro, Cabela's).

According to a survey by *Sporting Goods Business* magazine in 2003, sales by the top 100 sporting goods retailers (including sporting goods, department and discount stores) were 37.2 billion dollars. Just 11 of these retailers (those listed in Table 2) represent nearly one-half of this total. The combined total of all storefronts owned by these 100 top chains equaled 24,075, equaling average sales per store of 1.5 million dollars. Thus, these chains represent 60 percent of all retailer storefronts in the industry, and their sales represent over 80 percent of all in-store (as opposed to mail order or online) consumer purchases of sporting goods equipment, apparel and footwear.

Selling to Retailers

The great majority of consumer-oriented sporting goods products are sold directly by vendors to retailers, using either their own fully employed sales representatives or independent sales representatives. Generally speaking, the larger the company, the more likely it is to employ their own field sales staff.

Some vendors have policies that limit the number and types of accounts that are permitted to sell their merchandise, although this policy is less restrictive than in the past. For example, until recently, most "pro" lines of golf equipment were sold only to "green grass" accounts, that is, shops located at golf courses. Now golf equipment, apparel and footwear vendors sell to off-course golf specialty shops and in many cases, to full-line sporting goods stores. In the ski and bicycle industries, some companies restrict sales to retail specialists in the category. Some vendors exercise these restrictions for all their products, others use it selectively, allowing full-line sporting goods stores to sell some products but restricting premium products to retailing specialists.

One primary reason that vendors would concentrate on sales to specialists is that selling higher-priced, more complex equipment to consumers requires a level of sales skills normally found in sports specialty stores. However, recently some chains have recognized the value of well-trained sales associates (as they are called in the industry), and these chains are raising their standards for hiring and training sales floor employees.

BUYING GROUPS

While larger retail chains tend to buy individually from vendors, smaller chains and independent retailers often buy through buying groups. Retailers often choose to belong to these groups because they often receive lower prices from vendors as part of a group than they would if they were to purchase independently. Among the major buying groups are Sports, Inc., National Buying Syndicate (NBS), Worldwide Distributors, SSL and SMC (specialty store groups). Combined, they represent over 1,000 retail accounts and over 2,000 storefronts (individual store locations).

Other buying groups, such as hardware co-ops Ace and True Value and team dealer buying groups—Athletic Dealers of America (ADA) and Team Athletic Goods (TAG)—purchase sporting goods products on behalf of their members.

INDEPENDENT SALES REPRESENTATIVES

Generally, the largest vendors tend to employ their own sales force. Smaller companies tend to use the services of independent sales representatives. Independent representatives will usually sell several different product lines, normally offering only one brand within any given product category. Independent representatives do not take title to the merchandise they sell — they solicit orders and pass them on to vendors whom they represent in return for a commission on sales. Some vendors reserve major retailers as "house accounts," that is, they sell directly to these retailers, leaving smaller and regional customers to be serviced by independent sales representatives.

WHOLESALERS

The use of wholesalers and distributors is relatively limited in the sporting goods industry, particularly in the recent past. One exception exists primarily for outdoor products, including hunting, fishing, and archery products. There are hundreds of small vendors making one or two products serving this market, e.g., duck calls, specialized fishing lures, etc., and there are still thousands of smaller, specialized retailers selling these products. As long as this pattern holds— many smaller vendors and a specialized retailer market — vendors of such products will be unable to sell these products to these retailers without the existence of wholesalers.

Traditionally, wholesalers have benefited smaller sporting goods vendors who cannot find adequate independent sales representation or who are not able to support the credit services needed by most retailers. Most of these vendor's products are highly specialized and again, it's not economical for independent representatives to provide the effort and widespread coverage needed to meet retail demand. These wholesalers tend to promote their products to retailers through non-personal channels (direct mail, etc.) rather than supporting a full-blown sales force. In selected cases, wholesalers will represent larger vendors in order to sell to smaller retailers, allowing vendors and independent sales reps to devote more time to larger retailers.

A third area where wholesalers are active is in certain specialized markets, such as golf and cycling. There are large numbers of specialty retailers in these categories. With hundreds of vendors providing some specialized products for these markets, wholesalers are necessary for smaller companies to distribute their products to specialty retail customers. Finally, product selection may be very regional, as in the cycling industry, making the wholesaler a more effective means of servicing such markets.

While there are no specific figures on the importance of wholesalers, industry experts indicate that wholesalers are most important in the fishing market, where an estimated 20 to 30 percent of all purchases for resale by retailers are made from wholesalers, the balance coming directly from vendors. In total, combining all sporting goods products, retailers purchase approximately 10 percent of their goods from wholesalers, with the remainder (90 percent) coming from vendors. As the sporting goods specialty and full-line retailing landscape becomes more and more dominated by chains, however, the need for wholesalers will decline. An example is the recent demise of a major general sporting goods and footwear wholesaler, Reda Sports.

TRADE SHOWS

Trade shows have long been an integral part of the sporting goods industry. A trade show is simply a place where a large number of vendors present their merchandise in one place at a given point in time, usually over a three to four day period. In recent years, there has been a marked decline in horizontal shows, that is, shows featuring many different sports and product categories, and a corresponding gain in vertical shows, which serve particular industry merchandise categories. A vertical show features one or two product categories, such as outdoor, action sports, exercise/fitness, skiing/snowboarding, ice hockey, cycling, hunting/shooting, golf, or fishing.

Some trade shows are sponsored by industry trade groups, such as the Shot Show, sponsored by the National Shooting Sports Foundation; the PGA Merchandise Show (golf), sponsored by the PGA of America; and the Ski Show, sponsored by SnowSports Industries America. The Super Show remains the only major horizontal show in the United States, that is, a show combining exhibitors for several different sporting goods categories. The ISPO is a major international horizontal trade show, produced in Munich, Germany, twice a year (winter and summer). Exhibitors at the Super Show and the ISPO show include major companies from all parts of the world.

The largest U.S. commercial producer of vertical trade shows is VNU, headquartered in Holland, with major U.S. offices in New York and Laguna Beach, California. VNU shows cover fitness, cycling, outdoor, surfing and action sports.

The primary function of trade shows in the sporting goods industry is to provide an opportunity for all retailers and others interested in the industry to look at new products, make product comparisons, meet company personnel, and find new suppliers. They also provide excellent opportunities for industry networking and communications.

Selling Directly to Consumers

Some vendors, primarily in the footwear and apparel segments, have opened factory outlet stores. Some of these are in warehouse-type locations and some are located in shopping malls and in high-traffic downtown retail locations. Non-athletic footwear and apparel companies have long practiced this type of direct selling, and it is now becoming more prevalent than ever in the sporting goods industry. It is estimated that at least 5 percent or more of all sales volume in the footwear and apparel categories is done through factory outlets.

Another form of direct selling to the consumer is the Infomercials (a televised commercial lasting for up to 30 minutes or longer promoting a product), used to sell directly to consumers on a selective basis for certain products, primarily fitness and specialized golf clubs. As online purchasing behavior expands and broadband is used on a more widespread basis, infomercials could play an even larger role in selling to the consumer.

A third form of direct selling to the consumer is online selling by vendors. This is a complicated issue because retailers become concerned when vendors begin selling directly to their customers. You'll read more about e-commerce in chapter 9.

Patterns of Retail Distribution

The type of retailer that dominates sales for any given product category depends on the product. The general rule is that higher-priced, performance-type products are sold predominantly through full-line sporting goods stores and sports specialty stores (including pro shops). Department and discount stores generally feature products at lower and mid-range price points. However, in recent years the dividing line has blurred between different outlet types. For example, department stores and mass merchants will often feature higher-priced, better equipment as well as medium to lower price lines.

Now let's take a closer look at the three different types of product categories—equipment, apparel and footwear. We'll identify the different patterns of retail distribution depending on the product.

SPORTS EQUIPMENT

There are significant variations in the outlet types offering products depending on the specific product and/or product category:

- Products in categories such as golf, scuba, climbing, boating, and ski equipment sell the majority of their high-end products through pro shops and specialty sport stores that deal almost exclusively with each product. This is less true for medium and lower-end priced products, which are often sold through full-line sporting goods stores and mass merchants.
- Products in camping, fishing and other outdoor recreation categories such as tents, sleeping bags, coolers, stoves, fishing rods and reels, and accessories, tend to be sold through mass merchants (except for the most sophisticated products in these categories).
- Fitness equipment enjoys significant sales in several different channels—mass merchants, specialty fitness stores and full-line sporting goods stores.
- Team sports products (including products for sports medicine) are primarily sold to consumers through full-line sporting goods and mass merchants.
- With regard to online sales, we'll deal with that in chapter 9.

ATHLETIC/SPORTS FOOTWEAR

There are six different types of retail outlets that dominate the athletic footwear market:

1. specialty athletic footwear stores (Foot Locker, The Finish Line, etc.)
2. full-line sporting goods stores (The Sports Authority, etc.)
3. department stores (Sears, Macy's, Kohl's, etc.)
4. discount stores (Wal-Mart, Target, etc.)
5. factory outlet stores
6. full-line shoe retailers (Payless and Famous Footwear)

Performance products, that is, shoes designed to appeal primarily to sports participants, sell for higher prices and are generally sold in sporting goods and sports specialty stores. Athletic footwear products that have more appeal to the casual market are generally purchased in department and discount stores.

For certain types of shoes, particularly running shoes, mail order, catalog and online sales are growing in importance as retail outlets. Recently, mail order and catalog specialists have expanded to include online marketing, and are experiencing sales growth beyond the industry average.

Table 3 reflects the distribution of sales for all types of sporting goods equipment,

---

Full-line sporting goods stores have increased their share of the total market by at least 25 percent since 1993, despite significant competition from discounters and sports specialty shops. Source: NSGA.

TABLE 3: CONSUMER EXPENDITURES BY OUTLET TYPE,
BY MAJOR CATEGORY (LATEST AVAILABLE DATA)

	% of Total Dollar Sales, by Major Category		
Item	*Equipment (2004)*	*Footwear (2004)*	*Apparel (1999)*
Sporting Goods Stores	22.5	15.2	16.3*
Specialty Athl. Footwear Stores	n/a	15.4	n/a
Specialty Sport Shops (incl. Fitness)	17.5	4.9	n/a
Pro Shops	7.9	1.2	n/a
Discount Stores	16.8	12.2	22.8
Department Stores	14.9	18.4	28.1
Family Footwear Stores	n/a	13.1	n/a
Factory Outlet Stores	n/a	7.5	n/a
Online (Internet)	7.3	3.4	n/a
Mail Order	1.6	4.0	6.2
Specialty Apparel	n/a	n/a	10.6
Off Price/Warehouse Club/Factory	3.1	n/a	10.0
Other Outlets	8.3	4.6	6.0
Total	100.0%	100.0%	100.0%

Includes sporting goods, athletic footwear, specialty sport and pro shops.
Source: NSGA.

apparel and footwear combined. As indicated in the table, there are five different types of stores (sporting goods, specialty athletic footwear, discount, department and family footwear) that have at least 12 percent of all shoe sales, reflecting the complexity of distribution for sports footwear compared with other types of shoes, which are primarily sold through general shoe, department and discount stores.

ATHLETIC APPAREL

Over 50 percent of all athletic apparel is sold through department or discount stores, compared with 35 percent of all equipment and 30 percent of footwear. Primary reasons for this phenomenon are: over 50 percent of all athletic apparel sales are for casual wear; athletic apparel is often featured in regular clothing departments within department and discount stores; and selling athletic apparel requires much less technical expertise than selling equipment or even athletic footwear.

Table 3 compares the percentage of sales for various outlet types for equipment vs. footwear vs. apparel.

Highlighting the major differences that appear in Table 3:

• Sporting goods outlets (full line, specialists and pro shops) are clearly much more important for sales of equipment (50 percent) than footwear (20 percent) or apparel (16 percent).

• Department and discount stores are more important for apparel (50 percent of all sales) compared with equipment (36 percent) and footwear (31 percent). One major cause is that footwear and equipment are more technically-oriented products, requiring more sales and product information support than is often available in department and discount stores.

• Online sales for equipment are nearly twice as important as they are for athletic footwear (figures are not available for the apparel market).

Selling to the Teams, Institutions, and Corporations

Team dealers sell products directly to sports teams of all types. Most schools and professional teams purchase their products from team dealers. Grassroots teams, such as youth soccer, baseball, football, basketball, and ice hockey, sometimes will purchase from team dealers and sometimes from a local sporting goods retailer directly. Team dealers are increasing their share of the grassroots market because locally owned retailers are shrinking in importance. One reason is because national or regional retail chains often choose not to invest heavily in the type of apparel screening equipment needed to apply numbers, names and/or logos on uniforms.

It's important to remember that team dealers concentrate on selling team sports equipment, which on a combined basis represents about 15 to 20 percent of the total sports equipment and apparel market. They do not sell outdoor, fitness, wheel sports, action sports, water sports or running products. While their potential is limited to team sports, they must provide comprehensive coverage of all the products needed by team sports participants.

According to the NSGA, there are approximately 400 core team dealers in the country. Sales range from less than $5,000,000 up to as much as $25,000,000 or more per year. Team dealers nearly always support their own sales force. Team sales are quite different from consumer sales. The product mix is narrower — primarily uniforms, field equipment, team equipment, training aids and sports medicine products. As would be expected, products are sold at lower prices on a per-unit basis than in regular retail outlets.

Larger team dealers usually belong to a buying group, which enables them to bulk purchase from vendors, thereby purchasing at lower costs than if each one purchased independently from a vendor. The two largest organizations are Team Athletic Dealers (TAG) and Athletic Dealers of America (ADA).

Team dealers normally have full-time sales representatives contacting all amateur and professional teams in the geographic area they serve. Team dealers try to carry as many different brands as they can so as to offer teams the widest possible choices. A key factor in their strategy is the effort they make to develop personal relationships with the individuals responsible for buying team equipment. Team dealers often support local athletic programs, and they are active in local organizations concerned with recreation and scholastic sports programs.

Sales of team dealers, while representing only about 5 percent of total dollar volume, exert a greater influence on consumer sales than this percentage would suggest. Team usage of a product tends to influence regular consumers favorably and inspire them to purchase the same products for their own use.

A recent development in the team dealer market is an acquisition surge by Collegiate Pacific. Collegiate functioned as a catalog team dealer for many years. Beginning in 2004, Collegiate embarked on an acquisition program, acquiring several team dealers by the fall of 2005: Dixie Sporting Goods, Kesslers Team Sports, Orlando Team Sports, Salkeld & Sons and a majority ownership position of Sport Supply Group. These acquisitions make Collegiate the dominant team dealer company in the field.

An important aspect of Collegiate's success was their early adoption of e-commerce as a part of their marketing program. Collegiate's marketing strategy combines three distinct marketing ingredients—catalog merchandising, e-commerce and a personal sales organization — making them a formidable competitor in the field. As in all aggressive acquisition programs, their future success depends on Collegiate's ability to digest and manage these various acquisitions as one profitable enterprise, but thus far they have met with success, projecting sales for FY06 in excess of $200 million.

The Commercial Market

The commercial market includes product sales for final use by such organizations as corporations (as premiums or for team or fitness equipment), health clubs, and college/university/high schools (the latter includes primarily fitness equipment — team equipment is sold by team dealers). For most sporting goods products (heavy-duty fitness equipment being the exception), commercial buyers represent a small portion of the market, estimated to be less than 3 percent of all purchases.

There is no particular common source of product for commercial purchases. Some commercial buyers purchase locally through sporting goods outlets, some buy from team dealers and some buy directly from vendors. Factors influencing where goods are purchased include the dollar amount of the purchase, whether or not it's for a single or multiple location, and whether the products purchased are in a retailer's inventory.

Vendor Relationships with Governing Bodies and Trade Associations

Many sporting goods product categories produce products which need to meet standards established and maintained by various outside organizations governing the sports for which their products are used. For example, the United States Golf Association (USGA) and the United States Tennis Association (USTA) have established performance and construction standards for golf and tennis balls, and balls must conform to these standards if they are to be used in USGA or USTA sponsored events. High school, collegiate and professional sports teams and leagues establish certain standards for equipment, such as the size of balls allowed for game use and the construction features of certain types of protective equipment.

Field equipment for nearly every sport must be produced in accordance with size and material specifications provided by the various governing bodies for those sports, or by high school, collegiate and professional governing bodies. Recreational sports products must meet standards specified by appropriate governing agencies such as the Consumer Product Safety Commission (more about CPSC in chapter 5).

The purposes of these standards are twofold. The first purpose is to establish safety standards for participants. The second purpose is to foster competition within the sport by requiring that the physical characteristics of a product do not make it materially better than other products.

How American Sports Consumers Shop

In November 2003, *Sporting Goods Business* magazine sponsored a major survey by Nielsen Media to measure changing spending patterns of American sports consumers. While this study is somewhat dated, industry experts would agree that the basic principles discovered in this research still hold true today. Results of this survey are summarized below.

How America Shops: A Special Research Report Conducted Exclusively for SGB by Nielsen Media Research
(Sporting Goods Business, *November 2003*)

The most powerful person in the sporting goods industry likes to buy on sale. This person is not too interested in browsing, though his wife is, and is increasingly sophisticated on how and where to do his pre-purchase research.

The most powerful person in the sporting goods industry is, of course, the consumer. And what appears in the following pages is an up-to-date profile of today's sports consumers: where and when they shop, what motivates them to get to the store and what moves them to buy once they are there.

Also, SGB didn't want to talk to just any Tom, Dick or Harriet. The intent of this research was to talk to consumers who had actually purchased sports equipment, footwear or apparel in the past six months. The data in this report is compiled only from consumers who forked over their hard-earned cash to buy a piece of garb or gear in the past six months.

In an exclusive study created and conducted for SGB by Nielsen Media Research, the following portrait of today's sporting goods consumer emerged:

- Today's consumer is time-crunched and men, in particular, view shopping as a commando raid. They want to get in, find it, buy it, and get out.
- Conventional wisdom is validated in many areas. Conventional wisdom says consumers want brands at a good price. The research confirms it.
- Consumers want convenience. They want advertised items in-stock.
- Consumers are price-conscious; research always says they are, but they're not nuts about it. They want the best price, but they won't drive all over town to find it. And they're not going to use coupons to get discounts.
- Consumers trust in brands and increasingly, the store is the brand. Sixty percent of all those surveyed said the store's image and reputation was key in determining where they shopped for sporting goods.
- Sports consumers are no longer stigmatized by Wal-Mart. The store rated high as an intended destination to purchase apparel, footwear and equipment.
- Consumers are Web-savvy. Eighty-four percent of all sporting goods consumers in this study access the web regularly, 70 percent on a daily basis. Fifty-four percent of them and 66 percent of all males 16- to 34-years-old in the sample use it to access information on sporting goods.

When and How We Shop
- During the week, at what time of day are you most likely to shop for sporting goods?
  After 6 p.m.: 42%   1–6 p.m.: 30%   Before 12 noon: 19%   12–1 p.m.: 6%

- When shopping for sporting goods, do you prefer to browse or decide ahead of time exactly what you want?
  Decide ahead of time: 49%   Browse: 39%

- When shopping for sporting goods, do you prefer to browse or decide ahead of time exactly what you want?
  Women 16–34 years old: Browse 49%
  Analysis: Shopping has become a commando operation. Consumers go into the store on a mission, and are focused on getting in and out. This may hurt the opportunity for add-on sales and make an argument for express checkout—except when it comes to women 16–34, who still seem to view shopping as sport and recreation.

- How often do you shop for sporting goods?
  Once a week: 2.6%   Once every two or three weeks: 7.4%   Once a month: 15.2%
  Once every two to three months: 30.3%

Analysis: More than half the shoppers are in stores every 90 days, which under-scores the need to keep bringing in fresh merchandise on a regular basis.

• Who else do you usually shop for?
Husband: 31%   Son: 49.5%   Daughter: 34.8%
Analysis: This would seem to suggest that at least 31% of shoppers in sports stores are women.
What Gets Us In The Door—And What Motivates Us Once We're There
Top 10 Reasons Consumers Say They Buy

• How likely are you to make a purchase because of . . . ?
Store having item you're looking for: 93%
Good Prices: 86%
A great bargain: 79%
Good, knowledgeable sales help: 62%
Brand names: 59%
Special events or sales: 50%
Store having something new and different: 31%
Private sales or loyalty/frequency programs: 24%
Store displays: 23%
Signage: 17%
Analysis: No surprises here. Consumers typically overrate price and under-value logical factors like signage and sales help in research.
A Dozen Deciding Factors
Top 12 Reasons Consumers Say They Shop Where They Do

• How important are the following to you when deciding where to shop for sporting goods?

Store carries product I need: 91%   In-stock items: 87%
Prices of items: 81%   Informed, helpful staff: 73%
Low price guarantee: 66%   Store's image/reputation: 63%
Location of store: 66%   Brand name a store carries: 63%
Private sales/loyalty programs: 28%   Advertising: 34%
Store has a new, exciting look   Special promo event or sale: 58%
   every time I shop there: 16%

Analysis: The days of retail as theater are over. Have what they want, sell it to them at a good price, and be consistent are the underlying themes here.

What we think of the stores
• When shopping for sporting goods, what stores do you think of first?
The Sports Authority: 12.3%   Academy Sports & Outdoors: 6%
Dick's Sporting Goods: 10.6%   Big 5: 5%
Wal-Mart: 9.5%   Sportmart: 4%

• When shopping for sporting goods, what stores do you think of second?
Wal-Mart: 8.2%   Oshman's: 4.7
The Sports Authority: 6.2%   Modell's: 3.6%
Big 5: 5.3%   Kmart: 3.5%
• When shopping for athletic apparel, what stores do you think of first?
The Sports Authority: 9.9%   Foot Locker: 5.7%
Dick's Sporting Goods: 9.5% Academy Sports & Outdoors: 4.8%
Wal-Mart: 7.4%   Big 5: 4.8%
• When shopping for athletic apparel, what stores do you think of second?
The Sports Authority: 6.7%
Wal-Mart: 6%
Foot Locker: 4.5%
Oshman's: 3.7%

- When shopping for athletic footwear, what stores do you think of first?

  Foot Locker: 18.9%   Big 5: 4.8%
  The Sports Authority: 6.5%   Wal-Mart: 3.2%
  Dick's Sporting Goods: 5.9%

- When shopping for athletic footwear, what stores do you think of second?

  Foot Locker: 12.2%   The Sports Authority: 5.8%   Wal-Mart: 4.6%

  Analysis: If these Wal-Mart numbers don't sufficiently scare you, consider this fact from American Demographics: 84 percent of households with incomes of $70,000+ shopped at Wal-Mart, Kmart and Target in the past three months. The high consumer regard for The Sports Authority bodes well for the expansion of that nameplate across the country.

- Please tell me what a sporting goods store could do to get more of your business?

  Lower prices: 25.9%   Newest, latest merchandise: 7.1%
  More sales: 12.9%   More sales help: 6.8%
  More knowledgeable sales associates: 7.3%

  Analysis: Consumers typically rate price as the number one consideration, but logic would tell you that just because prices are lower doesn't mean consumers would necessarily buy more.

- What kind of sporting goods did you purchase in the past six months?

  Athletic footwear: 50.9 %   Fishing equipment: 10.5 %
  Workout clothes: 27.8 %   Exercise equipment: 10.2%
  Golf equipment: 11.6 %

What Else Do We Do?

- How often would you say you attend live sporting events?

  At least once a week: 16.6%   Several times a year: 36.4%
  Several times a month: 10.3%   At least once a year: 18%
  At least once a month: 14%

- Thinking about the past year, what types of live sporting events, if any, have you, yourself, attended?

  Major League Baseball game: 40.3% Children's events: 10.6%
  NFL football game: 25.4%   Soccer: 10.3%
  High school events: 24.7%   NBA game: 9.5%
  College football game: 19.2%   College basketball: 8.3%
  Hockey game: 13.7%

- Which pro sports do you typically watch on television?

  NFL football: 78%   Pro golf: 14.8%
  Major League Baseball: 43.2%   NHL hockey: 11.5%
  NBA basketball: 32.5%   NASCAR: 9.5%
  College basketball & football: 18.9%

  Analysis: Sporting goods shoppers attend more games and watch more televised sports than other fan groups surveyed by Nielsen.

Where We Get Our Information

- Do you have access to the Internet?

  Yes: 84%

- Have you accessed it in the past 24 hours?

  Overall sample: 70%
  HHI $80K+: 79%

- Do you use the Internet to access information about sporting goods equipment?

  Overall Sample: 54%   Men 16–34 years old: 66%

- Have you ever purchased sporting goods over the Internet?
  Yes: 38.2%

- What kind of sporting goods did you purchase over the Internet?
  Athletic footwear: 27.1%   Fishing: 9.7%
  Workout clothes: 23.7%   Bikes: 7.1%
  Hunting: 12.2%   Baseball equipment and apparel: 6.3%

- How often would you say you purchase sporting goods using the Internet?
  Several times a year: 43.9%   Less than once a year: 10 %
  At least once a year: 40%   At least once a month: 4.3%

- When deciding to shop for sporting goods, what sources of information do you typically use?
  Newspaper ads: 40%   Internet: 12.5%
  Word of mouth: 36%   Magazine ads/articles: 12%
  TV ads: 19%

- When deciding to shop for sporting goods, what sources of information do you typically use?
  Thirty-two percent of all men 16–34 year olds answered TV ads, almost twice the amount of the overall sample.

- Are you familiar with the store circulars in the Sunday paper?
  Yes: 89%

- Do they impact your purchase decisions?
  Yes: 45%

- Do Sunday circulars impact your purchasing decisions?
  Fifty-three percent of those in top 10 DMAs answered yes, 20 percent higher than the national sample.

- During a typical week, that is Monday through Saturday, how often do you read a daily newspaper?
  Everyday: 42.1%   Once a week: 20.4%
  4–5 days a week: 8.7%   Do not read a daily newspaper: 10.6%

- During a typical month, how often do you read a Sunday newspaper?
  Every Sunday: 57.3%   Do not read a Sunday newspaper: 13.3%
  2–3 times a month: 15.7%

- When reading the newspaper, what section of the paper do you typically read first?
  Main news: 38.7%   Sports: 17.8%   Local news: 11.8%

How the study was conducted

Nielsen Media Research conducted this study in conjunction with *Sporting Goods Business*. The survey was conducted via telephone from September 11 through 22nd across the continental United States and included more than 800 total respondents. The interviews were conducted among those respondents 16+ who had shopped for sporting goods at least once in the past six months.

Approximately 52 percent of those who were contacted for the study had shopped in the past six months for sporting goods and the data from those interviews make up the study.

The study was designed to gather information on sporting goods consumers' attitudes on shopping; likes and dislikes; reasons they shop in particular stores; reasons they decide to shop, etc.

Researchers over-sampled 14 cities (Cincinnati, Cleveland, Charlotte, Richmond, Va., Detroit, Philadelphia, Pittsburgh, Albany, Binghamton, Buffalo, Baltimore, Syracuse, Hartford and Louisville). The total data was then weighted back to produce a geographically accurate representation of the data.

Certain data presented in the study makes reference to the top 10 DMAs in the country. The Top 10 DMAs are:

- New York
- Los Angeles
- Chicago
- Philadelphia
- San Francisco
- Boston
- Dallas
- Washington, D.C.
- Atlanta
- Detroit

RELATED WEBSITES

Academy Sports & Outdoors: www.academy.com
The Athlete's Foot: www.theathletesfoot.com
Bass Pro Shops: www.basspro.com/servlet/catalog.OnlineShopping
Big 5 Sporting Goods: www.big5sportinggoods.com
Champs Sports: www.champssports.com
Dick's Sporting Goods: www.dickssportinggoods.com
The Finish Line: www.finishline.com/store
Foot Locker: www.footlocker.com
MC Sports: www.mcsports.com
Modell's Sporting Goods: www.modells.com
National Sporting Goods Association (NSGA): www.nsga.org
Pacific Sunwear: http://shop.pacsun.com
The Sports Authority: www.thesportsauthority.com
ZUMIEZ: www.zumiez.com

EXERCISES

1. Choose three retailers (larger ones, such as Dick's, Foot Locker, The Sports Authority, MC Sports, Big 5 Sporting Goods, the Athlete's Foot, The Finish Line) and review their websites. Analyze each site and compare them with respect to the following criteria:
- What you believe they are trying to accomplish
- How well they present their products
- How informative they are about the company
- Ease of navigation
- Ability to find what you might be looking for when visiting the site

2. Using the tables and information in the text for this chapter, answer the following questions:

a. In what circumstances are wholesalers an important part of the distribution chain? Approximately what percentage do wholesalers represent of all sales to sporting goods retailers?

b. What are the major types of outlets for sports footwear? Sports apparel? Why do you think department and discount stores are more important in sales of sports apparel than for sports footwear?

c. Provide a brief description of the relative importance of different types of retailers in the distribution of sporting goods equipment vs. sports apparel vs. sports/athletic footwear.

d. What is the difference between a team dealer and a regular retailer in terms of the market and the types of customers they serve?

3. Using Table 3 (which presents the distribution by outlet type for all equipment products, all footwear, and all apparel), together with other text you might find appropriate, write a brief summary of the differences in the distribution of sales by outlet type between the three different categories (equipment, footwear, apparel).

4. Describe the basic strategies used by team dealers to maximize their sales volumes. You'll find the information in the text and articles for this chapter.

5. Go to www.sbrnet.com. Click on "Basketball" under "Market Research Statistics" on the home page. Then click on "Basketball-Cons. Exp." on the menu, and print the series of tables. Find the "Outlet Type" tables. You'll find two tables—one for consumer expenditures and one with unit market share. After you've done this for basketball, go back to the home page and search under "Consolidated Market Research" and do the same thing for treadmills (under "Exercise/Fitness"), golf balls (under "Golf"), running shoes (under "Footwear"), and inline skates (under "Inline Skating"). Choose one of these products, and compare the percent by outlet type for units with the percent by outlet type for dollars. (Note: If the percentage of units for a particular outlet type is larger than the percentage of dollars for the same outlet type, that indicates the average unit price for that outlet type is below average. If the percentage of units is smaller than the percentage of dollars for the same outlet type, that indicates the average unit price for that outlet type is above average.) Answer the following questions:

a. For "Department Stores" is the average unit price for running shoes above or below average?

b. For "Sporting Goods Stores" is the average unit price for golf balls above or below average?

c. For "Discount Stores" is the average unit price for basketballs above or below average?

5

Sports Medicine and Product Liability

OVERVIEW

> Over the past two years, sports medicine has been the fastest growing category in all of sporting goods.

Nearly all sporting goods equipment and footwear products are used for activities requiring physical activity, with many involving physical contact with other participants. Sports medicine has evolved as a segment of the industry to serve the needs and issues occurring as a result of this activity and physical contact. Sporting goods companies recognize that their very survival depends on producing products that enjoy consumer confidence with respect to injury prevention.

Accordingly, a wide array of vendors offer products such as athletic tape, protective equipment for all parts of the body, rehabilitative and support products for injury protection and treatment, therapeutic products, sports facility–related products, orthotics, pain-relieving products, and educational products. Some of these are totally involved in sports medicine or product liability, but most are involved in broader sports, medical- and health-related issues within which sports medicine and product liability is a segment of their total responsibilities.

Consumers of sports medicine products include not only individual sports and recreational participants but also athletic trainers, physical therapists, doctors, coaches, and administrators at all levels of sports including youth, collegiate and professional. Products for consumers are sold primarily through traditional full-line and specialty sporting goods stores, whereas medical supply houses and team dealers serve the sports team marketplace. Vendors use independent sales representatives to call on their customer base, whether it be retailers, medical supply houses or team dealers.

Sports medicine is one aspect of a broader, health-related industry dimension, which involves industry efforts related to promoting health and well-being in the general marketplace. The sporting goods industry's future is significantly related to the overall health of the American consumer. With this in mind, sporting goods companies have sponsored a Physical Education initiative entitled *PE4LIFE*, a completely separate organization whose primary mission is to "inspire active, healthy living by advancing the development of quality, daily physical education programs for all children." *PE4LIFE*'s founding sponsors include a blue-chip list of sporting goods companies.

At the end of this chapter, you should be able to:

• Identify the role of sports medicine and product liability in the sporting goods industry.

- Understand the synergistic relationships between sports medicine product vendors and trade associations dealing exclusively or partially with sports medical issues.
- Understand the role of government in sports medicine.
- Identify changes that have occurred as the industry has become increasingly active in promoting and supporting programs designed to reduce the dangers involved in sports and recreation participation.
- Understand the types of products that are most directly related to product liability issues.
- Understand the broad scope of the industry's efforts to protect consumers from injury while participating in sports and to enhance the overall well-being of consumers.

DISCUSSION

Sports medicine products are predominantly used by individuals participating in team sports activities—baseball, basketball, field hockey, football, ice hockey, lacrosse, soccer, softball and volleyball. Other important market segments include participants in activities such as running, weightlifting, ice skating and tennis which require substantial physical activity, resulting in the obvious need for products such as braces, supports, tape and orthotic products.

Sales volume is estimated to be slightly less than $1 billion, including traditional sports medicine products and orthotics. Sports medicine products are used by almost every participant in these sports—children, and high school and college students represent the primary market. Given increasing sports involvement and activity among older people, sports medicine promises to enjoy above-average market growth for the foreseeable future.

The trade association most directly related to and interested in sports medicine products is the National Athletic Trainers Association (NATA), founded in the 1950s and originally funded by Cramer Products, Inc., a leading producer of sports medicine products in today's marketplace. NATA members come primarily from schools with team sports athletic programs. Other organizations with significant interests in sports medicine include the American Physical Therapy Association (APTA) which has a separate section devoted to Sports Physical Therapy, and the National Association for Sport and Physical Education (NASPE). These organizations sponsor programs directly related to sports physical therapy and physical education, and resources of valuable information of interest to sports medicine product vendors and retailers.

In addition, the sporting goods industry, through its trade associations (SGMA, NSSF and NSGA), counsels with college athletic administrators (NCAA, NAIA, NJCAA), high school athletic administrators (NFSHSA), and youth sports administrators such as Little League and Pop Warner Football on the subject of sports medicine and product liability issues.

Equipment Standards

In the interest of reducing, if not eliminating athletic injuries, the sporting goods industry has established a close working relationship with the National Operating Committee on Standards for Athletic Equipment (NOCSAE). While NOCSAE's stated purpose is protective athletic equipment, it devotes the majority of its efforts from a product standpoint to football, baseball and lacrosse helmets.

The overall objective of NOCSAE, as stated on its website, is "to commission research on and, where feasible, establish standards for protective athletic equipment. In its efforts in this field the Committee fosters and encourages the dissemination of information on research findings on athletic equipment, injury data, and other closely related areas of inquiry through the organizations represented on the NOCSAE Board of Directors, and other entities in the fields of athletic and sports medicine."

Since its inception in 1969, NOCSAE has been a leading force in the effort to improve athletic equipment and as a result, reduce injuries. Some of the efforts of NOCSAE include the development of test standards for football helmets, baseball/softball batting helmets, baseballs/softballs, lacrosse helmets/face masks and football face masks. NOCSAE research efforts have also led to a better understanding of the mechanism and tolerance of head and neck injuries and more knowledge concerning the design and structure of football helmets, football face masks and lacrosse protective headgear and face masks.

NOCSAE's board includes representation from all organizations involved with team sports, including the American College Health Association, the American College of Sports Medicine, the American Orthopedic Society for Sports Medicine, the American Football Coaches Association, the American Medical Society for Sports Medicine, the Athletic Equipment Managers Association, the National Athletic Equipment Reconditioners Association, the National Athletic Trainers Association, the Sporting Goods Manufacturers Association, Riddell and Oklahoma State University.

NOCSAE has created standards and certification requirements for helmets for football, baseball, and lacrosse. These standards are designed to protect both the consumer from unsafe products and to significantly reduce, if not eliminate, product liability suits resulting from athletic injuries

Institutions that purchase helmets that meet NOCSAE standards are not immune from litigation. However, purchasing products that meet NOCSAE standards "is an indication that the institution has taken steps to safeguard its student athletes by purchasing helmets which meet the best available helmet standards."

Consumer Product Safety Commission

Nearly every sport and recreational activity that requires physical activity carries with it the risk of injury. In our society, it is incumbent on producers of every product to ensure that their products are designed for maximum safety of the consumer. The Consumer Product Safety Commission (CPSC) was established to ensure that consumers are protected from companies and individuals who produce products that can intentionally or even accidentally cause injury to users. Even for apparel products, inflammability is a potential risk. So basically no sporting goods product, whether it be equipment, footwear or apparel, is immune to risks associated with sports participation.

The CPSC is responsible for evaluating consumer products to ensure that they do not endanger the public, and if they do, to require appropriate labeling to that effect. The CPSC requires companies to recall products if they do not meet CPSC standards. Sport-

"The American Dental Association has identified 40 sports in which wearing a mouthguard is recommended. They include soccer, volleyball, rugby, baseball, softball, shotput, wrestling, weightlifting, judo, karate, motocross and racquetball." *Sporting Goods Dealer*, May/June 2004.

ing goods products most often involved in CPSC monitoring and recall programs are those posing the highest risks to consumers, including but not necessarily limited to firearms, fitness equipment, baseball bats, bicycles and certain types of outdoor camping equipment.

There has been a significant reduction in product liability suits over the past 25 years. For example, Sturm Ruger, a leading firearms manufacturer, reported that the number of product liability lawsuits dropped from 69 cases in 1979 to four cases pending in 2004.

As a result of product liability lawsuits, nearly all manufacturers of football helmets stopped producing this product. Today, the market is dominated by Riddell, Schutt and Adams USA, in addition to a small list of companies who sell reconditioned helmets. Two leading helmet producers, Riddell (team sports) and Bell (bicycle helmets) are owned by a private equity company, Fenway Partners.

Sports Medicine Vendor Products and Practices

Sports medicine product vendors sell their products through three distinct trade channels: (1) retailers selling directly to individual consumers; (2) medical supply houses selling to all types of institutions, including schools, hospitals, doctors, laboratories, nursing homes; and (3) sporting goods team dealers, who sell directly to scholastic institutions of all types as well as local, regional and national youth and adult teams and organizations. As is the case with the majority of all sporting goods vendors, sports medicine vendors contact potential customers using independent sales representatives who call on prospects in all three segments.

At least 50 companies offer sports medicine products. Among the leading vendors are Becton Dickinson, Cramer Products, Inc., Johnson & Johnson, McDavid Sports Medical Products, Mueller Sports Medicine, and Tru-Fit. In addition, some selected sports medicine products are also sold by vendors who specialize in other sporting goods products. The vendors market the sports medicine products under their own brand name even though most are often produced by another company.

Specific sports medicine product categories include:

- analgesics
- athletic/sports tapes and wraps
- bottles/carriers/coolers
- braces and supports for all parts of the body
- cleaners/disinfectants
- first aid kits

- hot and cold therapeutics
- mouthguards
- ointments
- orthotic products
- protective pads

These products have historically been the major components of the sports medicine market. However, new types of protective apparel, such as those provided by Under Armour, are considered by many industry experts to be in the sports medicine genre, because to a certain degree they protect consumers from injury and potential respiratory problems and diseases.

The Market

There are two major market segments for sports medicine products: individual consumers and institutions (scholastic and health-related). Consumers represent the largest segment of the market for sports medicine products. While specific industry figures are not available, as it was astutely stated by Curt Mueller, president of Mueller Sports Medicine way back in 1985, "It's a matter of sheer numbers. In a football stadium, there may be 200 people suited for football, but there are 60,000 people in the stands—many of them are weekend athletes." (*Sporting Goods Dealer*, April 1985.)

Publications

Two leading publications serving the field of sports medicine are *The Physician and Sportsmedicine* and *Medicine & Science in Sports & Exercise* (official publication of the American College of Sports Medicine). These publications deal with all aspects of sports medicine and a significant part of their editorial has to do with sports-related injuries and applicable scientific issues related to sports injuries and treatment programs. These publications serve as valuable resources for sports medicine product vendors and retailers, often stimulating new product development related to incidents reported in the publications.

RELATED WEBSITES

PUBLICATIONS:

Medicine & Science in Sports & Exercise: www.acsm.org/publications/MSSE.htm
The Physician and Sportsmedicine: www.physsportsmed.com

TRADE ASSOCIATIONS:

American Physical Therapy Association: www.nata.org
National Association for Sport and Physical Education (NASPE): www.naspe.org
National Athletic Trainers Association: www.nata.org
National Operating Committee on Standards for Athletes Equipment: www.nocsae.org
PE4LIFE: www.pe4life.org
Sports Physical Therapy Association: www.spts.org

VENDORS:

Cramer Products, Inc: www.cramersportsmed.com
McDavid Sports Medical Products: http://mcdavidusa.com
Mueller Sports Medicine: www.muellersportsmed.com
Spenco Medical Corp: www.spenco.com

EXERCISES

1. What organization is significantly involved in establishing standards for sports helmets? Describe their role in creating standards.

2. What role does the Consumer Product Safety Commission play in the sporting goods industry?

3. What are the three trade channels for sports medicine products?

4. What is the largest market segment for sports medicine products?

5. Are long-term prospects better or worse for sports medicine products than for other sporting goods products? Why do you think this is so?

6

Sports Marketing: Licensing, Endorsement and Sponsorship

OVERVIEW

> In addition to bringing significant dollars to the industry, licensing is a critical contributor to the industry's consumer visibility.

Licensing, sponsorship and endorsement dominate the sports marketing landscape of the sporting goods industry. Roots of these programs go back to the late 1800s, and it's almost impossible for a sporting goods company to exist without utilizing these programs in one form or another. The primary focus of all these programs is to enhance the credibility and visibility of sporting goods products, as well as to stimulate actual sales, within their core markets.

Licensing is a process whereby an organization or individual (the licensor) allows their name to be used by another organization or individual (the licensee), in return for some form of payment, which in most cases is in the form of royalties based on the amount of products sold with the licensor's name. Endorsement is similar to licensing except that the endorser's name is used to promote a company or a brand; as opposed to having his name on the product. Another difference between licensing and endorsement is that fees are most often based on a predetermined negotiated amount, rather than being dependent on how much merchandise is sold. Sponsorship is a process whereby a sporting goods company associates their name with a particular sporting event, league, team, or athlete. Very often, licensing, endorsement and sponsorship programs are combined in one relationship. For example, a company can sponsor an athlete by paying his costs to participate, they can produce certain products bearing his or her name, and they can feature the athlete in advertising promoting the total brand.

Licensing is done by many different types of organizations and individuals—professional and amateur leagues and teams, professional athletes, governing bodies, sports trade associations, team coaches, and of course, sporting goods vendors and retailers. The emphasis of this chapter is on how the licensing process works, what factors determine whether a product is licensed, and the risks and rewards of licensing. Licensing is sometimes used interchangeably with the term *endorsement*. However, in reality there is an important distinction. With licensing, a vendor pays for the right to use the name of the licensor (a team, league, athlete, etc.) on his product. The term *endorsement* is most often used in situations whereby the endorser (team, league, or athlete) is associated with a vendor's products but the products do not bear the actual name of the endorser.

Sponsorship can be defined as a program to enhance a brand or product image through association. In the sporting goods industry, sponsorship associations most often occur for sports events, professional and amateur sports teams, leagues and associations, and professional athletes. Sponsorship programs range in magnitude from local grassroots activities such as a local youth softball team, to international events such as the Summer or Winter Olympics. Sponsorships offer sporting goods companies unique opportunities because their products are often used in events or by professional athletes, making them highly visible to spectators.

At the end of this chapter, you should be able to:

- Identify the two major types of licensing.
- Identify the kinds of sporting goods products that are licensed.
- Describe the factors that influence consumer demand for licensed sporting goods products.
- Describe recent developments that have influenced consumer demand for licensed products.
- Understand how professional sports leagues manage their licensing programs.
- Identify the different ways that sporting goods products become licensed products.
- Understand how the sporting goods industry's use of sports marketing differs from other industries.
- Understand what endorsement is, and how it differs from licensing.
- Understand the benefits and risks associated with endorsement.
- Identify and understand the three basic types of sponsorship.
- Understand how sponsorship by sporting goods companies differs from sponsorship by non-sporting goods companies.

DISCUSSION

Licensing

The term *licensed product* in the sporting goods industry usually includes products licensed by sports institutions and organizations, as well as products that carry the name of a particular athlete. Most sporting goods products are licensed by professional or collegiate sports leagues, organizations and teams—among the most prominent being the National Football League (NFL), the National Basketball Association (NBA), Major League Baseball (MLB), the National Hockey League (NHL), Major League Soccer (MLS), and the National Collegiate Athletic Association (NCAA). Recently, other sports organizations, notably the National Association for Stock Car Automobile Racing (NASCAR) and the World Wrestling Federation (WWF), have established licensing programs. In recent years, fashion-clothing designers such as Polo, Tommy Hilfiger, and Nautica have licensed their names to sporting goods companies to produce products designed specifically for sports participants.

What Is Licensing?

Simply defined, licensing is a process whereby the licensor allows use of their name for marketing and promotion purposes by a licensee, who generally pays royalties in return for this right.

Major sporting goods products that bear names of licensors include:

- athletic apparel (athletic jackets, T-shirts, fleece bottoms and tops, athletic socks, warm-up suits, athletic shirts/tops, caps/hats, uniforms, golf apparel, etc.)
- athletic footwear
- sports balls (basketballs, footballs, soccer balls, volleyballs, baseballs, tennis balls, etc.)
- other team sports equipment (baseball bats, hockey sticks, basketball standards, etc.)

Many products such as baseball equipment, athletic footwear and to a lesser extent, golf clubs, are more likely to bear names of professional athletes.

The name of the licensor is expected to significantly enhance the appeal of the licensed product to consumers. Licensees are willing to pay royalty fees because they judge these fees to be justified by the attendant marketing benefits. Benefits can be in the form of increased revenues or the enhancement of the overall appeal of the licensee's complete product line, including licensed and non-licensed products.

According to industry experts, licensed sports apparel represents approximately 50 percent of all licensed sports products sales, with the remainder represented by sales of licensed sports equipment and footwear and non-sports products such as coffee mugs, towels, and a myriad of other non-sports products.

There are two major forms of licensing: (1) licensing by teams, leagues, organizations and athletes; and (2) licensing of their name by sporting goods vendors (licensors) to other companies (licensees) who would produce and sell products bearing the licensor's name.

Licensing by Teams, Leagues, Organizations and Athletes

Until the middle 1960s, most licensing was done by athletes — and, to a lesser extent, teams — to manufacturers; sports organizations, such as professional leagues and college conferences, devoted most of their energy to overseeing competition among member teams. Over the past 35 years, however, a seismic centralizing shift has occurred in the policies of leagues and organizations. Most professional leagues have set up licensing arms, such as NFL Properties, Major League Baseball Properties, Soccer United Marketing, and NBA Properties. Players associations have similarly created an arm for licensing purposes. They coordinate licensing activities and programs for all teams (or players) in the league, including contracting with suppliers for licensed products and distributing all royalties evenly among all teams in the league, regardless of the varying popularity of sales of products for different teams. These licensing arms are staffed with highly skilled marketing professionals, whose role is to ensure that all merchandise sold by the teams meets their standards of quality and value.

Professional leagues vary with regard to their licensing strategies. The NFL and NBA have each licensed Reebok to be their exclusive uniform and apparel supplier, with various types of equipment licensed to other companies, such as Wilson as their exclusive football, Riddell as the exclusive helmet supplier, and Spalding as the official NBA basketball. Major League Baseball awarded an exclusive license to Majestic for uniforms, but other companies hold other apparel product licenses, Rawlings is the official ball supplier. Major League Soccer does not have an exclusive supplier for any product line.

College sports licensing operates in a different way. An NCAA license allows licensees to produce products leading up to and during its 87 championship events. The NCAA does not manage or monitor the licensing agreements of the conferences, schools or its other member institutions. Individual schools and conferences contract for their own licensed products. Two organizations represent the great majority of larger colleges and universities in licensing programs: the Collegiate Licensing Company and the Licensing Resource Group. These organizations arrange for the creation and production of products bearing the school name, negotiating directly with sporting goods companies (and other types of companies as well).

Athletes also play a major role in product licensing. Prominent athletes license their names for a wide range of equipment and footwear products, including but not limited to team sports, golf, tennis, winter sports, extreme sports and outdoor sports. A very select number of high-profile athletes are involved in both licensing (for products bearing their name) and endorsement (promoting a company-wide product line). Michael Jordan is the best-known athlete in this category.

Sporting goods companies pay significant sums of money to earn the right to be a licensee of professional and collegiate sports organizations and athletes. Licensing agreements have a wide variety of features. Rarely is a license allowed in perpetuity, that is, forever. There is usually a predetermined time frame for the license, after which it can be either extended or cancelled. Some licensing agreements have performance clauses, whereby the licensee is required to produce a certain amount of revenue for the licensor or the license automatically expires. Some licenses are exclusive for the licensee's product category, others are non-exclusive. Most licensors require their licensees to meet certain product performance standards. These standards can include such areas as revenue minimums, product quality, moral image, minimum pricing, and advertising campaign approval.

While licensing is a major factor in the sale of sporting goods products—equipment, apparel and footwear—there is substantial risk associated with this form of marketing. For example, there are obvious risks involved with athletes who license their name and then get into personal trouble of one kind or another. While licensing companies are often able to cancel agreements when this happens, the company needs to replace the athlete, and this can take some time, particularly if the athlete's licensed products were an important part of a company's sales. The most serious situation of this type occurs when an athlete's name is on the product and serves as the basis for marketing that product, and the athlete misbehaves in such a way as to generate a lot of bad publicity. Not only has the company lost the opportunity to use the athlete because of the behavior, but they can have great difficulty in selling products that have already been produced bearing the athlete's name. This aspect of licensing is one reason why sporting goods companies have embraced league, team and organization licensing opportunities, mitigating the potential problems associated with individual athletes or performers from other entertainment categories such as music or film.

Finally, an important licensing consideration for sporting goods companies is the type of appeal of an athlete or organization. For example, some athletes might have a following within certain market segments but no appeal, or perhaps even a negative appeal, to other segments. Sporting goods companies will tend to contract with athletes whose appeal is universal and generally positive both from skill and character standpoints. Contracting

According to a report published by EPM Communications, Inc., when commenting on growth in licensing, "the highest rate of increase was seen in China where sales of licensed merchandise increased nearly 70% between 2001 and 2004, reaching $1 billion for the first time and representing the fastest growing market in the world for licensed goods." *NSGA Research Newsletter,* January 27, 2005.

with an athlete who has a bad-boy image may seem on the surface to be an effective attention-getting device, but the downside is potentially offending some segments of the market.

Licensing by Vendors

Another type of license is one offered by sporting goods vendors who are either unable or unwilling to produce and market a product or products that differ from their products either by type or by price point. These licenses can be offered to other sporting goods companies or to manufacturers of non-sports products such as children's products, bathroom accessories, eyewear, coffee mugs, etc. In these situations, the licensee (producer) bears the responsibility to actually market the product, although the licensor may assist in the marketing.

Most often a vendor acting as a licensor will restrict their licensees from selling products in trade channels that could conflict with sales of a similar product offered by the licensor. For example, a company may license lower-priced products to other vendors but keep the higher-priced products to sell themselves.

The primary reason for this type of licensing is that a sporting goods company may not be familiar with the distribution channels or the marketing strategies utilized for the product they license. They want to generate revenues from the category, and they believe that their name on a product in that category will result in additional sales, but they're unfamiliar with the distribution channels and marketing strategies required to be successful in that category. Sporting goods companies receive less revenue than if they produced the product themselves, but they avoid the need to invest in production and marketing.

CONTRACT PRODUCTION

Using a contractor to produce a product is not licensing. For example, a sporting goods company may contract with a producer to manufacture a product or products under the name of the sporting goods company. The vendor (sporting goods company) contracts with the producer to manufacture products to their desired specifications; these products bear the name of the sporting goods company, and the sporting goods company does all sales and marketing. Most often the sporting goods company will seek out companies to produce other products for them that adhere to their own high standards. The consumer is unaware (unless they look at the fine print on the label) that the product was made by a company other than the sporting goods company. This type of production is generally called *contract* or *private-label* production and is not to be confused with licensing.

Advantages and Disadvantages of Licensing

The major advantages of licensing are:

• To enhance the marketing appeal of a product by capitalizing on the appeal of profes-

> "For retailers, the toughest job is deciding how much inventory to commit to a specific player or team, and that task ultimately involves correctly forecasting a team's or player's fortunes." *Sporting Goods Business,* April 2004.

sional leagues and athletes to the youth market, particularly young children and
teenagers.
• To generate revenues for the licensing organization (licensor) without incurring additional marketing or manufacturing costs.

As for disadvantages, licensing is sometimes not successful financially; it often carries a large element of risk. Perhaps the most difficult aspect of successful licensing is determining if the potential licensor's name will indeed appeal to the public. An athlete or
organization may be flying high at the time they provide the license but they may lose their
place in the market, creating major problems for their licensee. Examples are a team that
experiences a winning season one year, but falls back into the "also-rans" in future years;
and athletes who experience a poor performance year or conduct themselves improperly
in their private or even athletic life.

Another element of risk is changing fashion preferences—licensed products are very
much a fashion item, particularly apparel, and a change in consumer tastes such as occurred
in the late 1990s and early 2000s can create major problems. Two notable victims of such
a trend were Starter and Pro Player.

Product pricing has been a major consideration throughout the growth of licensed
products. Many industry experts feel that professional sports leagues rode their success
for too long—requiring licensees to incur royalty and other exclusivity costs that forced
vendors to price their merchandise at levels higher than could be sustained by market
demand.

Size of the Licensing Market

Figures available to define the licensing market are readily available through 1999.
While we acknowledge the value of more current information, which is not available, we
are including this information to provide some licensing market parameters with regard
to relative importance of different categories.

For example, in 1999 total licensing sales were $13.1 billion, or approximately 18 per-
cent of all consumer expenditures for sporting goods equipment, apparel and footwear.
According to Table 1, beginning in 1999, licensed products lost their appeal as a fashion
item, and sales declined steadily for a two-year period.

Since MLB and NBA exhibited growth between 2003 and 2004 (see sidebar below),
one can hypothesize from these admittedly scattered numbers that the licensing market
has changed shape considerably since 1999 (MLB, NFL and NASCAR doing well, NHL and
Collegiate down). However, total dollar growth has grown only slightly since then, while
unit sales declined steadily through 2004. This would suggest that more expensive licensed
products are holding their own, even increasing, but the middle, lower-priced market is
losing ground.

"'04 was an up and down year for licensed apparel and products. From a league stand-
point, here are the overall comps for '04 vs. '03, based on dollars generated at retail:
NBA +3.30%, NFL +7.83%, MLB +15.17%, NHL -58.99% and NCAA -13.66%."
(SportSCANInfo Research / *Inside Sporting Goods*).

The Collegiate Licensing Corp. has found that women's events don't generate the
sales dollars of men's events when it comes to commemorative apparel or licensed
souvenirs. *SGB's Inside Sporting Goods*, January 21, 2003.

TABLE 1: DOLLAR SALES OF LICENSED PRODUCTS
(IN BILLIONS OF DOLLARS)

	1999	2002
NASCAR	1.1	1.4
Total Collegiate	2.5	2.5
NFL	3.1	2.9
NHL	1.6	1.1
MLB	2.9	NA
NBA	1.8	NA
Total	13.0 (8.3 exc. MLB, NBA)	7.9 (exc. MLB, NBA)

Source: Sporting Goods Business.

TABLE 2: CHANGE IN UNIT AND DOLLARS SALES
OF LICENSED APPAREL AND PRODUCTS

	Units—% Change	Dollars—% Change
2005 (January-May)	+7.63	+ 2.79
Year 2004	-2.71	-0.71
Year 2003	-8.4	+ 6.3

One final note. A separate study by the *Licensing Letter*, a leading publication serving the licensing market, reported that total sports licensing in 2004 was $12.7 billion, suggesting that the market today is about the same as it was five years ago.

Profiling the Licensing Market

In March 2002, *Sporting Goods Business* magazine reported results of a major study of licensed product buyers conducted by a prominent New York research firm, Scarborough Research. While the study is a few years old, we are reporting it because we believe these profiles provide a basic framework illustrating the differences between buyers for different sports.

Here is a summary of the report, excerpted from *SGB*:

Sports fans are all the same, right? They're all crazy, they love to go to the games and they can't get enough info on their teams. That's not quite true, as this in-depth data from Scarborough Research (which is owned by SGB's parent, VNU) indicates. Fans of the NBA are the youngest, NHL fans tend to be the best-educated and most Web-savvy, and fans of all sports are avid shoppers—especially for licensed apparel.

Here, courtesy of Scarborough, are profiles of seven key fan groups that make up an important part of the sporting goods consumer base. [Editor's Note: the data doesn't measure the behavior of those under 18 years of age, so the numbers skew a bit.]

NBA Fans
Age: 37% are between 18–34.
Education: 62% attended or graduated college
Income: 48% make $50K+ annually

With the advent of large regional and national retailers, expect to see growth in the number of products from major brands that are made specifically for and exclusively licensed to a single retailing chain.

Gender: 59% male/41% female
Shopped for sporting goods in past three months: 54%
Purchased Licensed apparel in past 12 months: 45%
Stores Shopped: Wal-Mart 25%; Kmart 15%; Target 11%; TSA 7%
Brands Purchased: Nike 43%; Adidas 20%; Reebok 20%; Champion 11%, Russell 7%
Access Internet Regularly: 66%
Internet Purchase in past 12 months: 38%
Own a Video Game System: 46%

WNBA Fans
Age: 35% are between 18–34; 41% between 35–54*
Education: 58% attended or graduated college
Income: 40% make $50K+ annually
Gender: 42% male/58% female
Shopped for sporting goods in past three months: 51%
Purchased Licensed Apparel in past 12 months: 43%
Stores Shopped: Wal-Mart 27%; Kmart 16%; Target 10%; TSA 6%
Brands Purchased: Nike 45%; Reebok 22%; Adidas 21%; Champion 11%; Russell 8%
Access Internet Regularly: 62%
Internet Purchase in past 12 months: 33%
Own a Video Game system: 45%
*(most likely representing the parents of young girls who are fans)

NHL Fans
Age: 41% are between 18–34; 42% between 35–54
Education: 63% attended or graduated college
Income: 55% earn $50K+ annually
Gender: 64% male/36% female
Shopped for sporting goods in past three months: 58%
Purchased Licensed Apparel in past 12 months: 52%
Stores Shopped: Wal-Mart 23%; Kmart 15%; TSA 11%; Target 9%
Brands Purchased: Nike 39%; Adidas 20%; Reebok 19%; Champion 13%; Russell 9%
Access Internet Regularly: 73%
Internet Purchase in past 12 months: 46%
Own a Video Game System: 50%

NFL Fans
Age: 33% are between 18–34; 41% are between 35–54; 27% are 55+
Education: 60% attended or graduated college
Income: 49% earn $50K+ annually
Gender: 64% male/36% female
Shopped for sporting goods in past three months: 58%
Purchased Licensed Apparel in past 12 months: 43%
Stores Shopped: Wal-Mart 26%; Kmart 16%; Target 9%; TSA 7%
Brands Purchased: Nike 35%; Reebok 18%; Adidas 16%; Champion 9%; Russell 7%
Access Internet Regularly: 65%
Internet Purchase in past 12 months: 38%
Own a Video Game System: 43%

MLB Fans
Age: 28% are between 18–34; 30% are 55+
Education: 59% attended or graduated college
Income: 49% earn 50K+ annually
Gender: 60% male/40% female
Shopped for sporting goods in past three months: 52%
Purchased Licensed Apparel in past 12 months: 42%

Stores Shopped: Wal-Mart 24%; Kmart 15%; TSA 8%; Target 8%
Brands Purchased: Nike 35%; Reebok 18%; Adidas 17%; Champion 9%; Russell 7%
Access Internet Regularly: 64%
Internet Purchase in past 12 months: 37%
Own a Video Game System: 42%

MLS Fans
Age: 44% are between 18–34
Education: 59% attended or graduated college
Income: 43% make $50K+ annually
Gender: 61% male/39% female
Shopped for sporting goods in past three months: 59%
Purchased Licensed Apparel in past 12 months: 43%
Stores Shopped: Wal-Mart 24%; Kmart 17%; TSA 9%; Target 9%; Sears 8%
Brands Purchased: Nike 45%; Adidas 32%; Reebok 22%; Champion 11%; Russell 5%
Access Internet Regularly: 68%
Internet Purchase in past 12 months: 40%
Own a Video Game System: 46%

NASCAR Fans
Age: 32% are between 18–34
Education: 53% attended or graduated college
Income: 43% earn $50K+ annually
Gender: 66% male/34% female
Shopped for sporting goods in past three months: 57%
Purchased Licensed Apparel in past 12 months: 46%
Stores Shopped: Wal-Mart 34%; Kmart 20%; Target 9%; TSA 6%
Brands Purchased: Nike 33%; Reebok 20%; Adidas 16%; Champion 8%; Russell 6%
Access Internet Regularly: 60%
Internet Purchase in past 12 months: 33%
Own a Video Game System: 49%

Scarborough USA+ is an aggregate of 75 local markets that Scarborough currently surveys along with an additional sample representing the balance of the U.S. The data was collected from adults 18+ via telephone interview, product booklet and TV diary. Over 100,000 respondents were surveyed August 2000 through March 2001. Scarborough USA+ enables you to compare and contrast the American consumer lifestyle on local, regional and national levels.

Endorsement

Endorsements are situations whereby the endorser — an individual or an organization — promotes the merits of a particular product or company to potential consumers of that product or company. Endorsers receive remuneration, either financial or in-kind with products, in return for their endorsement of products or brands.

While endorsements have been a mainstay for sporting goods companies since the industry's inception, outside forces have significantly influenced an athlete's potential as an endorser in recent years. One of these forces has been the news media's relatively recent (over the past 30 years) penchant to write about an athlete's personal behavior. Historically, an athlete's bad habits were largely unknown to anyone except those very close to him or her. And even if they were known, they tended to be overshadowed by the athlete's skill and performance, largely because their bad habits rarely, if ever, made headlines.

That's not the case today. Most athletes' behavior is scrutinized from almost every angle. Drug testing is prevalent throughout all professional and amateur sports, and a failed drug test receives widespread publicity. Temper tantrums, either on or off the field, inevitably lead to bad publicity, often with serious consequences for an athlete's endorsement potential. The result of all this is that choosing athletes and teams as endorsers in today's environment is much more complicated than it was in the past. Sporting goods companies, whose livelihood depends a great deal on these endorsements, have had to develop far more rigorous evaluation procedures than they ever used in the past to chose their endorsers.

Just as for licensing, achieving maximum credibility and visibility is the benefit to the company receiving the endorsement. Endorsements by athletes, leagues and teams are usually presented to consumers in broadcast and print advertising, and also by providing athletes (or leagues or teams) with the company's equipment (or apparel or footwear) to use when competing. One clear example of an endorsement is Easton Sports' comments on a new television campaign, reported in *Sporting Goods Business Daily Dispatch*, May 23, 2005:

> The new television campaign is an evolution of our previous work for Easton," said Kyle Horn, vice president of account and business development at The Ballpark, Easton's advertising agency of record. "Previous 'PLAY WITH IT. OR AGAINST IT.' print campaigns emphasized different aspects of the brand, such as authenticity and product quality. This new television series pulls each of these threads together along with athlete endorsements and specific technology benefits surrounding CNT. We're really happy with how the new campaign turned out and believe it delivers a technological, contemporary feel that matches Easton's new product line.

Another example:

> To support the launch of the apparel, Body Glove plans to implement a national advertising campaign in Spring 2006, and will utilize sponsorships of prominent surfers such as Beck and Adam Robertson, and top AVP beach volleyball players Sean Rosenthal and Larry Witt, to endorse and promote the sportswear collection [*Sporting Goods Business*, April 2005].

A perceived company endorsement is often a desired result of a licensing arrangement. For example, if a company has a licensing arrangement with the NFL on a particular product, it's possible for the NFL image to be perceived by consumers as enhancing all their products, not just the products that are licensed. Achieving this kind of result requires expert marketing and promotion skills on the part of the company receiving the endorsement.

Endorsement negotiations between sporting goods companies and athletes require a great deal of skill and judgement on the part of both parties. Endorsement relationships are fraught with risks for both parties. The most successful relationships usually evolve over a period of time as the company and the endorser get to know one another's needs and personality. Even when this happens, the financial arrangements of the relationship must suit both parties.

Very often people will ask whether athletes are really worth the millions of dollars they are paid to endorse sporting goods products. The answer to that question is obvi-

---

"NFL quarterback Brett Favre has teamed up with Starter, which was acquired by Nike last year, to endorse the brand's full line of athletic footwear and apparel for the value retail channel." *Sporting Goods Business Daily Dispatch*, March 15, 2005.

ous—you can't pay an athlete too much for an endorsement, as long as sales and profits of the products produced are sufficient to pay the athlete and still generate a profit for the company.

The value of endorsements in the sporting goods industry are judged on a bottom-line basis, rather than on the absolute amount of money spent for the endorsement. The highly competitive environment in collegiate and professional sports, the chance for physical injury, potential morality problems and the ability to spend enough money to achieve consumer awareness of the endorsement are all major considerations in the endorsement process. It's much more complicated than just picking up the phone and hiring an athlete to endorse your product.

Endorsements are generally (although not always) used by larger companies who can afford to sufficiently advertise the existence of the endorsement and who can afford to pay the high fees associated with widely popular athletes. Smaller companies benefit when athletes are seen participating in events wearing company logos or otherwise communicating that they are a spokesperson for the company's products.

The following quote, from an article in the May 2005 issue of *Sporting Goods Business,* best exemplifies the value of endorsement in sporting goods:

> Promoting that way of life and creating a strong tie-in between cars, fashion, sports and celebrities is the foundation of 310 Motoring's (a footwear brand) marketing agenda. Broadcast and print campaigns, product placement — in movies, primetime sitcoms, and on the feet of a growing list of "influencers"— keeps 310 Motoring top-of-mind with the 18- to 36-year-old male demographic. "The advertising, the marketing . . . it's extremely important," offers Munaker. "But then, the Greenbergs are famous for that."
> TV and print is very important," concurs Quinn, "*but what Marc does with the athletes, celebrities and other influencers is really the heart of it*" [emphasis added].

Entertainment Personalities As Endorsers

Very recently, within the past three years, selected sporting goods companies, particularly in apparel and footwear, began hiring popular entertainment personalities to endorse their products. Clearly, the purpose of this effort is to present their products in a "hip" or "cool" environment, appealing to the market segments where the entertainers are popular. Young, popular musicians are most often chosen. It remains to be seen whether this effort is an effective stimulant to sales. To the extent that product style and brand image become more important in the basic appeal of sporting goods products, even for high-performance categories, this approach may serve the industry well.

Sponsorship

Sponsorships provide similar benefits to the sponsor as do licensing and endorsement. They call attention to a company's products or services in a favorable environment, adding product credibility and visibility. If event participants are looked up to by spectators (either at the event or on air), credibility and visibility occur when the sponsor's products are associated with the event in the minds of spectators and viewers.

Licensing and endorsement costs consume a major portion of marketing budgets for most sporting goods companies. Consequently, funds available for sponsorship are more limited than might exist in other industries. Very often, sporting goods companies therefore provide sponsorship in the form of no-charge or low-cost equipment, apparel or footwear to event participants, which would otherwise be paid for by the event management.

Historically, sporting goods companies were considered as the primary sponsors of sports events. It was more or less expected since the companies had established close relationships with teams, leagues and organizations while conducting business. Their association with the events served much the same purpose as did licensing and endorsements —calling favorable attention to their products.

However, over the past 30 years or so, event and league sponsorship has exploded as a marketing medium. Companies in nearly every market segment —consumer and business products and services— are heavily investing in sponsorship. Events and leagues are becoming much more sophisticated, and they've found ways to greatly enhance the commercial appeal of their services. The net result leaves the sporting goods companies— except the very largest — in the lurch since sponsorship costs have increased significantly.

The great majority of sponsorship activity by sporting goods sponsorship programs is and always has been devoted to sports events, teams and athletes. However, in recent years, some of the larger companies have become involved in sponsorship of concerts and cultural events, particularly those appealing to youth and young adult markets.

Forms of Sponsorship

Sporting goods sponsorships involve some combination of the following:

- in-kind merchandise (exchanging products/services for sponsorship benefits)
- fees
- advertising/promotional support

Sporting goods companies tend to search for opportunities to achieve measurable benefits from their sponsorships. They are less inclined to pursue sponsorships whose main promise is exposure of their product. Most often, sporting goods companies will want marketing rights for their products to the team's or event's audience or fan base. For example, company X might be a well-known sports brand, so sponsorship of a team or event won't significantly enhance awareness of their products. However, if company X sells athletic jackets and they are worn by individuals or participants in the team or event's fans or coverage area, the sponsorship is much more attractive.

Sponsorship often takes the shape of becoming the "official" product for the sponsored organization — such as the official baseball or the official uniform. Sometimes this requirement stands for all competition — such as for all NBA games. Other times, the events covered by the sponsorship are limited. For example, an NCAA sponsor is entitled to representation in predetermined NCAA championships, but not for regular season college games. Companies with "official" recognition often acquire licensing rights for their products from the team, league or event.

Thus, as we see, sponsorship, licensing and endorsement are often combined in order to maximize the value of a relationship with a team, league, event or athlete.

Sponsorship Opportunities

There are seven major types of sponsorship opportunities. Each of these exist internationally, nationally, regionally and/or locally. These types are:

1. individual events
2. professional leagues/organizations
3. professional teams
4. youth leagues

5. youth teams   7. college teams
6. college organizations

Almost every sporting goods vendor and many sporting goods retailers become involved in some aspect of national, regional or local sports event, team or league sponsorships, providing funding, personnel and/or promotional activities. Depending on the size of the company, they will usually become involved in sponsoring one or more of the following types of organizations and/or events, listed in order of importance:

- grassroots youth leagues such as Little League Baseball, Pop Warner Football, or local recreational programs
- collegiate sports teams, conferences, and events
- professional sports leagues and events

Grassroots events are the most widely used form of event sponsorship for retailers, whereas vendors are more likely to sponsor programs at all levels of competition. Grassroots event participants are all prime prospects for the products of sporting goods companies. Sponsoring companies provide free products or funds to promote attendance and participation in the event.

Sporting goods vendors and retailers will use their own employees or hire local individuals to help implement the sponsorship to maximize its effectiveness by working with event managers to develop and promote the event.

Larger companies, particularly footwear companies, who can afford it will sometimes sponsor collegiate sports events. These events would include such events as NCAA, conference or regional championships for specific sports, or a specific event featuring long-standing rivals. Some of these companies will also sponsor athletic programs at specific colleges, providing equipment, apparel and footwear for selected or all varsity athletic teams.

Professional sports events are rarely sponsored by sporting goods companies. The relatively high cost and the fleeting nature of any one event makes professional sports events an inefficient investment. Only the largest companies can afford the significant costs associated with this type of sponsorship. The same holds true for professional teams, particularly major-league teams. Again, only the largest companies can afford the investment required. One example of this type of sponsorship is Adidas' sponsorship of the New York Yankees.

However, team sponsorships do not override league sponsorships, preventing Adidas from the right to produce Yankee uniforms used on the field. Major League Baseball contracts with uniform producers for all uniforms worn by their member teams. This kind of limitation reduces the value of a professional team sponsorship for sporting goods companies.

Large retailers often sponsor both professional and grassroots sports event related to products they sell in their stores. A good example is Cabela's Sportsman's Quest, Inc., a company set up by Cabela's (a major retailer of outdoor sports equipment in Sydney, Nebraska). Their website (www.sportsmansquest.com) features a magazine and results from the various events they sponsor throughout the year.

Evaluating Sponsorship Opportunities

As we've already indicated, sponsorship offers a wide range of opportunities. However, no matter the order of magnitude of a sponsorship program — local, regional, national or international—there are certain fundamentals related to the evaluation of any sponsorship program. These principles are very well documented in an article in the May 2005 issue of *SportBusiness International*, a leading publication serving the worldwide sport sponsorship market. This article is reproduced below in its entirety.

TV Exposure Isn't Everything
By Kevin Roberts
(*SportBusiness International*, May 2005; www.sportbusiness.com)

Giles Morgan, new managing director of the European sports marketing division unit at PR heavyweights Hill & Knowlton, is currently in his second stint with the company which, as part of the WPP marketing services group, sees itself at the leading edge of sponsorship integration within a broader marketing environment.

Morgan, who returned the H&K fold after a lengthy stint with Craigie Taylor, subsequently the GEM Group, is eloquently passionate about the role of PR in sports marketing and sponsorship.

"We all understand that investment in the major sports such as football and F1 is about connecting with customers through a shared passion in sport but I'm not so sure that marketers are thinking hard enough about the way that people actually and realistically engage in their sporting passions. Whilst live events are at the heart of the sporting experience, the reality is that for 85 per cent of people, the day-to-day link to their passion is through the media coverage of sport—whether it be in the newspapers, live broadcast or online.

"Once you understand that, the role of PR and media communications for major international sports sponsorship is the ability to inform and influence so the media agenda becomes clearer and more comprehensible," he said.

Morgan also takes a pragmatic view of the 21st century sponsorship environment and is quietly despairing of those who equate sponsorship opportunity and value solely to television exposure.

"It's not the case now and it never had been," he said.

"To understand sponsorship you have to understand that it is all about matching client's objectives with third party marketing assets. Sponsorship is not a one-size-fits-all marketing solution. Sponsorship is about building partnerships that create opportunities to meet quite specific business and brand objectives.

"On one hand the objective might well just be about brand visibility—about getting your logo in front of as many people as possible—a straightforward media buy. This is the traditional sponsorship model and whilst there are far fewer sponsors like that around today, these brands should have done a thorough analysis of their brand objectives and the sponsorship, and concluded that they will get value for their money.

"On the other hand there are those companies who might have a target audience of as few as, say, 200 highly influential customers or influencers throughout the world. They too may find that an appropriate sponsorship provides the best way of achieving their objective of communicating with their target audience via meaningful dialogue through an association. Brand awareness is more or less an irrelevance so far as they are concerned."

Morgan believes that understanding these disparate objectives is key to understanding the role of sponsorship in a changing media environment.

"While it is the case that major sports are all about engaging with their fan base through their consumption of media, and in particular about television, that's not the case elsewhere in minor sports. There are millions of people whose lives are touched by sports that cannot guarantee even a tiny percentage of the coverage that football and other premier tier sports take for granted.

"That doesn't mean that they have no value for sponsors. The key element is the way that they can engage with their participants or fans and create an opportunity for sponsors to engage with customers. The next important thing is the creativity and expertise with which that passion can be harnessed to achieve set sponsor objectives. With secondary or tertiary sports, that is far less likely to be left to television coverage and will depend on communication achieved across a wide range of other media, both in specialist publications, newspapers and in the new media channels which have become such a central part of our lives.

"We have to understand that big properties have an inherent media value and that others simply don't and it's frustrating to see secondary sports putting too much emphasis and value on media value when, in fact, there are other means of activating and delivering hugely successful sponsorship programmes."

INTEGRATION

Morgan's return to Hill & Knowlton sees him back in the orbit of a company that has invested to develop its sports expertise alongside other specialist areas including healthcare and public affairs.

But while H&K is among the world's leading PR brands, Morgan is aware that its greatest strength will increasingly be found in its relationships with WPP, which also includes sports aligned brands such as Global Sportnet and Performance.

"All forms of marketing are, ultimately, about aligning brands to customers," he said.

"To do that you have to have a clear understanding of both brand objectives and more specific business objectives and, within those, to understand what success actually looks like. Once you have that you have the starting point.

"Within a major marketing services group we have the breadth of skills and experience to be able to understand what a client's brand and business require and develop programmes to get them to where they need to be. There are many different pieces to all this and you can be sure that no single agency has all of the skills or all of the answers. It's often a question of drawing in the relevant skills, whether they are PR, advertising, hospitality, experiential marketing, sales promotion or whatever else it takes to achieve objectives."

That said, Morgan is only too aware that is not necessary to activate every trick in the marketing services book to make a sponsorship work.

"There are so many reasons to get involved in sponsorship that it is extremely unwise to generalise," he said.

"If your business objective is to develop relationships with just 150 extremely influential people, you may well decide to take the sponsorship route but have no reason for activating anything other than the hospitality rights. You only need to activate across the entire marketing mix if it makes sense."

There are many reasons for getting involved in sponsorship. Morgan well recalls one former client who became the sponsor of a major international property not because of any intrinsic interest in the property or broad marketing objective.

"The brand agreed to pay a considerable sponsorship fee because they had been approached by a customer which spends many millions of dollars with them each year. They did the sums and took the view that despite the size of the sponsorship, it would secure the longer-term relationships with a valuable client and was worth every cent for that reason alone.

"Likewise, sponsorship can be the right investment for multinational businesses that are wishing to engage with their workforce to instill a sense of pride, loyalty and focus as it can be for a brand that wishes to communicate with a multinational mass consumer market through football."

The message from Morgan is loud and clear. "Investment in third party marketing assets can be an extremely useful weapon in the war-chest of corporate brands. The key to success is to pre-rationalise before embarking on relationships as to what are the objectives of the business and brand, and identifying who and where is the target market. Armed with this information, there is a raft of opportunity to associate with all manner of properties."

Market research can be used generally in basically two ways to help evaluate the benefits of sports marketing programs. One is changes in sales that result from sports marketing; the second is the degree to which a company's image improves among existing and potential customers as a result of the sports marketing program. Sporting goods companies have long been aware, based largely on experience, that sports marketing is more effective for them than any other form of marketing — whether it be advertising or promotion. Thus, within the industry, sporting goods companies are most often evaluating sales to detect any changes that occur if they change the nature of their sports marketing program. Changing consumer perceptions are less important to sporting goods companies, since any change in consumer perceptions is likely to have a reasonably quick influence on positive (or negative) sales results.

Sports Marketing Program Variation Within the Industry

Sports marketing is an integral part of every segment of the industry; however usage patterns vary in form depending on several factors, which are sales volume, sports for which the product is used, and the market segment to which the product appeals.

Company Sales Volume

Larger companies can afford to invest more heavily in national and international programs than can smaller companies. The larger the company, the more it can devote necessary financial resources to the most desirable form of sports marketing — coordinated licensing, endorsement and sponsorship programs, each element of which enhances the other elements.

Sports for Which the Product Is Used

Competitive sports such as team sports, golf and tennis are extremely desirable avenues for sports marketing. Winning teams or athletes are highly publicized within the sports community, and to the extent that their names are associated with a product, clearly that product is a prime beneficiary. Even within the recreational sports market, there are competitive events, such as fishing tournaments or bicycle races, which also lend themselves to sports marketing, particularly sponsorships. Outdoor and fitness products are less likely to benefit from sports marketing programs.

Market Segment to Which the Product Appeals

The most obvious example of a market segment to which a product appeals is the role model appeal of athletes and leagues to young people, particularly children and teenagers. The youth market comprises the largest segment of most team sports products, including equipment, footwear and apparel. Sporting goods marketers are acutely aware of this basic phenomenon, and for most products appealing to this segment, sports marketing is the major, if not only, form of marketing used for these products. Another market segment for which sports marketing is most important is comprised of individuals who are constantly striving to perform at higher levels within a sport. In general, it can be said that the importance of sports marketing depends on how deeply individual participants are involved in their sports activities.

Why Sports Marketing Is More Important in Sporting Goods than in Other Industries

There are several fundamental differences between sports marketing in the sporting goods industry and sports marketing in non-sports companies and industries. The most obvious difference are the products produced by sports marketers—for sporting goods companies, the product has a direct role in the sport, whether it be for athletes, teams, organizations or events. For other types of companies using sports marketing, the products or services range from having a tangential relationship to being totally unrelated to athletes, teams, organizations or events.

As a result of this basic differentiation, sports marketing programs for sporting goods companies operate differently from those utilized by non-sporting goods companies in several ways.

- Most marketing expenditures in the sporting goods industry are devoted to sports marketing. In contrast, sports marketing represents a relatively minor part of marketing budgets for non-sporting goods companies, with the possible exception of beer producers. This distinction manifests itself in several ways: senior executives at sporting goods companies are much more likely to be involved in the decision-making process and management efforts related to sports marketing, financial fortunes of sporting goods companies are more closely tied to the success of their sports marketing programs, and sporting goods brand names are much more closely associated with athletes or organizations with whom they are involved.
- Sporting goods products are very often used during competition by athletes or in the events with which they are associated. Not so in the case of non-sporting goods companies. Many times this creates a unique risk-reward situation for the sporting goods companies. If athletes or teams use their products and win—clearly the vendor benefits—but if they don't, the vendor doesn't benefit nearly as much.
- Performance-related marketing strategies are common in the sporting goods industry; vendors often depend on athlete usage and endorsement to communicate the superior performance of their products. It's a lot easier to convince a golfer that if Tiger Woods plays with Nike clubs and balls, that the equipment is superior, than it is to use sports marketing to convince a consumer that Visa is really better than American Express.
- Sporting goods companies are most likely to manage their sports marketing programs in house; whereas non-sporting goods companies will most likely engage the services of sports marketing agencies.
- Sporting goods companies are much more likely to evaluate sports marketing programs based on product sales. Non-sporting goods companies generally use more broadly-based criteria such as the enhancement of corporate image perceptions among their current and potential customers.

RELATED WEBSITES

PROFESSIONAL AND COLLEGIATE SPORTS ORGANIZATIONS DEALING WITH LICENSING:

Collegiate Licensing Company: www.clc.com
Indy Racing League: www.indycar.com

Licensing Resource Group: www.lrgusa.com
Major League Baseball Authentic Licensed Products: http://shop.mlb.com
Major League Soccer: www.mlsgear.com
NASCAR: www.nascar.com
National Basketball Association: http://store.nba.com
National Football League: www.nflshop.com
National Hockey League: http://nhl.com/shop
World Wrestling Federation: www.wwf.com

ONLINE LICENSED PRODUCTS RETAILERS:

Fans Edge (online licensed product retailer): www.fansedge.com
Lids (brick-and-mortar/online retailer): www.lids.com
New Era Cap Co. (major licensed product supplier): www.neweracap.com
Sporting Goods Business (covers licensing): www.sportinggoodsbusiness.com

SPORTS MARKETING AGENCIES:

IMG: www.imgworld.com
Octagon: www.octagon.com/clients/athletes.php

SPONSORSHIP PROGRAMS:

New Balance: www.newbalance.com/eventsteamnb/index.html

EXERCISES

1. Explain the role of sporting goods companies in licensing vs. endorsements vs. sponsorship, and discuss how sporting goods companies benefit from each of these sports marketing activities.

2. Prepare a summary of the different types of licensing and how they differ. The types are discussed in this chapter.

3. Write a brief summary of the major benefits of licensing.

4. Describe the difference between licensing and endorsement.

5. Explain how you would evaluate the results of a sports marketing program.

6. Describe the basic difference between professional sports licensing policies and NCAA licensing policies.

7. Compare the benefits and risks involved with athlete endorsements.

8. Briefly describe the three types of sponsorships and the role of sporting goods vendors and retailers in each type of sponsorship.

9. Is sports marketing more or less important in sporting goods than in other industries? Why?

7

Broadcast and Print Advertising and Market Research

OVERVIEW

Because of the value endorsements play in sporting goods marketing, athletes and teams are often used to convey the product or company's message in the advertising.

Media advertising in any industry exists to create awareness of the industry's products among the consuming public and to motivate consumers to purchase the industry's products. In the sporting goods industry, traditional advertising is much less important than in most other consumer product industries. For most consumer products, consumer media advertising is a major factor in the process of generating sales. In sporting goods, however, several factors combine to limit or even eliminate the value of an investment by sporting goods vendors in traditional media advertising.

One major factor inhibiting the value of media advertising is the relatively short buying season for products in any one sport. The industry is really a potpourri of many different sports with different seasons. For most equipment products, as much as 80 percent of purchases are made within a 60 to 90 day period immediately preceding or in the very early stages of the season when that sport is played. Given that consumer advertising's impact is generally more cumulative than immediate, there isn't enough time for media advertising to be effective. Other inhibiting factors include the relatively small size of the hundreds, even thousands, of companies serving the sporting goods marketplace, and the fact that sports marketing is generally more effective and therefore receives most marketing dollars invested by sporting goods companies.

Athletic footwear vendors dominate consumer advertising within the industry, and only the giant companies, notably Nike and Adidas (now including Reebok), are significant advertisers in general national media. Most sporting goods companies, if they invest in advertising at all, do so using vertical media vehicles. Vertical media is comprised of (a) any magazine or broadcast program directed specifically at participants in a particular sport, or (b) any magazine or broadcast program focused on a specific sport., such as a televised golf tournament.

Within the sporting goods industry, three factors play an uppermost role in the selection process of media vehicles used, as well as actual advertising content. These factors are

1. product performance and the ability of the product to enhance the athlete's performance will strongly influence a consumer's preference for a particular brand;
2. there are really two basic markets for sporting goods products ... a market among athletes and a much broader market for sports apparel and footwear; and

3. a wide range of demand for price and quality between sports participants and casual or activewear buyers. As a result, media selection for sports equipment and for performance-related apparel and footwear, is highly targeted to reach participants, particularly those most actively involved in the sport for which the equipment is used. Advertising content, whether direct or subtle, is focused on product performance and the ability of the product to enhance an athlete's performance. Since athlete endorsement, and the attendant relatively high costs, is often an essential ingredient in advertising content, the amount spent on traditional advertising media is less than for most consumer product categories.

With rare exceptions, a typical sporting goods vendor will spend less than 2% of their revenues on traditional advertising. Only a handful of companies, such as Nike, Reebok, Icon Health & Fitness, and Adidas spend more. Many smaller sporting goods companies don't do any consumer advertising at all.

At the end of this chapter, you should be able to:

• Identify the factors which influence the relative importance of traditional consumer and trade advertising in sporting goods vs. other marketing techniques.
• Describe how sporting goods companies choose media advertising media.

Identify the difference between mass and vertical or targeted media forms, and the relative importance of each in sporting goods.

Identify how the recent explosion of the market for athletic apparel and footwear has influenced sporting goods advertising.

Understand the influence of market segmentation in the use of traditional consumer and trade advertising in sporting goods.

DISCUSSION

Advertising

The great majority of sporting goods vendors and retailers spend relatively modest amounts of money on advertising as a group, far less as a percentage of total sales than do most other consumer product companies. Advertising for many consumer product categories averages 5 percent or more of total sales, whereas in the sporting goods industry, total consumer advertising is less than 2 percent of sales. Many sporting goods vendors, particular medium- and small-size companies, do not sponsor any consumer advertising in any form.

In 2004, Nike, the world's largest sporting goods company, was the only sporting goods company among the top 100 national advertisers (ranking 65th), with estimated total expenditures of $573.9 million (*Advertising Age*, June 27, 2005). Considering measured media expenditures only (magazine, newspaper, outdoor, TV, radio and Internet), Nike ranked even lower (88th) among the top 100 advertisers, with expenditures of $220.1 million.

In 2004, sporting goods measured media advertising totaled $492.2 million, ranking 25th among all product categories. The major portion of this amount was spent in magazines, followed by 22 percent in TV and 6 percent in all other measured media forms.

Based on these statistics, Nike's expenditures represented nearly 45 percent of all measured media expenditures. Consumer advertising in traditional media, including TV, print and radio, is sponsored primarily by major footwear firms (Nike, Adidas, Reebok and New Balance), leading golf companies (Titleist, TaylorMade and Callaway), and fitness companies (Icon Health & Fitness, Brunswick and Nautilus). That's because, while the overall market for sporting goods products is in total a mass market, there are literally thousands of different products that serve this market, each with its own niche. For most consumer products—such as toiletries, cosmetics, automobiles, food, drugs, or electronics —almost everyone is a potential buyer. Choices between products relate primarily to how much the individual buyer can afford. Everybody eats. Everybody brushes their teeth (let's hope so!). Everybody drives a car. Everybody watches television. Everybody washes their hands. Everybody drinks soda.

Not so are these generalities in the sporting goods market. While most consumers use at least one sporting goods product, whether it be for fitness, golf, camping, running, baseball, basketball, soccer, hockey, volleyball, boating, hunting, bicycling, archery, tennis, skiing, fishing, or any one of hundreds of sports activities, the market for any one product represents a tiny portion, often less than one-tenth of one percent, of the total population. Each product is produced and marketed in a different way, so the advantage of large volume sales for one product that normally applies to consumer products rarely exists for sporting goods products. This factor inhibits the ability of vendors to devote enough funds to make consumer advertising by itself an effective or efficient medium for most companies and most products.

Another factor which weighs heavily on the amount of money sporting goods vendors can spend is that a lot of factors are involved that influence a sporting goods consumer's perception of a branded product. Word of mouth among consumers, team, league and athlete endorsements, availability in retail stores, and consumer experience with and acceptance of other products offered by the company, all play heavily in the marketing mix for sporting goods products. No matter how effective the advertising, the weight of all these other factors will go a long way toward determining a company or product's success in the marketplace, and if these factors aren't positive, no amount of advertising can overcome the negatives. Media forms most often used by the industry include print (magazines and catalogs) and electronic (network TV, cable TV, radio, infomercials and online).

Advertising Content Orientation

Sporting goods advertising is not usually theme or image oriented, with the exception of ads sponsored by major footwear companies such as Nike ("Just Do It"), Reebok ("I Am What I Am") and New Balance ("For Love Or Money"). The great majority of advertising sponsored by sporting goods vendors and retailers will focus on specific, timely situations related to an event or an athlete.

Even campaigns by the largest companies in the industry which are theme oriented often include copy interwoven with a specific product, event or athlete. This represents an attempt to implant the image of a brand together with the benefits of a particular product or company-sponsored event.

One important thing to recognize is that the use of athletes does two things. It gives the advertiser credibility for the product being advertised, and it allows the sporting goods company to benefit from the athlete's exposure when he or she is performing or promoting other products. Athletes carry a lot more exposure value in an advertisement than do models or announcers who are otherwise unknown to consumers.

Budgeting for advertising is, therefore, most often done on a project-by-project basis.

A vendor who has a new product, decides to expand marketing to new heretofore neglected market segments, joins forces with a new athlete endorser, signs on as a sponsor for a major event or program, or establishes a relationship with a sports governing body will usually require some form of media campaign, most often as a part of a multimedia program involving advertising, promotion, in-store displays, catalog mailings and other types of marketing tools. Since it's often difficult to predict opportunities which may suddenly appear, budgeting for advertising campaigns is more fluid, opportunistic and less consistent than in most other industries. The discussion below includes a brief list of several opportunistic advertising campaigns.

Seasonality

Most sporting goods products are highly seasonal — they are purchased within a two to three month period immediately preceding a sport's season and through the season's early stages. Vendors and retailers are well aware of this and they plan their advertising and promotion efforts accordingly. Even advertising in publications that are exclusively devoted to a sport will be significantly curtailed during the "non-buying" season.

Here are some examples reflecting the high degree of specificity in sporting goods advertising:

- Under Armour promoting a line of products for women.
- Nike's Brett Favre endorsing Starter, a brand Nike recently purchased.
- Shoe Carnival using an advertising campaign to announce their redesigned store look.
- Reebok promoting it's sponsorship of an event — tying in with it's overall national campaign.
- Reebok supporting its acquisition of The Hockey Company.
- Puma promoting its new products as being cool with interesting graphics.
- Nike using NBA players to promote its marketing partnership with the NBA.
- Quiksilver and DC using a tie-in with ESPN's Winter X Games to launch a national advertising campaign with athletes from both brands featured in new ads set to debut during the games.
- FootJoy launching a new advertising campaign featuring SignBoy, the golf fanatic.
- Adidas supporting its newly-signed relationship with MLS with a national advertising campaign.

Consumer Magazines

Which is cause and which is effect, no one knows for certain, but certainly interest in sports has played a major role in spawning the enormous consumer demand for specialty magazines and broadcast programming directed at specific market segments (commonly identified as vertical media). There is at least one consumer magazine for nearly every sport; and for many sports, there are several. These publications appeal primarily to individuals who are very serious about the sport, and who tend to spend the most money for equipment and related products. Thus, these publications are natural places where marketers of specific sporting goods products will invest in advertising. Because the circulation of the magazine is limited to those deeply interested in the sport, the audience is relatively small, making advertising much more affordable while at the same time targeted to the precise potential market for a specific sporting goods product. With the exception of the leading vendors (Nike, Adidas, Reebok, Titleist, Callaway and TaylorMade), most consumer advertising is done in vertical media. The more general magazines and television programs (so-called mass media) are much too expensive on a cost per prospect basis because most of the people they reach do not participate in any one sport in large enough numbers to justify an advertising investment.

Listed below are some of the more popular independent consumer magazines for sports. Most sporting goods companies with products in the category, except for the smallest companies, will do some advertising in these publications. In addition to the publications listed below, several companies, such as Athlon and Street & Smith, publish annual magazines, primarily for various team sports, focused on the upcoming season. Finally, most governing bodies for amateur sports will publish one or more magazines focused on their sport.

- Adventure Sports: *Adventure Sports* (new in 2005)
- Archery: *Bowhunting.net* (online)
- Baseball: *Baseball America*; *Baseball Digest*
- Basketball: *Basketball Times*: *Hoop*
- Bicycling: *Bicycling Magazine*; *Mountain Bike*
- Billiards: *Billiards Digest*; *Pool and Billiard Magazine*
- Boating: *Motor Boating & Sailing*; *Power & Motoryacht*; *Sailing*
- Fishing: *Bassmaster*; *Fly Fisherman*; *Salt Water Sportsman*
- Fitness: *Men's Fitness*; *Muscle & Fitness*; *Shape*
- General: *ESPN The Magazine*; *Sports Illustrated*
- Golf: *Golf Digest*; *Golf For Women*; *Golf Magazine*; *Golf Plus (Sports Illustrated)*
- Gymnastics: *International Gymnast*
- Hunting: *Peterson's Hunting*
- Running: *Runner's World*
- Scuba: *Scuba Diving*
- Skateboarding: *Transworld Skateboarding*
- Skiing: *Ski Magazine*; *Skiing*
- Snowboarding: *Snowboarder Magazine*; *Transworld Snowboarding*
- Soccer: *Soccer America*
- Tennis: *Tennis*; *Tennis Week*
- Track & Field: *Track & Field News*

Another economic inhibition to advertising expenditures in the sporting goods industry is that consumer advertising often requires the use of athletes to demonstrate that a product is superior in performance. Fees for the services of prominent athletes are considerably higher than actors typically working in consumer commercials. This has the effect of raising the cost to produce ads and commercials to much higher levels than they might be for most consumer products.

Some sporting goods products such as basketballs, soccer balls, baseballs, and certain sports medicine products sell in quantities of millions and could be considered mass. On the surface, one could expect consumer advertising would be productive. However, looks are deceiving. Most of these products require costly athlete endorsement or league sponsorships to succeed in the marketplace; thus precluding the availability of enough advertising funds to successfully mount an effective consumer advertising campaign.

Trade Publications

Trade publications (magazines and newsletters) in the sporting goods industry serve readers primarily involved in the businesses of sporting goods retailing, wholesaling, and manufacturing. Retailers represent the primary audience for all trade publications in the industry; thus the great majority of advertising carried by these publications is directed at these retailers. No trade publications are designed to specifically serve sporting goods vendors. However, information they carry is often of considerable interest not only to vendors but also to allied services such as advertising agencies, financial analysts, technology providers and marketing consultants. These magazines deal extensively with news and features related to new products, fashion trends within the industry, financial trends and developments, new media and technology as it relates to the industry, market research survey results, retailer directories, retailing and merchandising programs, trade shows and other similar subjects. They are a vital part of the chain of communication between retailers and vendors.

Currently, there are three general magazines that cover the industry, *Sporting Goods Business* (monthly; a VNU publication), *NSGA Focus* (bi-monthly; published by the NSGA), and *Sporting Goods Dealer* (bi-monthly, a VNU publication). *Sporting Goods Business*, founded in 1965, the oldest and largest publication of the three, has been archived by SBRnet, a leading online industry database, since 1996. These archives provide a veritable treasure-trove of industry history, having reported on all major industry activities during that period. Two major newsletters serve the industry — VNU's weekly *SGB's Inside Sporting Goods* and *Sporting Goods Intelligence*, published by Sporting Goods Intelligence, Inc.

Several other trade publications serve various market segments. They include but are not limited to: *Archery Business, Bicycle Retailer & Industry News, Bowling Industry, Club Business, Fishing Tackle Retailer, Golf Shop Operations, Golf Product News, Health & Fitness Business, Hunting Business, Outdoor Business, Shooting Sports Retailer,* and *Tennis Industry.*

Trade magazines often serve as a marketing tool for trade shows. They provide an ongoing communications vehicle for trade show producers, since they are read by potential exhibitors and show attendees.

One factor significantly impacting trade magazines is rapid retail consolidation. Trade magazines were originally developed to serve the needs of thousands of individual retailers, providing a vehicle for vendors to communicate with potential customers on a regular basis. However, in recent years, retailers have consolidated to a point where over 50 percent of the business is done with fewer than 100 retailers. One major result of this consolidation is that trade magazines and newsletters focus less on new product features, and more on industry trends and financial developments.

Catalogs

Catalogs are used by retailers to reach consumers, by vendors to reach retailers, and by team dealers to reach team and institutional customers.

Catalogs represent a major marketing ingredient for athletic footwear and outdoor sports retailers. In the outdoor market, dominant retailers such as Bass Pro Shops, Cabela's, Campmor, Eastern Mountain Sports, L.L.Bean, Orvis, and REI all provide catalogs, chock-full of merchandise. In the athletic footwear market, Foot Locker and The Finish Line, the two leading athletic footwear retailers, mail millions of catalogs annually, as do Eastbay and Road Runner Sports, among the first catalog producers serving the footwear market. Catalogs are also used, but to a lesser extent than outdoor and footwear, by baseball, fitness, golf, track and field, and women's product retailers.

Some mid-size and small sports equipment, apparel and footwear vendors use catalogs to market their products to retailers. Although actual numbers of catalogs mailed are not available for most companies, Cabela's is most likely among the most active, sending out over 150 million catalogs annually.

When the Internet first came on the scene in the late 1990s, many industry experts thought it might sink the value of catalogs. While this has, indeed, happened, this phenomenon did not result in the disappearance of catalogs. Rather, retailers have discovered that a combination of Internet and catalog merchandising has enabled retailers to equal, and often significantly increase, catalog-only sales prior to the Internet's appearance. Two factors help to explain this evolution:

1. Some people simply don't like using the Internet for shopping, because they are hesitant to use credit cards online, they just aren't skilled enough online, they feel that catalogs are more personal, or they still like the shopping comfort zone experienced with catalogs.
2. Catalogs enable consumers to shop and view many different products at one time much more easily, and often in a more visually attractive setting, than is possible online.

A good example of success achieved by merging catalog and Internet marketing is The Sportsman's Guide (TSG), originally an outdoor market catalog company that began using the Internet early on. As reflected in Table 1, 2004 sales recently increased at a much higher rate than previous year-to-year comparisons. The results suggest that early on, the Internet was basically making up for lost catalog sales, but in 2004, the picture changed dramatically.

TABLE 1: THE SPORTSMAN'S GUIDE
TOTAL SALES, 2000–2004 ($ IN MIL.)

Year	Total	Year	Total
2004	$237.5	2001	$169.7
2003	194.7	2000	$154.9
2002	180.3		

TSG acquired the Golf Warehouse in late 2004, an online retailer that also features a catalog, thus merging two retailing companies with the same dual strategy—catalog and Internet marketing.

Team dealers use catalogs extensively to supplement and support their personal sales representatives. For team dealers, catalogs serve as an effective continuous reminder about their products and services for their customers. While schools and institutions tend to consolidate the majority of purchases at certain times of the year, catalogs are an effective stimulus featuring new products and fill-in needs throughout the year.

Here is a list of several leading sporting goods retail and vendor company that offer catalogs:

- Aetrex Worldwide, Inc. (Health and performance footwear)
- Athleta (women)
- Austad's (golf)
- Bacharach Rasin (lacrosse)
- Baseball Warehouse (baseball)
- Bass Pro Shops (outdoor)
- Cabela's (outdoor)
- Campmor (outdoor)
- Collegiate Sports/Sports Supply (team)
- Decker's Outdoor (footwear)
- Delta Apparel (apparel)
- Eastbay (apparel, footwear)
- Eastern Mountain Sports (outdoor)
- Edwin Watts Golf (golf)
- ESPN (apparel, equipment, footwear)
- Eurosport (soccer)
- The Finish Line (apparel, footwear)
- Fitness Quest (fitness)
- Foot Locker (apparel, footwear)
- Gill Athletics (track and field)
- Golf 'n Gals (women's golf)
- Golfsmith (golf)
- The Golf Warehouse (golf)
- L.L.Bean (outdoor)
- Laxworld.com (lacrosse)
- Markwort Sporting Goods (baseball)
- M-F Athletic (track and field)
- Nautilus (fitness)
- Nike (women's)
- Orvis (outdoor)
- Patagonia (outdoor)
- Performance, Inc. (cycling)
- Road Runner Sports (apparel, footwear)
- Sears (fitness)
- Sierra Trading Post (outdoor)
- The Sportsman's Guide (outdoor)
- Terry Precision Cycling (women's cycling)
- Title Nine Sports (women's apparel, footwear)
- West Marine (boating)
- Woolrich (outdoor)

Network/Cable TV Advertising

Again reflecting modest sporting goods expenditures, in 2004 Nike ranked 88th among the top 100 advertisers in broadcast advertising expenditures (*Advertising Age*, June 27, 2005), with no other sporting goods company among the top 100. Television commercials for sporting goods products, primarily footwear and golf, are most likely to be aired with sports-related programming, such as golf and tennis tournaments, the Olympics, or televised collegiate or professional sports events. These events provide an opportunity for sporting goods advertisers to present their product in an environment conducive to their product and sport, and to an audience that's most likely to participate in the sport. This vertical approach, which also includes advertising on specialized cable channels devoted to a particular sport, such as the Golf Channel or the Tennis Channel, is similar to that described earlier in this chapter for print media.

Most advertising campaigns for sporting goods companies, whether image oriented or more product specific will most often include athletes or personalities. Here's an example of such a campaign, with the purpose explained by Reebok:

Reebok Launches "I Am What I Am" Campaign
(Sporting Goods Business Daily Dispatch, February 10, 2005)

Reebok International has launched its new global advertising campaign, "I Am What I Am," starring athletes and celebrities including Allen Iverson, Jay-Z, and Lucy Liu.

> "The Finish Line partners with vendors on traditional advertising. The company has been doing some TV advertising since the mid-90s, but in 2000 shifted to a consistent three or four flights a year." *Sporting Goods Business*, October, 2004.

Reebok said the multi-faceted campaign links all of the brand's marketing and advertising efforts under the "I Am What I Am" umbrella, and is supported by the company's largest advertising spend in nearly a decade. Created by New York advertising agency mcgarrybowen, "I Am What I Am" launches globally this month on TV, cinema, in key print publications and on billboards in target cities such as New York, Los Angeles, Chicago, Paris, London and Tokyo. The television spots debut during the NBA All-Star Game on February 20, 2005, and the print ads hit in March publications.

Reebok said the campaign encourages young people to embrace their own individuality by celebrating their contemporary heroes including: music icons Jay-Z and 50 Cent; top athletes Allen Iverson, Andy Roddick, Kelly Holmes, and Yao Ming; screen star Lucy Liu, skateboarder Stevie Williams, and soccer star Iker Casillas.

"The 'I Am What I Am' marketing campaign which celebrates authenticity and individuality is both relevant and inspiring for young consumers," said Dennis Baldwin, Reebok's global chief marketing officer. "We understand the struggle for today's youth to both fit in and stand out as individuals. Through this campaign, we hope to encourage young people to find their own voice by celebrating contemporary icons who have accomplished their dreams by being true to themselves and following their own unique path to greatness."

Again it's the high cost of national broadcast advertising, not only for an individual ad but also because of the need for repeated messages to be effective, relative to the limited market, that makes widespread broadcast advertising financially prohibitive for most sporting goods products."

In some instances, sporting goods retailers will partner with a vendor to create a campaign stressing the vendor's products. For example, recently The Finish Line, an athletic footwear retailer, launched a new TV campaign in conjunction with Nike. The campaign featured the new Nike Shox running shoe, and ran primarily on national cable television including ESPN, ESPN2, ESPN News, MTV, MTV2, Comedy Central, Spike, BET, G4, and the Cartoon Network. The ads also appeared online via Yahoo! Music, ESPN Motion, Gamespot, MTV and Maxim. The commercial depicted three runners on separate treadmills with various scenarios projecting behind them.

OTHER FORMS OF TV ADVERTISING

Many sporting goods companies sponsor athletes who are likely to appear on television when they are in competition. Whenever possible, these products (primarily apparel, footwear, uniforms, and balls) are worn or used by athletes in such a way that the sponsor's logo appears on the TV screen when they compete. This is a form of paid advertising, not in the traditional sense, but nevertheless often effective because most sports participants are familiar with sporting goods company logos. Prime examples of this would be golfers, tennis players, or team sports players wearing apparel with the Nike "Swoosh," the Adidas three-stripe logo, Riddell's name on NFL football helmets, Wilson's name on NFL game balls, or Spalding's name on NBA balls.

Another unique form of broadcast is the infomercial, which is an important tool for fitness companies, notably Icon Health & Fitness and Fitness Quest. Infomercials are also used to a certain extent by several smaller golf companies who produce special-purpose clubs or balls. Infomercials are targeted at prime prospects who are highly motivated to participate in the sport or fitness activity. They can last up to one-half hour or more and they are both motivating and highly instructional in their content. The usually appear on cable television channels.

Radio Advertising

Satellite radio program producers, notably XM Radio and Sirius, now broadcast a multitude of sports events across a broad sports broadcasting spectrum — including but not limited to golf, tennis, and team sports. To the extent that they target specific sporting goods audiences— golfers, tennis players, etc — these programming opportunities present sporting goods companies with the opportunity to reach their target market. Historically, radio has not been a widely used medium for sporting goods vendors, largely because product visibility is a critical ingredient in order to differentiate sporting goods products from one another.

Online Advertising

Sporting goods vendors and major retailers are most likely to advertise on websites which are offshoots of sports-oriented broadcast programming or consumer magazines. Two prominent examples of these are Foot Locker's association with ESPN.com, and The Finish Line's association with SI.com. To a limited extent, vendors will also advertise on sites devoted to a specific sports event that is consistent with their product lines.

However, to date, online advertising is a relatively minor part of a sporting goods vendor's overall marketing budget. Most sporting goods companies are testing the waters with limited budgets and are in the process of evaluating the effectiveness of this advertising.

Sporting goods vendors and retailers are increasingly active in creating their own websites. Most vendor sites focus on their product lines; although some sell products on their sites, nearly all vendors will use their sites to support local retailers who carry their products by providing a "Dealer Locator" feature on the site. Nearly every major retailer has a site, featuring their product offerings. Many offer consumers the choice of buying online for direct shipment or purchasing online and picking up their purchases at a retail location.

Newspaper Advertising

As in other industries, sporting goods retailers will use newspaper advertising to augment their promotional efforts with catalogs. Newspaper advertising is a staple medium for retailers, primarily because of its immediacy, serving as the best way to promote price savings, new product acquisitions, and special offers relating to specific brands or product categories.

Market Research

As an industry driven by entrepreneurship and creativity, and in many ways fashion, the sporting goods industry would normally fall in the "relatively little research available" category. However, this isn't the case, primarily because of the leadership exhibited by the National Sporting Goods Association (NSGA). The NSGA has sponsored research programs almost from its inception in 1929. Beginning in the 1970s, the NSGA provided industrywide coverage with a major annual consumer study of the market. This study continues to this day. The study measures consumer purchasing behavior, including distribution channels, pricing, brand preferences and demographics for all major sporting goods equipment and footwear categories, as well as, on a more limited basis, sports apparel. The

NSGA also publishes customized reports focusing on fitness and sports apparel. In 1984, the NSGA introduced their annual study of sports participation, which again continues to this day. The study covers detailed participation in every sport, including demographics and, for the most popular sports, state-by-state participation data.

Other reports provided by the NSGA include the "Cost of Doing Business" survey, "Used Sports Equipment Market" survey, and "Sporting Goods Stores— Sales, Number & Distribution."

One of the difficulties in measuring the total market for any one sporting goods category is that team sports equipment is sold directly to schools, and to this day the industry hasn't found a cost-effective way to measure the size of this market on a product-by-product or sport-by-sport basis. The NSGA has developed a method to estimate total expenditures, but not on a single-sport basis.

Another difficulty faced when researching the consumer market for sporting goods generally is the relatively small incidence of participation (percent of total U.S. population participating) for many sports. Sports that fall in this category include, but aren't limited to, water sports such as scuba diving, surfing and wakeboarding; team sports such as gymnastics, ice hockey, and lacrosse; and individual sports such as bow hunting, cross-country skiing, fencing, and snowboarding. Only a massive study such as the NSGA conducts every year is able to make even reasonable estimates as to the size of the market for these sports.

One excellent measure of the true size of the sporting goods market and the market for various product categories is government import statistics, because most sporting goods products in all three major categories— equipment, footwear and apparel — are imported. All importers are required to provide precise data to the government related to the amount of merchandise they import, and the price they pay to overseas producers. This information is published by the government. It is more specific for some products than for others. For example, government import statistics for bicycles are divided into categories according to wheel size, whereas basketball imports are reported in total, with no differentiation according to specific price point or other distinction.

In the late 1980s, the Sporting Goods Manufacturers Association (SGMA) began conducting syndicated market studies similar to those conducted by the NSGA. While it's rare that different organizations with national stature compete by trying to emulate each other, it's obvious that the competitive nature that pervades all of sports isn't limited to just to sporting goods vendors and retailers. Additional SGMA studies include reports on sports apparel, licensing and international markets

Types of Research

Research conducted by sporting goods companies serves two basic functions. One is to track and measure the magnitude of overall trends in purchasing behavior, consumer attitudes and facility development, focusing on changes in the popularity of specific sports and the underlying reasons for the changes. Consumer studies are the best source for this

> "Data analysis or data mining that enables the retailer to pull information on customer demands for products and services so the store can better meet each shopper's needs and wishes, results in higher customer loyalty." *Sporting Goods Business*, April 2005.

information, because, properly conducted, they allow researchers to measure several different aspects of behavior—for example, participation and purchasing, in one study.
Leading providers of this type of research include:

- American Sports Data: Provides syndicated and customer studies; serves as a primary supplier for SGMA studies.
- Irwin Broh & Associates: Provides syndicated and customer studies; serves as a primary supplier for NSGA studies.
- Leisure Trends: Provides syndicated and customized studies of consumer behavior and point-of-sale statistics serving the ski industry.
- Sports Marketing Surveys: Specializes in *media research* and *market research*.

The second function of research conducted by sporting goods companies is to track consumer purchases of specific products in the marketplace. Point-of-sale research is best suited for this purpose, and while this is a relatively expensive service to produce, more and more companies look to point-of-sale tracking research not only for specific products, but also for category trends such as licensed products, outerwear, team sports purchases, and purchases by price point. Another form of tracking specific product sales is a consumer diary panel. For this type of research, a national or regional cross section of consumers is preselected and asked to keep a diary of their purchases of products of interest to the research organization or company.
Leading providers of this type of research include:

- NPD: Provides syndicated and customized studies based on consumer diary panels and point-of-sale information drawn directly from sporting goods retailer records.
- SportScanINFO: Provides syndicated and customized studies reporting point-of-sale statistics for all products sold by retailers who participate in the survey, including many major sporting goods and discount store chains.

Company Research Management

Very few sporting goods vendors and retailers actually maintain a separate market research department. Nike and Reebok are among the very few companies that do. For the great majority of companies, market research is handled by marketing or product management directors, along with their other duties. They establish the overall goals of the research, thereafter depending on research expertise of market research suppliers, such as the companies listed above, to provide the information they need.

RELATED WEBSITES

American Sports Data: www.americansportsdata.com
Irwin Broh & Associates: www.irwinbroh.com
Leisure Trends: www.leisuretrends.com
NPD: www.npd.com
SportScanINFO: www.sportscaninfo.com
Sports Marketing Surveys: www.sportsmarketingsurveys.com

EXERCISES

1. Review a recent issue of four of the following six consumer publications: *Sports Illustrated, Baseball America, Golf Digest, Peterson's Hunting, Runner's World,* and *Snowboarder* (you should be able to find copies in most libraries). Make a list of the sporting goods companies sponsoring ads in each issue. What percentage of all ads feature an athlete or an athlete's endorsement using the product in some part of the ad?

2. Obtain a catalog from a major retailer such as Foot Locker or Dick's. Then compare the breadth of merchandise in the catalog to the merchandise offered for sale on the same company's website. If you have the opportunity, also visit one of the company's stores and make some comparisons. The purpose of this exercise is to examine the extent that the web is being used as another forum for merchandise promoted in the store and in advertising, or whether different approaches are used for each medium for the same product category.

3. Is consumer advertising generally more important or less important for sporting goods than for other consumer products? What are the primary reasons for this difference?

4. Explain the difference between consumer magazines and trade magazines for the sporting goods industry.

5. Describe the types of broadcast programs and online sites where sporting goods companies are most likely to place their broadcast advertising. Explain why the companies would choose these types of programs and sites.

6. What type of content (pictures and text) are most often featured by sporting goods vendors in their advertisements?

7. Why have catalogs survived after the introduction of online selling? What company or companies represent a good example of how catalogs are still important?

8. Briefly describe the two basic functions of market research in the sporting goods industry, and briefly discuss the purpose of each type.

9. Describe two difficulties related to market research that are unique to the sporting goods industry.

8

Financial Dimensions: Sales Trends and Profitability

OVERVIEW

Amer Group, K2 Corp., Russell, Nike, VF Inc., Dick's, and Adidas lead the booming sporting goods acquisition parade.

In this chapter, we deal with corporate sales and profits in various segments of the sporting goods industry. Recent developments, such as acquisitions and mergers, have significantly impacted the financial health of the sporting goods industry, and these factors play an important role as the industry strives to maximize profitability. This chapter focuses on various sales and profit summaries for companies in the industry and then reviews the underlying factors that affect their profitability. It's evident in the data shown that financial trends vary by company in different product categories. Variations also exist even among companies in the same category. Based on data for the past two years, sporting goods equipment profits expressed as a percentage of sales are generally less than profits of other comparable industries, whereas retailers and apparel and footwear vendors tend to experience similar profit margins when compared with similar categories in other industries.

At the end of this chapter, you should be able to:

• Identify the recent trends in overall industry sales and profits.
• Describe factors that influence industry sales and profits.
• Describe how companies take steps to maximize sales and profits.
• Describe the variations in profit trends between retailers and vendors.
• Identify future trends most likely to influence sales and profit.

DISCUSSION

Analysis of Financial Trends

Until the late 1970s and early 1980s, sporting goods companies were privately owned. Little was generally known about the industry's financial performance except, of course, to those working in the industry. Furthermore, equipment was the dominant vendor category—apparel and footwear enjoyed only a modest share of all sales.

Two developments since that time served to significantly change the financial structure of the industry. First, footwear and apparel products now represent nearly half of all industry sales, and footwear and apparel companies are significantly more profitable than equipment companies, at least based on profits-to-sales ratios. Second, since 1980, there's been a dramatic upheaval in the industry with respect to transparency, in both retailing and among vendors. Slowly, then rapidly, more and more companies in the industry have shifted to public ownership. Today, most leading names in the industry such as Nike, Reebok, Vans, K-Swiss, Callaway, Titleist (Fortune Brands), Adidas, Russell, Fila, The Finish Line, Foot Locker, The Sports Authority, and Hibbett Sporting Goods are all publicly owned and their financial information is available to the general public.

Industry experts have long been aware that sporting goods equipment vendor profitability was below that of most other business categories, whether industrial or consumer, and now it's there for all the world to see.

Coincidental with steady sales growth in recent years, the overexpansion of retail stores and floor space became a significant industry problem. Thousands of smaller full-line stores dominated the sporting goods retail landscape until the early 1980s, and when the industry transitioned to big-box retailers with large stores, many in the 75,000+ square foot range, the amount of retail floor space increased much more rapidly than corresponding sales did. Sportmart (now a division of The Sports Authority) was the first big-box retailer chain. Now nearly every full-line sporting goods store is a big box retailer.

Another development that accompanied sales growth has been a continuing shift of consumer preferences for apparel, footwear and equipment, based on fashion preferences; the introduction of new sports categories; and the introduction of new technologies, such as oversized golf clubs. Towards the end of the 1990s, the industry was in a major phase of expansion. Demand for licensed sports apparel flourished, inspiring a market boom for sports apparel as it became fashionable for everyday casual wear. Thus, you have the makings of an exploding sports apparel industry, which is what happened. By 2000, however, the market for sports footwear and apparel lost its luster among consumers as a fashion item. Also, after an initial surge, extreme sports growth slowed, and preferences changed within the category from rollerblading to skateboarding and water sports.

Companies positioned in the fastest growing segments, such as those producing and retailing footwear and casual wear related to extreme sports for younger age groups (Quiksilver and Pacific Sunwear) have benefitted from the trend. Companies positioned in traditional, team sports market segments (Russell and G III Apparel) struggle to maintain profits and sales. Competition has become more intense with Nike, Reebok and Under Armour becoming increasingly active in the team sports market. Parts of this market (team purchases) are growing, but consumer spending for team sports products has remained stagnant or even declined for some categories in recent years.

This continuous evolution and pressure on many existing companies resulted in rapid consolidation within the industry among vendors and retailers and in extremely varied financial results between companies.

In recent years, industry sales remain at a high level, with relatively modest growth rates. Reverberations throughout vendor and retailing market segments have diminished from the rough period when leading companies such as Starter and Nutmeg Mills, whose sales had reached the hundreds of millions of dollars, suddenly went into bankruptcy, as a result of the decline in demand for licensed products. In order to examine trends more closely, the discussion and tables below reflect sales and profit trends over the past two years for companies in four different categories: equipment vendors, footwear vendors, apparel vendors and retailers.

Sporting Goods Equipment Vendors

As might be expected, financial fortunes of sporting goods companies are inevitably susceptible to changes in the changing popularity of various sports. As indicated in Table 1, comparing 2004 to 2003, revenue growth was 13.7 percent, whereas profits declined 6.6 percent, reflecting the difficulty of achieving desirable profit levels in stagnant markets even when sales increase. The reason — most often sales increases in stagnant markets result from "fire sale" pricing, that is, selling goods below prices needed to maintain normal profit levels.

Overall equipment profits as a percent of sales declined from 3.7 percent in 2003 to 3.0 percent in 2004. However, there are significant variations depending on a vendor's product lines. For example, reflecting the recent softness in the market for golf and tennis equipment, profit levels for Head (tennis and ski) and Callaway (golf) declined significantly in 2004. In early 2005, the Salomon Ski division of Adidas was sold to Amer Group; Salomon has been a drag on Adidas sales recently, again reflecting softness in the so-called individual sport category (golf, tennis and ski market segments).

Footwear Vendors

Recently, the footwear industry was largely free of consolidation. Most footwear vendor consolidations occurred when smaller brands such as Converse were purchased by larger companies.

Over the past two years, financial results for vendors in this category are generally positive across the board. However, different companies experienced widely different sales growth and profitability. Smaller companies in growing categories such as outdoor and casual footwear experienced strong gains in sales and profits. Larger companies had solid gains, but at expectedly lower levels of change because of their sheer size.

Foreign sales are an important contributor to footwear sales and profits for smaller companies because of the growth potential from a very low base and for larger companies producing performance and casual athletic footwear such as Nike and Adidas.

Sports Apparel Vendors

Financial results for sports apparel vendors have recently become more positive than at any time in the past five years. At least two factors contribute to this profitability: a revitalized consumer demand for licensed sports team products and recent industry consolidation (primarily Russell's acquisitions of Bike, Spalding, and Moving Comfort).

Another factor influencing the market is growing demand for undergarments worn for participation, a market first served by Under Armour (see results in Table 3). Perspiration is an ongoing demon of the athlete and recent apparel technology has resulted in products that greatly reduce negative affects of perspiration on the athlete's performance. As this market grows, it is not unlikely to expect these products to have a positive effect on sales of larger athletic apparel vendors as they develop similar products for the marketplace.

> "The annual financial performance survey by SGMA found that the industry hit new lows for profitability and sales growth in '79. Return on sales was just 2.4% vs. 5.3% for all manufacturers." *Sporting Goods Dealer*, August 1980.

TABLE 1: SPORTING GOODS EQUIPMENT VENDORS
SUMMARY OF SALES AND PROFITS FY2003–FY2004

VENDOR	Dollars (in mil.)				% Change				Profit: % of Sls	
	Sales		Net Profit		Sales		Net Profit			
	'04	'03	'04	'03	'04 vs '03	'03 vs '02	'04 vs '03	'03 vs '02	'04	'03
Aldila	52.8	37.9	9.3	-1.7	+39.6	+0.9		-$2.8†	17.6	--
Amer*	1,312.9	1,369.5	104.8	80.2	-4.1	+0.2	+30.7	-1.3	8.0	5.9
Brunswick	558.3	n/a	45.2‡	n/a	+14.7	n/a	+51.7	n/a	8.1	n/a
Callaway	934.6	814.0	-10.1	45.5	+14.8	+2.6		-34.4	--	5.6
Cybex	103.0	90.2	3.2	-1.8	+14.3	+10.6			3.1	--
Everlast	45.0	64.7	-1.0	-0.955	+13.1	+11.3			--	--
GolfGear Intl.	0.7	2.0	-1.8	-4.2	-63.1	+27.6				
Head NV	479.1	431.2	-36.9	-14.7	+10.7	+11.3		-$2.6†	--	--
Icon**	1,095.7	1,011.5	23.4	26.7	+8.3	+16.1	-12.4	+37.6	2.1	2.6
Johnson	355.3	315.9	8.7	5.4	+12.5	-7.8	+61.1	-31.6	2.4	1.7
K2	1,200.7	718.5	38.9	11.4	+67.1	+23.4	+240.9	-5.3	3.2	1.6
Lowrance	111.9	88.3	8.8	4.6	+26.7	+91.3	+88.5	+94.4	7.9	5.2
Nautilus	523.8	498.8	30.0	34.4	+5.0	-14.7	-12.8	-64.9	5.7	6.9
Oakley	585.5	521.5	41.6	38.2	+10.9	+6.5	+8.8	-6.0	7.1	7.3
Sturm Ruger	145.6	147.9	4.3	12.4	-1.6	-8.4	-65.2	+36.0	3.0	8.4
Remington	393.0	360.7	-4.0	-3.2	+9.0	-6.0	+$20.0**	--	--	
TOTAL††	7,339.6	6,472.6	219.2	232.3	+13.7		-6.6		3.0	3.7

*Includes Wilson, Atomic, plus non-sports and is based on a conversion rate of 1.24 $ to 1.00 euro.
†Actual dollars for FY2002.
‡Operating earnings.
**Year ending May '04 vs. May '03.
††Excludes Brunswick.
Source: SGB's Inside Sporting Goods.

TABLE 2: FOOTWEAR VENDORS
SUMMARY OF SALES AND PROFITS FY2003–FY2004

VENDOR	Dollars (in mil.)				% Change				Profit: % of Sls	
	Sales		Net Profit		Sales		Net Profit			
	'04	'03	'04	'03	'04 vs '03	'03 vs '02	'04 vs '03	'03 vs '02	'04	'03
Adidas-Salomon*†	8,032.7	7,771.1	389.4	259.0	+3.4	-3.9	+50.3	-8.8	4.8	3.3
Deckers	214.8	121.1	25.5	9.2	+77.4	+22.1	+179.0	-$7.4*	11.9	7.6
Lacrosse	105.5	95.7	7.0	2.6	+10.2	-2.2	+169.2	-$4.1*	6.6	2.7
Nike‡	13,700.0	12,300.0	1,200.0	945.6	+11.4	+15.0	+26.9	+27.8	8.8	7.7
Puma*	1,897.6	1,579.8	319.1	222.3	+20.1	+40.0	+43.6	+111.3	16.8	14.1
Reebok	3,785.3	3,485.0	192.4	157.0	+8.6	+11.4	+22.5	+23.1	5.1	4.5
Rocky	132.2	106.2	8.6	6.0	+24.6	+19.3	+43.3	+112.4	6.5	5.6
Skechers	920.3	835.0	23.6	-11.9	+10.2	-11.5		+$47.0*	2.6	--
Stride-Rite	558.3	550.1	25.7	25.5	+1.5	+3.3	+0.8	+5.7	4.6	4.6
Timberland	1,501.0	1,342.0	152.7	117.9	+11.8	12.7	+21.0	+23.9	10.2	8.8
Wolverine	991.9	888.9	65.9	51.7	+11.6	7.5	+27.5	+7.9	6.6	5.8
TOTAL*	31,839.6	29,074.9	2,409.9	1,784.9	+9.5		+34.5		7.6	6.1

*Figures based on a conversion rate of 1.24 $ to 1.00 euro.
†Includes TaylorMade (golf), Salomon (skis).
‡FY ending May 2005.
Source: SGB's Inside Sporting Goods.

Retailers

Clearly, retailing is a profitable segment of the industry. With rare exceptions, over the past two years, major retailers have experienced steady increases in sales and profits,

TABLE 3: SPORTS APPAREL VENDORS
(EXCLUDES FOOTWEAR-ALSO COMPANIES)
SUMMARY OF SALES AND PROFITS
FY2003–FY2004

VENDOR	Dollars (in mil.) Sales		Net Profit		% Change Sales		Net Profit		Profit: % of Sls	
	'04	'03	'04	'03	'04 vs '03	'03 vs '02	'04 vs '03	'03 vs '02	'04	'03
Ashworth	173.1	149.3	8.2	7.3	+15.8	+15.5	+11.9	192.1	4.7	4.9
Cherokee*	38.9	36.3	17.2	14.2	+7.2	+9.6	+21.2	+8.8	44.2	39.1
Columbia	1,095.3	951.8	138.6	120.1	+15.1	+16.6	+15.4	+17.2	12.7	12.6
G-III	214.3	224.1	0.7	8.4	-4.4	+10.6	-91.7	+2,092.6	0.3	3.7
Quiksilver†	1,266.9	975.0	81.4	58.5	+29.9	+38.2	+39.1	+55.6	6.4	6.0
Russell†	1,298.2	1,186.2	47.9	43.0	+9.4	+1.9	+11.4	+25.5	3.7	3.6
Under Armour	205.1	115.4	14.3	5.3	+77.7	+132.7	+169.8	+89.3	7.0	4.6
TOTAL	4,281.8	3,538.1	308.3	256.8	+21.0		+20.1		7.2	7.3

*Licensing revenues only.
†In 2005, Quiksilver and Russell acquired significant companies producing sporting goods equipment.
Source: SGB's Inside Sporting Goods.

and as indicated in Table 6, sporting goods retailers enjoy profit margins consistent with retails in other specialty categories.

Two major retailers, Dick's and The Sports Authority, grew exponentially from acquisitions (Dick's combined with Galyan's and The Sports Authority combined with Gart's). Discounting these chains, Pacific Sunwear and The Finish Line led most other retailers in terms of growth of sales and profits. Pacific Sunwear capitalized on their unique appeal to teenagers and young adults and The Finish Line capitalized on Nike's disagreement with Foot Locker (that disagreement has since been resolved).

One exception to the big-box retailer phenomenon is Hibbett Sporting Goods, a retail chain located primarily in the southeastern United States. Hibbett stores are much smaller than usual, usually less than 15,000 square feet. They are located primarily in smaller southern communities, serving a 12-month season for outdoor team sports, and largely avoiding big-city metropolitan locations. Hibbett's growth in sales and profits is commensurate with big-box retailers, despite the fact that they serve the slower-growth team sports market.

Full-line retailers generally fared better during the past two years than retail specialists, with a notable exception, Pacific Sunwear. Pac Sun, catering to the teenage and young adult markets with apparel and water sports products, experienced significantly above-average growth in both sales and profits. On the other hand, more traditional outdoor retail specialists such as Gander Mountain and REI (similarly for Galyan's before it was absorbed by Dick's), grew rapidly but had difficulty earning a profit. Golfsmith, a specialty retailer, also experienced below-average profits despite enjoying significant sales growth.

This situation is one that often occurs in the sporting goods market. Full-line sporting goods retailers have, of necessity, learned to be agile and alert to changing consumer trends, and they often find ways to adapt to these changing conditions, often to the detriment of retailers who specialize in a particular market segment. A good example is the golf equipment market. Until recently, the golf retail specialist category grew at a rapid pace — but with full-line sporting goods retailers, particular Dick's and The Sports Authority, becoming more aggressive in the golf marketplace, some golf specialist chains have gone into bankruptcy and most others are experiencing slow growth.

Overall, sales of leading retailers increased 18.4 percent in 2004 vs. 2003, a much faster

TABLE 4: SPORTING GOODS RETAILERS
SUMMARY OF SALES AND PROFITS
FY2004–FY2005

| | Dollars (in mil.) | | | | % Change | | | | Profit: | |
| | Sales | | Net Profit | | Sales | | Net Profit | | % of Sls | |
VENDOR	'04	'03	'04	'03	'04 vs '03	'03 vs '02	'04 vs '03	'03 vs '02	'04	'03
Big 5	778.9	709.7	34.3	26.3	+9.8	+6.3	+30.4	+137.2	4.4	3.7
Dick's*	2,109.4	1,470.8	66.9	52.8	+43.4	+15.6	+26.7	+38.0	3.2	3.6
The Finish Line	1,166.8	985.9	61.3	47.3	+18.3	+30.2	+29.4	+88.8	5.3	4.8
Foot Locker	5,355.0	4,779.0	293.0	207.0	+10.0	+6.0	+41.5	+35.3	5.5	4.3
Gander Mountain	642.1	489.4	-3.5	-15.8	+31.2	n/a			—	—
Golf Galaxy	133.1	99.6	7.5	7.4	+33.1	n/a	+0.5	n/a	5.6	7.4
Golfsmith	295.2	257.7	-4.8	1.1	+14.6	+1.1		n/a	—	0.4
Hibbett	377.5	321.0	25.6	20.3	+17.6	+15.0	+26.1	+38.1	6.8	6.3
Pacific Sunwear	1,229.8	1,040.3	106.9	80.2	+18.2	+22.9	+32.0	+61.5	8.6	7.7
REI‡	887.8	805.3	25.3	19.1	+10.2	n/a	+32.5	n/a	2.8	2.4
Shoe Carnival	590.2	557.9	12.5	12.2	+5.8	+7.4	+2.5	-22.8	2.1	2.2
Sport Chalet	309.1	264.2	6.2	4.6	+17.0	+11.0	+32.9	+11.6	2.0	1.7
Forzani (Can.)	985.1	968.1	22.9	28.0	+1.8	+4.7	-18.2	-6.7	2.3	2.9
Sports Auth.†	2,435.9	1,800.0	34.2	16.4	+38.3	n/a	+108.7	n/a	1.4	0.9
Sptsmn's Guide **	237.5	194.7	7.6	6.2	+22.0	+8.6	+22.6	+53.3	3.2	3.2
TOTAL	17,533.4	14,743.6	695.9	513.1	+18.9		+35.4		4.0	3.5

*Includes Galyan's.
†The Sports Authority merged with Gart in 2004 (FY '05). Resulting chain kept The Sports Authority name.
‡Years 2003, 2004.
**Online- and catalog-only retailer.
Source: SGB's Inside Sporting Goods.

rate than the industry in general (+6.1 percent), reflecting increasing dominance of major retail chains. Profits as a percent of sales increased in 2004 to 4.0 percent vs. 3.5 percent in 2003. Table 4 reflects sales and profits for sporting goods retailers.

Table 5 summarizes profits as a percentage of sales for the four major categories: equipment vendors, footwear vendors, apparel vendors and retailers. Footwear and apparel companies as a group are the most profitable by this measure, with equipment vendors showing significantly lower profit margins.

It is interesting to compare sporting goods industry profitability with profitability by category with other industries. As reflected in Table 6, sporting goods retailing's profits are generally comparable with those of other retailing categories. Sporting goods apparel and footwear vendor profitability is above average for that category compared with general apparel and footwear companies. For sporting goods equipment vendors, profitability is below that of vendors of most other leading consumer product categories.

Factors Influencing Profitability

Acquisitions

Acquisitions can have significant impact on a company's profitability. This can occur if either company acquired in the transaction is significantly more or less profitable than the buyer, or if apparel or footwear companies acquire equipment companies (because of the normal variation in profit margins between the categories—see tables above), or if synergies usually anticipated in acquisitions do not materialize. In sporting goods, since

TABLE 5: SPORTING GOODS CATEGORIES
SUMMARY OF PROFITS AS A PERCENT OF SALES
FY2004–FY2005

SG Company Type	Profits as % of Sales	
	FY 2004	FY 2003
Equipment Vendors	3.0	3.7
Footwear Vendors	7.5	6.1
Apparel Vendors	7.2	7.3
Retailers	4.0	3.5

TABLE 6: INDUSTRY PROFITABILITY, SPORTING
GOODS VS. OTHER SELECTED INDUSTRIES
PROFITS AS A PERCENT OF SALES, FY 2004

Industry	Profits as Percent of Sales
RETAILERS	
Sporting Goods	4.1
Specialty Total	4.4
General Merchandise	3.6
Food & Drug	1.6
EQUIPMENT VENDORS	
Sporting Goods	3.0
Household, Other Personal Products	11.5
Beverages*	11.3
Entertainment Service*	9.2
Electronics, Electrical Equipment*	5.3
Food Production*	1.9
APPAREL VENDORS	
Sporting Goods	7.2
General Apparel†	5.9
FOOTWEAR VENDORS	
Sporting Goods	7.5

*Source: Fortune.
†Includes Nike, Reebok, Timberland, VF

"merger mania" has only recently become significant in sporting goods, it's not possible to anticipate long-term effects of acquisitions on the acquirers' profitability.

Russell's recent acquisitions make the company an interesting one to watch — an apparel company that has acquired other apparel companies (Bike) and equipment companies (Spalding and Worth). Apparel profit margins are traditionally above equipment companies, but not so with Russell, who has experienced very low margins for several years. The question is: Can resulting synergies in the merger overcome traditionally lower profit margins for equipment, thereby increasing Russell's margins overall?

Percent of Sales in Foreign Countries

Given the global expansion of the industry, foreign currency fluctuations and relationships can play a significant role in a vendor or retailer's profit margins. Companies such as Nike, Reebok, Adidas, Amer Group, Titleist, Foot Locker, Callaway, K2 and Head have significant overseas sales volumes, and other companies are moving in that direction, attempting to capitalize on the strength of American brand names around the world.

Footwear and footwear/apparel companies have been particularly active in foreign markets. Given the relatively stagnant market for athletic footwear in America, these companies' continued ability to grow sales overseas will significantly impact their bottom lines over the next several years.

Companies expanding globally need to carefully assess the costs involved in developing overseas markets. Decisions need to be made whether to staff their own offices or work through existing agents or distributors in foreign countries. The largest sporting goods companies tend to open and staff their own offices, particularly in larger markets, including but not limited to such countries as Japan, China, Germany, France, India, England and Russia. Smaller companies normally work with local representatives or distributors in each country, except in isolated cases where their brand is particularly strong.

New Product Development

So far, we've emphasized that the sporting goods industry is very much driven by new products. Genuine new products have been largely missing (Under Armour the exception) in sporting goods for several years; the result has been a market with relatively limited growth. The dynamics of the golf industry since Callaway introduced the large-size clubhead are interesting to observe. Callaway, with current sales of nearly $1 billion, significantly impacted traditional brands, particularly Wilson, MacGregor and Spalding, when it was introduced in the early 1990s. TaylorMade was also affected, but has rebounded by introducing products that are very competitive with those offered by Callaway. Other companies have introduced large-headed clubs, and success now depends on a firm's ability to make a better large-headed club.

Documenting this golf industry phenomenon, total golf industry sales surged from $2.7 billion in 1993 to $3.7 billion in 1997. However, since then sales have declined. Total industry sales in 2004 were $3.1 billion. This is a clear example of how a new product can have a remarkable impact — overall industry sales significantly increase to a point, but if nothing new comes along again, growth quickly stagnates. Clearly, this will significantly affect profit margins, both for companies successful with the new product and for companies failing to capitalize on the demand.

Relationships Between Vendors and Retailers

Much was made of the celebrated rift between Nike and Foot Locker, which occurred primarily during calendar year 2003. Several retailers, notably The Finish Line, took advantage of Nike's decision to allow some retailers to feature their premium product lines, while for a variety of reasons, Foot Locker was not permitted to carry some of these same products.

Clearly, an analysis of sales and profits suggests that The Finish Line benefited from Nike's decision. However, Foot Locker's sales were not rising before the rift, probably affected by other more consequential factors. The only clear conclusion from this data is that The Finish Line clearly benefited, whereas one cannot ascertain, but only speculate, that Foot Locker would have grown at a more rapid rate had they also been able to feature Nike's premium products.

Table 7 reflects sales of Foot Locker and The Finish Line, beginning with the year prior to the rift.

TABLE 7: SALES AND NET PROFITS,
FOOT LOCKER AND THE FINISH LINE
FY 2002–FY 2005

| Year Ending | Foot Locker | | The Finish Line | |
	Sales (mil. of $)	Profit (mil. of $)	Sales (mil. of $)	Profit (mil. of $)
Jan 31, 2005	5,355	293	1,167	61.3
Jan 31, 2004	4,779	207	986	47.3
Jan 31, 2003	4,509	160	757	25.0
Jan 31, 2002	4,325	142	701	18.4
Jan 31, 2001	4,356	111	664	4.7

Source: SGB's Inside Sporting Goods.

Foreign Market Product Sourcing

Most sporting goods products are manufactured overseas, primarily in far eastern countries, with China rapidly becoming the leading location of offshore production of all product categories: equipment, apparel and footwear. Since this move by the industry to offshore production has been going on now for 20 years, most industry vendors are familiar with the processes involved in managing overseas production, obviating the prospect of a return to American production of sporting goods. Even if China became involved in war with Taiwan and the United States took strong steps to isolate China, there is probably enough production technology in other far eastern countries to take up the slack, with minimal disruption.

The question then becomes: Is the industry capable of managing foreign producers who violate child labor laws or who have other social issues that aren't acceptable to American Consumers. The industry is acutely aware of consumer perceptions, particularly since a substantial market for sporting goods exists among young people whose preferences are more defined. It is a credit to sporting goods vendors that they maintain a leadership position in establishing standards for producers that are consistent with American's social values.

This can affect industry profitability particularly for new companies entering the business, although they can seek out and usually find industry experts available on a consulting basis who can guide them through the process of overseas sourcing.

Relatively Limited Economies of Scale

Even for a single product category, such as tennis racquets, skis or basketballs, sporting goods vendors must produce a large number of items in order to serve market needs. Differences in physical size, performance ability and ages among participants require vendors to offer a wide range of products. Whether it be shoulder pads, ice skates, golf clubs, tennis racquets or even outdoor camping equipment, economy of scale for any single product within these categories is often difficult, if not impossible to achieve.

For example, on its website, Dick's currently offers 30 different "Official Size" footballs—14 Wilson, three Spalding, nine Rawlings, two Champion, one MacGregor and one Tachikara—as well as 40 different "Youth Size" balls. MC Sports, another major sporting goods retailer, offers 31 different "Official Size" footballs and 39 different "Youth Size" footballs on their website.

Yet collectively, football producers offer at least 300 different balls—some for individual consumers to be purchased in retail sporting goods outlets and others for team dealers selling to youth, high school, collegiate and professional teams. Slightly more than 13 million footballs were imported in 2004; thus, average sales per model would be 40,000. However, some models will outsell others by a significant amount, suggesting that a wide range of profitability exists for various footballs.

Another factor inhibiting economy of scale is how easy it is to enter the market. Outside production sourcing is widely available, and raw materials usually don't require significant financial resources to begin production. Vendors need to "protect their flanks" by offering enough different products to at least inhibit, if not prevent, other vendors or new companies from filling market voids.

Significant Sports Marketing Costs

While traditional advertising and promotional costs and benefits can be reasonably controlled, sports marketing costs are subject to wide ranges of effectiveness. Since these costs often represent a significant portion of total marketing costs for sporting goods companies, overall profitability is much more susceptible to the risks associated with sports marketing programs. One recent example is the NHL lockout of the 2004–05 season. Any company offering licensed hockey products was victimized by the lockout, clearly something the hockey equipment and apparel vendors were not able to control.

This is all the more reason for vendors to protect themselves by offering products for several different sports in order to hedge against future problems associated with a particular sport. This in turn forces vendors to be subject to the problems discussed above relating to the relative lack of economics of scale within the industry.

New Product Introductions with Widespread Appeal

Few industries are as affected as quickly as sporting goods to the introduction of a new product. An automobile manufacturer can introduce an automobile with a new design, but the scope and size of the market makes it unlikely that all car producers will be significantly affected. New hair sprays or new drugs, rarely if ever obsolete all current products on the market. Revolutionary new electronic products will eventually obsolete other products, but the time frame for this to happen is normally several years.

But a new sporting goods product will often immediately affect existing products on the market. The introduction of the Callaway large-headed golf clubs, for example, basically made every other driver on the market obsolete. The company grew almost overnight from nothing to the second largest producer of golf equipment. Golfers of all kinds constantly seek equipment that enhances their ability to perform, and any product that comes along that performs that function will quickly change the entire complexion of the marketplace. Even more unique, in sporting goods, as often as not the new product is developed by an individual who has no historical experience in the sport for which the product was developed; so there's very little warning when it's about to happen, further complicating the everyday modus operandi of sporting goods companies. Examples of this abound — Callaway in golf, Howard Head in ski and tennis equipment, and Easton with the metal bat (Easton was experienced in archery, but not in baseball).

Clearly, this complicates a sporting goods equipment company's ability to continually improve profitability. What is happening is that sporting goods companies are merging, and larger companies are more capable of moving quickly to adopt the new product or develop products with similar functions. Thus, to the extent that the trend toward size and increased capital resources continues, its increased ability to respond to dramatic new products should improve overall profitability.

Labor Unrest Within Professional Sports Organizations

Sporting goods companies are, to some extent, at the mercy of labor contractual relationships with professional sports organizations. Short-term strikes or lockouts of professional athletes have a relatively minor effect on sales of sporting goods companies making equipment or apparel for those sports, but extended labor strife will eventually take its toll on industry sales. Licensed apparel normally suffers the worst losses, although basic equipment sales to consumers (as opposed to sales to high school and collegiate teams, which are less affected) can also experience slowdowns in sales.

The following article appearing in the December, 2004 issue of *Sporting Goods Business*, provides a summary review of major developments within the industry occurring during the year. It reflects situations alluded to in the preceding text and provides a real-life excursion through the dynamics of the industry's financial and economic experiences.

Looking Back at 2004
By Bob Carr
(Sporting Goods Business, December, 2004)

Consolidation, megastore expansion, and the growing importance of industry conferences will continue to make their mark in 2005.

Looking back at the past year's top news, I think there were three top trends. The first, and most obvious, was continued consolidation at every level. The growth of outdoor megastores such as Bass Pro Shops, Cabela's and Gander Mountain, was another key development. Third was the growth of conferences and their increasing importance as networking events.

The year started off with the financial problems of Footstar, the number two athletic shoe retailer in the U.S. Footstar's Just For Feet doors are long gone. It was an acquisition that never worked. The Footaction units, which were viable, were the subject of a bidding war between Foot Locker and The Finish Line. It looked like Foot Locker was vying for the Bottom Fisher of the Year Award, when The Finish Line entered the bankruptcy court and drove up Foot Locker's bid, much to the thanks of Footaction's creditors. Foot Locker has managed to come up with a merchandising strategy that separates the new acquisition from the other Foot Locker units.

Dick's Sporting Goods picked up what was once a jewel, Galyan's. The latter became another example of how difficult it is to run a sporting goods chain from a department store mentality. I've talked this over many times, but it's almost a self-fulfilling prophecy that new management from the department store sector will run into problems of one kind or another. While these managers can bring in some ideas on controls or systems, there doesn't seem be the same realization that sporting goods is still a relationship business, and that the retailer is less the brand than the core offerings. The regional nature of the business and its margins make it daunting, as well.

Collegiate Pacific did not make the mistake of Sport Supply Group when it bought out team dealers and chased away the road sales force. Collegiate CEO Michael Blumenfeld seems to have realized the importance of face-to-face relationships. For years, while CEO of BSN, he bad-mouthed team dealers. But with Collegiate's acquisitions of Kessler's Team Sports and Dixie Sporting Goods (and their respective salespeople), Blumenfeld saw an opportunity to increase profits through the normal business of the dealers, and also saw the opportunity to boost Collegiate's proprietary product sales through these dealers.

Our vendor community also went on a buying spree. K2, VF Corp. and Russell led the way, but there were others. Quiksilver bought DC Shoes. Nike found a way to sell into mass merchant channels with the acquisition of Starter. Reebok acquired The Hockey Co., but immediately faced the NHL lockout.

One interesting phenomenon is the surge of outdoor megastores, namely Bass Pro Shops, Gander Mountain and Cabela's. The latter two went public and immediately saw huge gains in their stocks' values. But as I write now, Cabala's is up 17.05 percent, while Gander, which warned of a terrible third quarter, is off 15.31 percent (since the IPOs of both companies this year). The retail expansions of all three retailers have helped consumers see and touch the rich variety of hunting and fishing merchandise that's available, but this sector is in for some problems. When will there be too many doors sitting bunched up in outdoor markets? It's already reminding me of the big box expansion fiasco of the last decade.

One trend that will continue, but goes relatively unnoticed, is the growth of conferences, as opposed to trade shows, for serious networking. The NSGA Management Conference & Team Dealer Summit is the grandfather of the industry conference, and is the most important networking event. Here at SGB, we've been hosting conferences by invitation only. Last week, SGB hosted a specialty running store conference. Tom Raynor, Fleet Feet chairman and CEO, mentioned at the podium that he had never seen so many specialty dealers under one roof in years, and the conference had already become a significant networking event among retailers and vendors at its debut.

RELATED WEBSITES

APPAREL/EQUIPMENT VENDORS:

Russell Athletic: www.corporate-ir.net/ireye/ir_site.zhtml?ticker=RML&script=950
Under Armour: www.underarmour.com

EQUIPMENT VENDORS:

Callaway Golf: www.callawaygolf.com
Icon Health & Fitness: www.iconfitness.com
K2 Corp.: www.k2sports.com

FOOTWEAR/FOOTWEAR AND APPAREL VENDORS:

Adidas: www.adidas.com
Nike: www.nikebiz.com

RETAILERS:

Dick's Sporting Goods: www.dickssportinggoods.com
The Sports Authority: www.sportsauthority.com

EXERCISES

1. Go to www.thesportsauthority.com and www.nikebiz.com and review the sites. Familiarize yourself with the reporting formats of these companies (see "Investor Relations" in the "About Us" section for The Sports Authority) and try to develop some interesting comparisons between the two companies.

2. Choose one company from each of the following categories and complete an analysis of their website: equipment vendors, footwear, footwear/apparel manufacturers and sporting goods retailers.

3. Over the long term, what two factors have had a major impact on industry profitability? Describe how the industry has been impacted by these factors.

4. Choose the two most profitable companies and two least profitable from Tables 1–4 (using the column on the far right of each table — profits percent change from previous year). What conclusions can you draw from this analysis?

5. Comparing four major categories of companies— equipment, footwear, apparel and retail — which category was the most profitable in 2004 and which category was the least profitable? Briefly explain why you think this is so.

6. What was the most profitable (profits as a percent of sales) equipment company in 2004? What equipment company was least profitable? Answer the same two questions for the footwear, apparel and retailing categories.

7. What single category of non-sporting goods vendor categories is less profitable than sporting goods equipment vendors as a group? See Table 6.

8. What factors influence sporting goods industry profitability? List the factors, choose two from among them and briefly describe how they affect industry profitability.

9

E-Commerce: Vendors, Brick-and-Mortar Retailers, E-Tailers

OVERVIEW

Among all sporting goods products, consumers were most likely to purchase golf, tennis and fitness equipment online in 2003.

(NSGA)

Since it began in the mid-1990s, online selling has been a major challenge for sporting goods vendors, retailers and team dealers. The primary reasons are the diversity of sporting goods products and the need of the sporting goods consumer to relate to the equipment, apparel and footwear. Many consumers, particularly those most seriously involved in sports participation, are simply unwilling to make any sporting goods purchase without personally examining and often trying a product. The most obvious example relates to athletic footwear, particularly among young people, whose shoe size changes continuously, making online purchasing often impractical. Considering that sporting goods products can have a major impact on the buyer's ability to improve and enhance their athletic or recreation experience, most participants will purchase in a store until online presentation more closely approximates a personal buying experience.

However, there are certain times when sporting goods buyers know exactly what they want, and they simply shop for the cheapest price online. These people are clearly prime prospects to become online buyers.

There is little if any evidence to suggest that online selling has expanded the market for sporting goods products, with the possible exception of licensed products. This complicates the decision-making process for online involvement. Online costs are significant, requiring companies to increase marketing costs while facing the risk that sales won't increase as a result. Furthermore, the question as to whether a more effective online site will attract customers away from competitors has yet to be convincingly demonstrated.

Despite the inhibitions and challenges currently associated with online selling, online selling is expected to expand as online technology improves, and also because some consumers are so certain of what they want to purchase that they will simply search for the best price and make their purchase online.

Research has shown that many consumers will research products in a retail store and then make their purchase online, looking for the best price. Also, it isn't any secret that for every online buyer, there are three retail store buyers who did their shopping online prior to purchasing at a store. As a result of all these dynamics, the industry needs to wake-up to the online challenge and integrate online selling as a fundamental dimension of their overall marketing programs, all the while searching for the most effective and profitable way to accomplish this objective.

- At the end of this chapter, you should be able to:
- Describe the different types of e-commerce strategies in the industry.
- Identify the rationale that underlies each e-commerce strategy.
- Analyze the progress of various strategies as they are developing.
- Describe the various ways that e-commerce is affecting the industry.
- Analyze the relative success of different products in e-commerce.

DISCUSSION

E-commerce emerged as a viable commercial entity in the early 1990s. For a variety of reasons, such as the industry's entrepreneurial bent, the relatively small size of most companies in the industry, and the personal involvement of sporting goods consumers with their equipment, apparel and footwear, the sporting goods industry paid little attention to e-commerce. Most industry experts felt at the time that the vast majority of consumers wanted to "touch and feel" products before they purchased. They found most consumers were skeptical of using credit cards online, and that many others didn't like the idea of waiting for their purchases to be delivered.

What went unrecognized at the time was that a number of scenarios were operating concurrently to favorably influence online purchasing. Consumers liked the idea of being able to search online to learn what kinds of products were available, even if they intended to purchase in a store, and although consumers continued to want the "touch-feel" aspect of buying in some product categories, they generally accepted online purchasing for many others such as golf, fitness and many types of camping and outdoor equipment because they were sufficiently familiar with the products. Individuals residing in relatively rural areas had limited access to most products, so many of them welcomed the opportunity to shop online, and online security was improving rapidly, greatly reducing early-on hesitation of consumers to use their credit cards online.

Early on there were a lot of other reasons for the industry to be skeptical Questions were being asked about whether online exposure would increase the industry's total sales volume, or whether it would function as a competitive advantage for individual companies. Still other considerations included whether online exposure for a sport would have a positive effect on participation and whether vendors should sell online and risk alienating their retail customers.

Finally, the issue of cost reared its ugly head. Originally thought to be relatively inexpensive, the opposite has proven to be the case for e-commerce. Effective new online marketing and product presentation technologies are costly, not only for the installation but also for the maintenance. The online environment offers consumers literally millions of choices, and breaking through this clutter for a single company has proven to be much more costly and challenging than originally assumed.

According to the National Golf Foundation, more than half of all core golfers say they researched golf equipment on the Web. Clubs were bought online by 21% of core golfers. A fifth of the core group have arranged tee times. Only 14% bought balls online. *Sporting Goods Business Daily Dispatch*, April 29, 2005.

These are the basic issues with which the industry is now dealing. There isn't much doubt in anyone's mind now that online selling and merchandising is a must for every retailer and vendor. How much it will grow remains to be seen, but the industry recognizes that the potential is yet to be realized, and it is working diligently, in some cases, feverishly, to establish a cost-effective, business-enhancing, online strategy, lest other industries get there first and inhibit the growth of sporting goods as an industry. Today, the industry is involved in e-commerce in two ways: e-commerce to consumers, which is the overwhelmingly dominant aspect of online usage by the sporting goods industry and e-commerce between team dealers and their customers.

Consumer E-Commerce

Consumer e-commerce has been the most widespread e-commerce activity in the sporting goods industry. There are hundreds, if not thousands, of sites offering sporting goods products for sale or providing information about their products, including where to purchase them.

During the early years of the Internet's commercial introduction, sporting goods retailers showed little interest, because they lacked familiarity with the Internet; the cost was high; it was unknown how many, if any, incremental sales would occur online; and there was the question of whether consumers would purchase sporting goods online, considering the technical nature of many products which is difficult to present online. The result was a proliferation of "pure-play" retail online sites. These sites did not have any traditional storefronts; their sole offerings are made online via the web. While pure-play sites experienced some sales success, they encountered many problems which resulted in significant financial losses for these companies. Major problems included:

- Some highly popular vendors refused to sell to these firms, fearing alienation with their regular retail customers.
- High delivery costs made it difficult, if not impossible, for online-only retailers to offer price advantages.
- A substantial portion of all consumers who visited pure-play sites spent their time learning about products on the sites, only to make the actual purchase from a store-front retailer.
- Traditional sporting goods retailers began to recognize that pure-play sites, whether they were financially successful or not, were selling products to their consumers, and that if the pure-play concept ultimately succeeded financially, it could have a significantly negative effect on their future opportunities.

For these and other reasons, the online sales of sporting goods is dominated today by existing store-front retailers and by professional sports organizations who sponsor their own websites. One early-on concern most retailers had was that they would be spending extra money — the cost of their site — without reason to expect sales increases to justify their online investment. However, they now realize that they have many advantages compared with pure-play retailers. They already have inventory and relationships with all major suppliers in the industry. They are already "branded," that is, consumers know who they are, eliminating the need for them to invest heavily in marketing just to identify themselves. They are familiar with consumer behavior and how consumers buy sporting goods. Dealing with returns requires no added cost since they are already doing this when necessary for their store-sold merchandise. And finally, they can offer goods for sale that can be purchased online but picked up at a local store location.

Now that retailers have embraced the Internet, perhaps now as a necessary evil, they are beginning to explore ways to use online merchandising to expand their existing customer base.

Using E-Commerce

E-commerce within the sporting goods industry has evolved and matured to a point where currently, there are three distinct applications: selling products online, presenting products online and driving the consumer to a retailer to make the purchase, and promoting participation in activities which lead to the purchase of related products. All retailers and catalog producers and some vendors sponsor sites which offer products for sale. Most vendors who sell products online do so selectively, promoting only certain products, to avoid creating disfavor among retailers who carry their products. Presenting products online and referring consumers to retailers is a strategy used by most sporting goods vendors. Vendor sites are designed to enhance the image of their products, explain product features, and include a list of retailers where their products can be purchased. Promoting participation is most effective for vendors who have a strong position in their category. An example of a firm using this strategy is the Coleman Company, who holds a dominant position in the outdoor camping equipment market. In addition to equipment vendors, associations that represent a segment of the industry (such as the National Shooting Sports Foundation or the National Golf Foundation), promote participation in the sport they represent, with the objective of increasing consumer purchases from their sporting goods vendor and retailer membership.

Products Selling Best Online

In 2004, online sales represented 7.4 percent of sporting goods equipment and 3.4 percent of athletic footwear, according to the National Sporting Goods Association (NSGA). While no figures are available for athletic apparel, early studies conducted by SBRnet indicate that licensed product apparel will sell very well online, and this has been confirmed, as reflected by the significant number of sites now promoting licensed products.

NSGA research portrays the wide disparity in the significance of online selling depending on the product category. Table 1 reflects the percentage of all consumer purchases made online in calendar year 2004, in units and dollars, for a wide range of sporting goods products. It is evident that consumers tend to spend more online, on average, than they do offline, because for nearly every product the percent of dollars is higher than the percent of units.

The onset of the Internet as a marketing tool required each segment of the industry to deal with heretofore nonexistent basic issues. As discussed earlier in this chapter, all segments had to consider whether online selling was necessary at all. Vendors had to confront the issue of whether to sell their products online directly to consumers or to avoid competing with their primary retail customers. Retailers had to consider how deeply to invest in the costly technology and maintenance involved, not knowing whether an Internet presence would increase sales at the expense of competitors. Team dealers had to con-

---

According to the NSGA, women increased their share of all sports footwear Internet purchases from 44.5 percent in 2003 to 51.4 percent in 2004.

TABLE 1: ONLINE CONSUMER PURCHASES, SELECTED PRODUCTS
PERCENT OF TOTAL CONSUMER PURCHASES MADE ONLINE, 2004
(RANKED BY PERCENT OF $ EXPENDITURES)

Product Category	*Percent of 2004 Consumer Purchases Made Online*	
	Percent of Units Purchased	*Percent of $ Expenditures*
Sleeping Bags	4.5	10.3
Golf Clubs (individual clubs)	10.7	9.7
Stationary Exercise Bicycles	8.3	9.6
Camping Tents (1–2 person)	3.6	9.6
Backpacks	3.4	7.5
Treadmills	4.8	7.4
Baseball Mitts	4.8	6.8
Running/Jogging Shoes	4.7	5.2
Scooters (non-motorized)	2.0	4.9
Tennis Racquets	2.8	4.8
Fashion Sneakers	3.3	4.2
Basketball Shoes	3.7	4.0
Inline Skates	3.4	3.9
Soccer Shoes	1.7	2.4
Golf Balls	2.0	2.4
Mountain Bicycles	1.1	1.8
Fishing Reels	1.7	1.7
Basketballs	1.1	1.5
Soccer Balls	0.4	0.9

Source: NSGA.

sider how to function online in a selling environment which is dominated by competitive bidding.

The question as to the necessity of producing an online presence, as it turns out, has been answered by the consumer. Millions responded favorably to the Internet. In addition to online purchasing, on average, there are three shoppers for every buyer. As a result, an online presence is a necessary fact of life in the industry, an essential ingredient that simply cannot be ignored or treated lightly.

Online sales are currently at modest levels, so the question can be asked, "Why so much effort for such a small result?" Most industry practitioners feel that the future potential of e-commerce is far greater than present-day experience, or at least they want to avoid losing out if e-commerce does expand significantly. Evidence substantiates growing interest levels in online sporting goods. For example, as reported in the July 20, 2005, issue of *Sporting Goods Business Daily Dispatch*, Media Metrix, a leading Internet audience measurement service, reported that in June 2005, the retail sports/outdoors category was the second-highest gaining category, rising 9 percent to 20.2 million visitors, second only to General Motors' new financing option. Furthermore, GSI Network, who produces online sites for several leading sporting goods retailers, was among the Internet's top-gaining properties in terms of traffic, climbing 18 percent to 5.3 million visitors.

At the moment, the industry is dealing with a number of key issues related to site development and management, whose resolution will strongly influence the future role of e-commerce. These issues include: how best to present products, the future potential of pure-play e-commerce sites (where no brick-and-mortar stores are involved) vs. brick-and-mortar retailers who have established sites, which products will be more or less successful than others in the e-commerce marketplace, the factors that inhibit consumers from using e-commerce for sporting goods, the viability of auction purchasing of sporting goods products, and how much vendors can or should sell their own products directly to consumers. It's too early to draw conclusions. Rather, the primary purpose of this chapter is to familiarize you with the nature of these issues, and to provide you with some guidelines on how to follow the issues as they develop. Two major industry newsletters, *SGB's Inside Sporting Goods* and *Sporting Goods Intelligence,* provide a continuous flow of news relating to e-commerce activities, and several industry trade magazines provide some e-commerce coverage in almost every issue.

Evaluating Online Sites

Establishing an online presence is still very much in the development stage for sporting goods companies. Sites which are graphically sensational may not be commercially viable, even to the point of hurting a company's sales. Sales can be hurt if an individual seeks out a site in order to find a product to purchase and they are driven away by a graphically exciting but time-consuming presentation that has nothing to do with the consumer's reason for visiting the site. Consumers normally visit a commercial site for a specific purpose — to buy something or to learn something about a product. If they can't accomplish that within a few seconds of arriving at the site, they will often turn away.

Consumers vary significantly on several dimensions:

- product knowledge
- skill level
- demographics (age, gender, income, etc.)
- reason for visiting the site (buyer vs. shopper)
- technical information requirements

Given that the Internet is an information-based medium, these factors must be considered carefully by site developers to be certain that their site meets the needs of individuals who are attracted to their site. For example, some sites provide a great deal of information right on the home page because visitors are there primarily to find a product to purchase. Within reason, the more popular product purchase opportunities that are offered on the home page, the better. This tends to be true for online sellers who also offer catalogs, and who specialize in a particular product or sports activity. Powerful graphic imagery in this situation would most likely get in the way of the ability to achieve immediate sales.

Full-line sporting goods retailers face major challenges with online selling because they offer many different products appealing to many different individuals for many different sports at many different skill levels. Their challenge is to appeal to all visitors, no matter their interest or skill level and to offer as much, if not more, than specialty stores. And they need to do it in a matter of seconds, if not milliseconds.

When evaluating a site, you must consider several factors, including:

- the objectives of the site (to sell a product, to create an image, to drive consumers to a store, to appeal to skilled participants only, etc.)
- whether the objectives are realistic given the constraints of online presentation
- what types of consumers are attracted to the store (skilled participants, new participants, older people, younger people, etc.)
- ease of finding relevant information related to a product (sizes and colors for apparel, equipment dimensions and quality, etc.)
- the range of choices available for a given product/product category (price, quality, etc.)
- the target audience (primarily current customers, primarily new customers, or both equally)

The answers to these questions are all important if one is to develop and maintain a productive investment in online selling and merchandising.

How Sporting Goods Vendors Use the Internet

As discussed above, after early struggles by all concerned, the "dealer confrontation" problem for vendors, that is, the question of whether vendors will offend and lose dealer support for their products if they sell online directly to consumers, has largely been resolved. Leading brands are so important to retailers that retailers can't really afford to discontinue selling them, even if vendors offer their products for sale directly. What has occurred is a compromise. Leading vendors tend to offer a selected list of products for sale on their sites, while at the same time directing consumers to local retailers who carry a much broader selection of their products. As for footwear, by tradition, leading vendors operate retail stores featuring their products exclusively or predominantly. For them, the problem of competing with their customers has already been dealt with and resolved, prior to the onset of direct online selling.

For smaller vendors, as a general rule, they simply present their products on their website along with the store locator feature, although some of them will also offer a limited selection of their products for sale online.

An interesting phenomenon related to online shopping has served to inhibit online selling by vendors. Most consumers look for a relatively wide selection of products when they shop, searching for different brands and types from which to select. Unless they (consumers) are deeply committed to a particular brand and specific product, buying at a specific company's website severely limits their opportunity to make the best choice for their needs. So the practical dynamics of shopping, combined with some consumer inhibitions about online purchasing, result in a very low level of consumer interest in purchasing from a vendor's website, thus minimizing the danger of plagiarism by vendors from their retail store customers.

Since direct selling is a relatively minor function of vendor websites, many use the latest site technologies to produce attractive, interesting, and image-building features. Some footwear sites allow consumers to design their own products online and then purchase them directly from the vendor. Other sites promote and glamorize athletes who endorse their products. Others visually present their products in "natural" environments—basketball shoes worn by players in a game, hiking shoes worn by hikers while trekking, and protective equipment worn by participants in a visualized game situation. Site graphics are designed to maximize viewer interest.

Using the latest glamorous technology may seem like the best thing to do, but it can conflict with a basic premise of online use — primarily as a source of information. Millions of consumers still use dial-up connections, which inhibit their ability to reap the benefits of flash technology, while spending a lot more time on a site than they originally hoped. Site sponsors have difficulty determining how much is enough of modern technology — technology producers want to sell their latest wares, while most consumers want a fast, easy and time-restricted experience online. Resolving this conflict is a major issue still facing sporting goods vendors as they try to evaluate the true benefits and most effective way to present and/or sell their products online.

Below are some examples of how different sporting goods vendors currently use the Internet. These examples reflect the variety of uses which, at the moment, are considered to be most effective for a company in achieving its particular objectives.

EVENT SPONSORSHIP

As reported in the August 9, 2005, issue of *SportsPipe*, Quiksilver (a leading apparel and ski company) will webcast five global extreme sports events that it sponsors from a new website created specifically for that purpose. The events are the Kelly Slater Invitational, Quiksilver Pro Japan, Boost Mobile Presented by Quiksilver, the Quiksilver Pro France and Quiksilver ISA World Junior Surfing Championships. These webcasts will incorporate video presentation, online chats and other features as well as text. Quiksilver's U.S. site will be provided in English and Spanish, and their European site will include French.

INCORPORATING REAL-TIME UPDATES

As reported in the July 25, 2005, issue of *Sporting Goods Business Daily Dispatch*, Fila will be incorporating on-demand web content into their site. "The goal is to put content in marketing's hands instead of the web development team," said Rob McClellan, general manager of Fila Online.

CUSTOMIZING PRODUCTS

Nike's "Nike ID" site allows the consumer to customize features of an existing product to their specifications. Customers can choose a specific product from many choices, then proceed through the site to select the colors and design configurations desired.

VENDOR-RETAILER SUPPORT

As reported in the June 9, 2005, issue of *Sporting Goods Business Daily Dispatch*, Brooks Sports launched online shopping on brooksrunning.com, but with a big twist. The new online service allows performance running stores to fulfill Brooks' online orders locally, maintaining the customer-retailer relationship. "Customers browse, learn about and order Brooks products online without ever leaving brooksrunning.com; participating retailers are notified daily of brooksrunning.com orders placed by customers located within a 250-mile radius of their store; retailers have the opportunity, if they have the requested product in stock, to fulfill each order, make a sale and gain a new customer; and through brooksrunning.com sales and inventory reports, retailers are capable of tracking individual product orders and sales trends in their area, allowing them to better match customer interests and more efficiently plan their own retail inventories."

How Sporting Goods Retailers Use the Internet

Basically there are four types of retailers who are presently selling sporting goods products online:

1. online sites maintained by storefront retailers
2. online-only multiproduct sites featuring several different product categories, including sporting goods
3. online-only exclusively sporting goods
4. sporting goods catalog retailers who have expanded their marketing to include online sales

Storefront Retailer Sites

Some leading retailers produce, sponsor and maintain their own sites, notably Recreational Equipment, Inc. (REI), The Finish Line, Hibbett Sporting Goods, Cabela's, Bass Pro Shops and Foot Locker. REI offers regular online merchandise for sale and also features REI.outlet.com which sells closeout merchandise. Some retailers, such as The Finish Line, serve as the shopping destination for other online sites such as *Sports Illustrated* (si.com) as well as having their own site.

Other retailers do not actually produce their own sites, but rather they outsource their site to, GSI Commerce, Inc. to produce, manage and host their site, as well as actually stock merchandise and fulfill orders. In return, GSI pays royalties for all sales. Retailers outsourcing to GSI earn less on a per-sale basis than they would if they made online sales themselves; however, their Internet business is cost free. Organizations working with GSI as of October 2005 are listed below.

Retailers (Storefront and Online-Only):

- Bally Total Fitness
- Blades Board & Skate
- City Sports
- Dick's Sporting Goods
- Dunham's Sports
- Fogdog Sports (online-only)
- G.I. Joe's

- MC Sports
- Modell's Sporting Goods
- Olympia Sports
- ProGolf.com
- Shoe Carnival
- Sport Chalet
- The Sports Authority

Professional Sports Organizations:

- Carolina Panthers
- Denver Broncos
- Houston Texans
- Major League Baseball (MLB)

- NASCAR
- San Diego Chargers
- San Francisco 49ers

Sporting Goods Vendors:

- Adidas
- Reebok (retail stores)
- Rockport (retail stores)

- Russell Athletic
- Timberland

For most retailers, their primary objective is to generate online purchases, although they also provide a store-locator feature that allows consumers to identify the store nearest to their home. Early in the life of online selling, sporting goods retailers approached the Internet with caution, concerned about consumer inhibitions to online purchasing such as a lack of credit card security, lack of a depth of choices, the need to have the product immediately, and the need to personally evaluate a product prior to purchase. With the passage of time and greatly improved online technology, these inhibitions have either disappeared or greatly diminished. This allows storefront retailers to focus on their primary objective of selling, rather than on presenting a more complicated site with two objectives— selling online and directing consumers to the store to purchase.

One major benefit of online selling for retailers is the opportunity to develop a valuable customer prospect list. The opportunity to communicate with customers by e-mail represents a potentially sizable opportunity for retailers to actually increase sales with existing customers. This was much more difficult and expensive to accomplish when direct mail was the only method available to use to communicate with customers.

Retailers use their sites not only to sell merchandise but also to provide other services. For example, G.I. Joe's, operating in Oregon and Washington, offers a certified fishing and hunting guide program through AdventuresExpress.com, an online outdoor travel and gear sales portal.

ONLINE-ONLY MULTIPRODUCT SITES

Among the leading companies in this category are eBay, Amazon.com and Overstock.com. Online-only companies use one or both of two basic strategies depending on the product and the market potential they consider to exist: (1) stocking merchandise that they offer for sale in their warehouse, or (2) using wholesalers, vendors or even other online-only sites to physically fulfill orders.

Who is the largest sporting goods e-tailer? It may surprise you. Here's what Bob Carr, editor and publisher of *SGB's Inside Sporting Goods* wrote in May 2004:

> Remember in the mid-'90s when we were told that online retailing would replace brick-and-mortar stores? That e-tail sites would be tomorrow's big box retailers? Since then, the Internet lost some of its selling glow and many dot-coms are history. There certainly have been successes. GSI Commerce isn't rolling in profits, but it has consistently grown and is expected to finish this year in the black. GSI's clients like the model, and the company has not lost any of its sporting goods partners–and that's saying something. REI, Foot Locker, The Sportsman's Guide, and a number of smaller, specialized companies have also been successful, if not profitable. But where is the megalith of sporting goods e-tail?
>
> It's on an auction site. In the sporting goods realm, eBay has changed over the years. It is now the largest e-tailer of bikes and golf clubs in the country. In prior years, consumers sold their used clubs on the site but today, eBay sells more new clubs than old. With hundreds of thousands of sporting goods products on eBay's site, sales of sporting goods, fan apparel and collectibles hit $1 billion last year ($1.8 billion worldwide). The three categories used to be ganged together, but now fan products and sporting goods are sold in one group.
>
> What's changed the model is the willingness of retailers to use the auction site to liquidate aged inventory at a profitable price. As shipping prices drop, a local retailer can develop an international business on eBay. It is now possible to ship a set of clubs to Australia for $20. Dozens of sporting goods sellers are doing $100,000 a month on the site. The deal with the PGA of America is increasing the relevance of the golf pro. PGA has established prices on used clubs. A consumer who wants to trade in old clubs goes to a participating pro who sells the clubs on eBay based on pre-set prices.
>
> Because there is no national sporting goods show that gives buyers any ideas of trends or hot new sports, eBay may be functioning that way. According to Drew Marich, eBay's director/sports, trade buyers visiting eBay can find new ideas based on what's going up for sale. He says eBay was quick to notice the trend toward motorized skateboards and scooters. The latest hot new product is Airsoft. Its "guns" fire paintballs and pellets. As of press time, there were 2,776 spring-loaded guns, 621 electric guns, 341 gas-powered guns and 69 others on eBay. Incidentally, paintball products are the seventh-largest category on eBay. The e-tailer is also working on better ways to sell sports apparel and footwear.

ONLINE-ONLY SPORTS-ONLY RETAILERS

During the early stages of the Internet, online-only sites were considered to show great promise, and hundreds, if not thousands, of sites sprung into being. Most of these sites had little if any credibility with consumers and were often managed by individuals without any sporting goods retail experience. By 2004, the great majority of these sites had disappeared. One major cause of their demise has been competition from storefront sporting goods retailers who are now aggressively pursuing online selling, as opposed to their hesitancy during the Internet's early days of existence. By 2005, the relatively few remaining online-only retailers, such as BoatersWorld and the Golf Warehouse, have educated themselves sufficiently in the needs and interests of sporting goods consumers, and their sites are serving the industry today.

FORMER CATALOG-ONLY RETAILERS

Former catalog-only retailers have been the most successful with online sites. Early-on conventional thinking that online sales would drive catalog retailers out of business has proved incorrect. Catalog retailers discovered that, while catalog sales suffered somewhat, overall sales combining online and catalog orders grew significantly. Examples of these retailers are The Sportsman's Guide (outdoor products) and Eastbay (footwear and apparel products). Illustrating their positive financial experience with the Internet, The Sportsman's Guide's sales rose from $170 million in 2001 to $240 million in 2004. Over this three year period, online sales doubled as a percent of total sales, increasing from 21 percent in 2001 to 42 percent in 2004.

One probable explanation for the positive relationship between online and catalog selling is that many online inhibitions related to the need to physically touch and feel products and hesitancies about using credit cards don't exist among historic catalog customers. Catalog customers were already conditioned to the absence of the touch-feel experience when purchasing. Industry experts speculate that many former catalog buyers still prefer to use catalogs to do their shopping, but they prefer making their purchases online.

How Sporting Goods Team Dealers Use the Internet

Team dealers, companies that sell team sports products to schools and recreational youth and adult leagues are rapidly finding their way in the online world. Even today, the team sales process creates several roadblocks to effective online applications. First of all, most high schools and colleges require bids for major purchases, and the bidding process doesn't lend itself easily to online technology. Second, team dealers have historic personal relationships which are a key factor in doing business with their prospects, while online selling is impersonal. Third, total revenues for most team dealers are less than $5 million; precluding their ability to invest significantly in developing an effective online presence, particularly since online activity cannot be expected to increase sales significantly, at least for the great majority of dealers.

As happened among vendors and retailers, however, as the Internet evolved, concurrent developments have increased online opportunities for team sales. While most major products are sold on a bid basis, a certain percentage, ranging from 10 to 25 percent, are not. And with more and more young, Internet-savvy people joining the coaching ranks, many of them turn to online purchasing whenever they can. Often they will search the Internet for products they need — searching not only team dealer sites but also sites sponsored by traditional sporting goods retailers. These same shoppers will search for the products they need and for the best price. In some cases, they'll discover that they can purchase the product they want, or a similar version, for less money from a traditional retailer than they can from the team dealer. Thus, the team dealer is often in a defensive position without an effective online presence. Perhaps for this reason, acquisition activity has rapidly expanded in the team dealer category, and most of these acquisitions are being made by one company, Collegiate Pacific. Coincidentally, Collegiate established an early online presence and it is expanding rapidly as their acquisition program grows.

Looking to the Future

The facts above lead one to conclude that online selling for sporting goods is still in its infancy. Some industry executives believe that the Internet's value should be measured in online sales, and that it will follow the catalog/direct mail buying pattern, that is, achieving a certain sales level and remaining there. Others feel differently. The reason — there is a major difference between catalog selling and online selling in one important respect. Online exposure reaches nearly every potential buyer, whereas catalogs most often reach only those individuals who have already made a catalog purchase.

As pointed out above, recent studies show that as many as three times the number of online buyers shop online before they make a store purchase. If this is true, then nearly 30 percent of all sporting goods equipment buyers shop online, a fact that demands increasing attention from the industry in the future.

As indicated in Table 1, online purchasing patterns vary significantly depending on the product. Based on experience thus far, fitness, golf, licensed apparel and outdoor products are likely to be the largest sellers in the future Vendors and retailers who aren't as well-known, who don't have as strong of a presence, or who simply haven't focused on these categories will need to reevaluate this situation if they want to make the most out of Internet opportunities.

The online competitive environment will undoubtedly lead to more sophisticated, more broad-ranging sites and seek new ways to attract online visitors, beyond simply offering products to sell. To date, vendors are more aggressive than retailers in broadening interest in their sites with information about events and effective use of flash technology, but that is likely to change.

Most likely, the scenarios described above are not unique to sporting goods. Other industries are dealing with the same strategic and philosophical issues with respect to the Internet. Sporting goods is not in imminent danger of losing position in the marketplace — as a matter of fact, the enormous appeal of sports sites such as ESPN, the NFL, MLB, and the NCAA are stimulating consumer interest in sports in general, thereby providing a significant platform for sporting goods companies to use to capitalize on the high interest levels reflected by the Internet/sports relationship.

RELATED WEBSITES

ONLINE-ONLY SPORTS-ONLY RETAILERS:

BoatersWorld.com: www.boatersworld.com
The Golf Warehouse: www.tgw.com

BRICK-AND-MORTAR (STOREFRONT) AND ONLINE/CATALOG RETAILER SITES:

Big 5 Sporting Goods: www.big5sportinggoods.com

Dick's Sporting Goods: http://www.dickssportinggoods.com
Eastbay: www.eastbay.com
Foot Locker: www.footlocker.com
GSI Commerce: www.gsicommerce.com
MC Sports: www.mcsports.com
REI: www.rei.com
The Sports Authority: www.thesportsauthority.com
The Sportsman's Guide: www.sportsmansguide.com

MULTI-CATEGORY ONLINE-ONLY RETAILERS:

Amazon.com: www.amazon.com
eBay.com: www.ebay.com
Overstock.com (check out the sports, travel and toys sections): www.overstock.com

VENDORS:

K-Swiss: www.kswiss.com
Nautilus: www.nautilus.com
New Balance: www.newbalance.com
New Era Cap: www.neweracap.com
Nike: www.nike.com
Wilson Sporting Goods Company: www.wilsonsports.com

PROFESSIONAL LEAGUES:

MLB Authentic Licensed Products: http://shop.mlb.com
NBA: http://store.nba.com
NFL: www.nflshop.com
NHL: http://nhl.com/shop/index.html?clk=001

EXERCISES

1. Choose three different retailer sites from those provided above and make a list of the similarities and differences between them. The factors to consider are:

- Variety of products offered
- Ease of finding what you want
- Selection offered within a product category, such as golf clubs, etc.
- Ability to pick up your purchase at a local store
- Information provided about products

Then choose three different vendor sites from above and do the same.

2. Go to www.sportsmansguide.com and www.rei.com. Prepare a summary analysis of these two sites, including their objectives and how well you feel they accomplished them. Do not use more than one-half page for each company.

3. Go to www.tgw.com or www.boatersworld.com. Prepare a summary analysis of the site you chose, including its objectives and how well you feel it accomplished them. Do not use more than one-half page.

Appendix

Leading Vendors, Retailers, and Multisport Media and Trade Associations

SPORTING GOODS VENDOR DIRECTORY

The information in this directory was accurate as of fall 2005.

ACCUSPLIT, INC.
6120 Stoneridge Mall Road, Ste 210
Pleasanton, CA 94566
925–226–0888
Fax: 925–463–0147
W. Ron Sutton, Pres/COB
Steve Simmons, VP Sls
Steve Yelta, CFO
Major Brands: Accusplit
www.accusplit.com
Timing Devices, Watches

ACUSHNET COMPANY/TITLEIST
(American Brands)
333 Bridge Street
PO Box 965
Fairhaven, MA 02719–0965
508–979–2000
Fax: 508–979–3909
Wally Uihlein, CEO/COB
Jim Conner, Pres Foot-Joy
Jerry Bellis, Exec VP Sls/Mktg
Dennis Doherty, Sr VP Human Resources
Major Brands: Cobra, Foot-Joy, Pinnacle,
  Titleist
www.titleist.com
Golf

ADAMS GOLF
2801 E. Plano Parkway
Plano, TX 75074–7497

972–673–9000
Fax: 972–398–8818
Oliver G. "Chip" Brewer III, Pres/CEO
Barney Adams, CEO/COB
Ann Neff, Mgr Human Resource
Major Brands: Adams
www.adamsgolf.com
Golf

ADAMS U.S.A., INC.
610 South Jefferson Ave
PO Box 489
Cookeville, TN 38503–0489
931–526–6857
Fax: 931–526–8357
Ray Abel, Pres
L. A. "Sonny" Allen, Mgr Sls/Mktg
Major Brands: Adams, Adidas, Neumann
www.adamsusa.com
Team Sports Equipment

ADIDAS
5055 N. Greeley Avenue
Portland, OR 97217–4139
971–234–2300
Fax: 971–234–2540
Herbert Hainer, CEO
Eric Stamminger, CEO Adidas America
Martin Brewer, Dir Sports Mktg
Bobbi B. Stedman, Dir of Human Resources
Major Brands: Adidas, TaylorMade

http://usa.adidas.com
Apparel, Footwear, Golf

AKADEMA
317 Midland Avenue
Garfield, NJ 07026
973–772–7669
Fax: 973–772–4839
Lawrence Gilligan, Pres
Joseph Gilligan, Sr., Sr VP
Joseph Gilligan, Jr., VP Sls/Mktg
Major Brands: Akadema
www.akademapro.com
Baseball

ALDILA, INC.
13450 Stowe Drive
Poway, CA 92064–6860
858–513–1801
Fax: 858–513–1972
Peter R. Mathewson, Pres/CEO/COO
Michael J. Rossi, VP Sls/Mktg
Maryann Jacob, Mgr Human Resource
Major Brands: Aldila
www.aldila.com
Golf, Ice Hockey

ALLESON ATHLETIC
2921 Brighton Henrietta Town Line Road
Rochester, NY 14623
585–272–0606
Fax: 585–272–9639
Ellie Oliveri, CEO
Todd Levine, VP Sls/Mktg
Michael Kretovic, Mgr Human Resources
Major Brands: DA Athletic
www.donalleson.com
Team Sports Apparel

ALL STAR DIV./AMPAC ENTERPRISES, INC.
1 Main Street
PO Box 1356
Shirley, MA 01464–1356
978–425–6266
Fax: 978–425–4068
David J. Holden, Pres
Stan Jurga, VP Sls
Jeff Johnson, Dir Opns
Carol Jurga, Human Resources

Major Brands: All-Star, MLB (Lic.)
www.all-starsports.com
Team Sports

AMEREX GROUP, INC.
350 Fifth Avenue, Ste 1401
New York, NY 10118
212–967–3330
Fax: 212–967–3352
Glenn Palmer, CEO
Monica Alberez, Mgr Sls/Mktg
Dorothea Walters, Human Resources
(732–587–1313)
Major Brands: Alpine Studio, Bombshell
www.amerexgroup.com
Outdoor Apparel

AMERICAN ATHLETIC
(Russell Athletic)

AMERICAN RECREATION PRODUCTS, INC.
1224 Fern Ridge Parkway
St. Louis, MO 63141–4451
314–576–8000
Fax: 314–576–8072
George J. Grabner, Jr., Pres American Rec. Products
Mike Billick, Pres Slumberjack
Mark Herbert, Pres Sierra Designs
Chuck Smith, Pres Wenzel
Bill Steele, Dir Human Resources
Major Brands: Kelty, Ridgeway (Lic.), Sierra Designs, Slumberjack, Trek (Lic.), Wenzel
www.kellwood.com/corporate/divO.asp?divID=2
Outdoor Products

AMERICAN SPORTING GOODS COMPANY
2323 Main Street
Irvine, CA 92614–6222
949–752–6688
Fax: 949–756–8609
Jerry Turner, Co-Chairman
Kevin Wulff, Pres/CEO
Margaret Oung, CEO
Ed Goldman, VP Mktg
Doug Vesling, VP Natl Sls

Natalie Avalos, Dir Human Resources
Major Brands: And 1, Apex, Avia, Turntec,
  Yukon
www.avia.com
Footwear

AMF BOWLING
8100 AMF Drive
Mechanicsville, VA 23111–3700
804–730–4000
Fax: 804–730–0652
Frederick Hipp, Pres/CEO
Chris Caesar, Exec VP/CFO
Merrill Wreden, Sr VP Mktg
Bethany Packet, Dir Human Resources
Major Brands: Accuscore, AMF
www.amf.com
Bowling

**ANTIGUA ENTERPRISES/ANTIGUA
  GROUP, INC.**
16651 N. 84th Avenue
Peoria, AZ 85382
623–523–6000
Fax: 623–523–6010
Ronald A. McPherson, Pres/CEO
Penny Larson, Dir Human Resources
Major Brands: Antigua
www.antiguasportswear.com
Apparel

ASHAWAY LINE & TWINE MFG.
24 Laurel Street
PO Box 549
Ashaway, RI 02804–1515
401–377–2221
Fax: 401–377–9091
Pamela Crandall, COB
Kathryn C. Crandall, Pres
Steven J. Crandall, VP Sls/Mktg
Barbara Lavalley, Dir Human Resources
www.ashawayusa.com
Racquet Sports

ASHWORTH SPORTSWEAR
2765 Loker Avenue West
Carlsbad, CA 92008–6601
760–438–6610
Fax: 760–438–6657
Randall Herrel, Pres/CEO

Rosie Rivera, Dir Human Resources
Major Brands: Ashworth
www.ashworthinc.com
Apparel, Callaway (Lic.)

ASICS AMERICA CORP.
16275 Laguna Canyon Road
Irvine, CA 92618–3603
949–453–8888
Fax: 949–453–0387
Richard Bourne, Pres/CEO
Eileen Schaaf, Mgr Human Resources
Major Brands: Asics, Tiger
www.asicstiger.com
Footwear

ATOMIC SKI
(Amer Sports Corporation)

BACHARACH RASIN
802 Gleneagles Court
Towson, MD 21286
410–825–6747
Fax: 410–321–0720
Chris Hutchins, Pres
Carol Donovan, Mgr Opns
Manufacturer, Distributor: Bacharach
  Rasin, Brian, DeBeer, STX, Warrior
www.bacharach.com
Lacrosse, Hockey

BADEN SPORTS, INC.
34114 21st Avenue South
Federal Way, WA 98003
253–925–0500
Fax: 253–925–0570
Michael J. Schindler, Pres/CEO
Laura Screiber, Mgr Human Resources
Major Brands: Baden
Inflatable Balls for Team Sports

**BECTON DICKINSON/BD
  WORLDWIDE**
1 Becton Drive, MC 376
Franklin Lakes, NJ 07417–1864
201–847–4000
Fax: 201–847–5487
Robert Singley, VP Sls/Mktg
Lynn Pagano, Dir Human Resources
Major Brands: Ace, Bauer & Black, Tru-Fit

www.bd.com/elastics
Sports Medicine

BELL SPORTS
(Fenway Partners, Inc.)
1924 County Road, 3000 North
Rantoul, IL 61866
217–893–9300
Fax: 217–892–8727
Bill Fry, Pres/CEO
Jackie Werblo, Human Resources
(469–417–6600)
Major Brands: Bell, Giro
www.bellsports.com
Cycling

BISON, INC.
603 L Street
Lincoln, NE 68508
402–474–3353
Fax: 402–474–6720
Nick Cosick, Pres
Laura Schwisow, VP Sls/Mktg
Sue White, Mgr Human Resources
Major Brands: Bison, Center Line
www.bisoninc.com
Basketball, Volleyball

BLACK DIAMOND EQUIPMENT
2084 E 3900 S
Salt Lake City, UT 84124–1723
801–278–5552
Fax: 801–278–5544
Peter Metcalf, Pres/CEO
Mille Buker, VP Mktg
Meredith Saarnen, VP Human Resources
Major Brands: Ascension, Black Diamond
www.blackdiamondequipment.com
Outdoor Equipment

BRASS EAGLE, INC.
(K2, Inc.)
1201 S.E. 30th Street
Bentonville, AR 72712
479–464–8700
Fax: 479–464–8701
Gary Remensnyder, Pres
David Jones, VP Mktg
Barbara Almond, Dir Human Resources
www.brasseagle.com
Paintball

BRIDGESTONE GOLF
14230 Lochridge Blvd., Ste G
Covington, GA 30014
770–787–7400
Fax: 770–786–6416
Keith Mineghshi, CEO/COB
Kelly Ellis, Sr Dir Sls/Comm
Bob Zillgitt, Mgr Human Resources
Major Brands: Firestone, Precept
www.preeptgolf.com
Golf

BRINE, INC.
47 Sumner Street
Milford, MA 01757–1696
508–478–3250
Fax: 508–478–2430
William McLean, Pres
Sean Fox, VP Sls/Mktg
Major Brands: Brine
www.brine.com
Lacrosse

BROOKS SPORTS, INC.
(Russell Athletic)
19820 North Creek Parkway, Ste 200
Bothell, WA 98011–8277
425–488–3131
Fax: 425–489–1975
Jim Weber, Pres/CEO
Scott Carey, VP Sls
Joanne Anderson, Dir Human Resources
Major Brands: Brooks
www.brookssports.com
Footwear

**BROWNING AND WINCHESTER
    FIREARMS**
1 Browning Place
Morgan, UT 84050–9326
801–876–2711
Fax: 801–876–3331
Charles Guevremont, Pres/CEO
Travis Hall, VP Sls/Mktg
David Rich, VP Human Resources
Major Brands: Browning, US Repeating
    Arms, Winchester
www.browning.com
Archery, Firearms

BRUNSWICK CORP.
1 North Field Court
Lake Forest, IL 6004
847–735–4700
Fax: 847–735–4765
George W. Buckley, COB
B. Russell Lockridge, VP/Chief Human
Resources Officer
Major Brands: Brunswick, Life Fitness,
    Mercury, Sea Ray
www.brunswick.com
Bowling, Fitness, Outdoor, Water Sports

BURTON SNOWBOARDS
80 Industrial Parkway
Burlington, VT 05401
802–862–4500
Fax: 802–651–4500
Jake Burton, CEO
Bryan Johnston, VP Mktg
Jim Boger, Dir Human Resources
Major Brands: Anon, Burton, Gravis, Optic
www.burton.com
Snowboarding

CALLAWAY GOLF CO.
2180 Rutherford Road
Carlsbad, CA 92008
760–931–1771
Fax: 760–931–8013
George Fellows, Pres/CEO/COB
Liz Weitzel, Dir Human Resources
Major Brands: Big Bertha, Callaway,
    Odyssey, Steelhead, Warbird
www.callawaygolf.com
Golf

CANNONDALE BICYCLE CORP.
16 Trowbridge Drive
PO Box 122
Bethel, CT 06801
203–749–7000
Fax: 203–748–4012
David Budd, Dir Mktg
Jean Benson, VP Human Resources
Major Brands: Cannondale
www.cannondale.com
Cycling

CCM
(Div. of Reebok at press time)
3400 Raymond Lasnier
Ville St-Laurent, Quebec Canada H4R 3L3
514–461–8000
Fax: 514–461–8020
Matt O'Toole, Pres/CEO
Len Rhodes, VP Global Mktg
Alain Larocque, Dir Human Resource
Major Brands: CCM, Heaton, Jofa, Koho
http://en.ccmsports.com/index.php
Ice Hockey

CHAMPION/SARA LEE BRANDED
    APPAREL
1000 E. Hanes Mill Road
Winston-Salem, NC 27105–1384
336–519–4400
Fax: 336–519–0554
Gerald Evans, Pres Champion Apparel
Larry French, VP Mktg
Lisa Purcell, VP Mktg
Manual Jassup, VP Human Resources
Major Brands: Champion, Champion Jog-
    bra, Duofold, Hanes, Starter (Lic.)
www.championusa.com
Team Sports/Cheerleading Apparel

CLEVELAND GOLF
(Quiksilver, Inc.)
5601 Skylab Road
Huntington Beach, CA 92647
714–889–1300
Fax: 714–236–9900
Greg Hopkins, Pres/COO
Todd Harmon, VP Prod Mktg
Steven Gingrich, VP Human Resources
Major Brands: Cleveland
www.clevelandgolf.com
Golf

CLIFF KEEN ATHLETIC
PO Box 1447
Ann Arbor, MI 48106
800–992–0799
Fax: 800–590–0759
Chad Clark, VP Sls
Barry Bellaire, Dir Human Resources
www.cliffkeen.com
Wrestling

THE COLEMAN COMPANY, INC.
3600 N. Hydraulic
Wichita, KS 67219
316–832–2653
Fax: 316–219–7540
Dave Kiedaisch, Pres/CEO
Randy Brillhart, Sr VP Sls/Mktg
Nancy Paulson, Sr VP Global Human Resources
Major Brands: Coleman, Peak 1
www.coleman.com
Outdoor Products

COLLEGIATE PACIFIC
532 Luck Ave S.W.
Roanoke, VA 24016
540–981–0281
Michael J Blumenfeld, COB
Adam L. Blumenfeld, Pres
Teresa Schneider, Mgr Human Resources
Major Brands/Subsidiaries: Dixie, Kessler's,
   Orlando Sports, Sport Supply Group
www.cpacsports.com
Team Sports, Team Dealer

COLUMBIA SPORTSWEAR COMPANY
14375 N.W. Science Park Drive
Portland, OR 97229–5418
503–985–4000
Fax: 503–985–5800
Tim Boyle, Pres/CEO
Bob Masin, Sr VP Sls/Mdsng
Susan Popp, Dir Personnel/Human
Resources
Major Brands: Columbia, Mountain
Hardware
www.columbia.com
Outdoor Apparel, Footwear

CONFLUENCE WATERSPORTS
   COMPANY
111 Kayaker Way
Easley, SC 29642
864–859–7518
Fax: 864–855–5995
Richard Feehan, CEO
Kelley Woolsey, VP Mktg/Sls
Major Brands: Mad River, Voyageur, Wave
   Sport, Wilderness, WindRider
www.confluencewatersports.com
Water Sports

CRAMER PRODUCTS, INC.
153 W. Warren Street
PO Box 1001
Gardner, KS 66030–1001
913–856–7511
Fax: 913–884–5626
Tom Rogge, Pres/CEO
Jack M. Patterson, Jr., VP Sls
Chris Waldeck, VP Mktg
Sharon Cramer, Mgr Human Resources
Major Brands: Cramer
www.cramersportsmed.com
Sports Medicine

CROSMAN CORP.
Routes 5 and 20
E. Bloomfield, NY 14443–9999
585–657–6161
Fax: 585–657–5405
Ken D'Arcy, Pres/CEO
Bob Hampton, VP Mktg
Kathy Chapman, Mgr Human Resources
Major Brands: Crosman
www.crosman.com
Airguns

CUTTER & BUCK
701 W. 34th Street, Ste 400
Seattle, WA 98108
206–622–4191
Fax: 206–448–0589
Fran Conley, CEO/COB
Sherry Randazzo, Sr VP Sls/Mktg
Theresa Treat, Dir Human Resources
Major Brands: Cutter & Buck, LPGA, PGA
www.cutterbuck.com
Apparel

CYBEX INTERNATIONAL
10 Trotter Drive
Medway, MA 021053–2299
508–533–4300
Fax: 508–533–1955
John Agliakoro, Pres/CEO
Roland Murray, VP WW Mktg
Carolyn Buckfeller, Dir Human Resources
Major Brands: Cybex, Trotter
www.ecybex.com
Fitness

DAIWA CORPORATION
12851 Midway Place
PO Box 6031
Cerritos, CA 90703
562–802–9589
Fax: 562–404–6212
Ted Suzuki, Pres
Terry Pederson, Mgr Natl Sls
Cyndy Tyler, Mgr Human Resources
Major Brands: Daiwa
www.daiwa.com
Fishing

DALCO ATHLETIC LETTERING, INC.
3719 Cavalier
Garland, TX 75042
972–487–1200
Fax: 972–276–9608
Gene Feil, Pres
Mike Carter, VP Sls/Mktg
www.dalcoathletic.com
Team Sports Apparel

DANSKIN, INC.
530 Seventh Avenue
New York, NY 10018
212–764–4630
Fax: 212–764–7265
Carol Hochman, Pres/CEO
Joyce Darkey, Sr VP Mktg
Lena Vladsky, Mgr Human Resources
Major Brands: Danskin
www.danskin.com
Apparel

DEBEER LACROSSE
(K2, Inc.)
5 Burdick Drive
PO Box 11570
Albany, NY 12211
518–438–7871
Fax: 518–438–7993
Paul Gait, Pres
Kim Allison, VP/Gen Mgr
Major Brands: DeBeer, Gait
www.debeerlacrosse.com
Lacrosse

DECKERS OUTDOOR CORPORATION
495-A South Fairview Avenue

Goleta, CA 93117
805–967–7611
Fax: 805–967–2982
Angel Martinez, Pres/CEO
Robert Orlando, Pres Teva
Nate Christensen, Dir Human Resources
Major Brands: Deckers, Simple, Teva, Ugg
www.deckers.com
Footwear

DIAMOND SPORTS COMPANY
11130 Warland Drive
Cypress, CA 90630
562–598–9717
Fax: 562–598–0906
Andrea Gordon, VP Sls/Mktg
Major Brands: Diamond
www.diamond-sports.com
Baseball

DODGER INDUSTRIES, INC.
1702 21st Street
Eldora, IA 50627
641–939–5464
Fax: 641–939–5185
Clark Lawler, CEO/Dir Human Resources
Bob Johns, Pres
Major Brands: Dodger, NCAA (Lic.)
www.dodgerindustries.com
Team Sports Apparel

**DUNLOP GOLF/FOCUS GOLF
  SYSTEMS**
25 Draper Street
PO Box 3070
Greenville, SC 29602–3070
864–271–0201
Fax: 864–241–2294
Andre Emery, Pres
Michele Jolly, Mgr Human Resources
Major Brands: Dunlop, DDH, Rebel
www.dunlopsports.com
Golf

DUNLOP SPORTS GROUP AMERICA
888–215–1530
Major Brands: Dunlop
www.dunlopsports.com
Squash, Tennis

EASTON SPORTS, INC.
7855 Haskell Avenue, Ste 200
Van Nuys, CA 91406–1900
818–781–1587
Fax: 818–782–0930
Jim Easton, COB
Anthony Palma, Pres/CEO
Jim Darby, VP Prom/Pub Rel
William Rojas, Mgr Human Resources
Major Brands: Easton
www.eastonsports.com
Archery, Baseball, Ice Hockey, Softball

EBONITE INTERNATIONAL, INC.
1813 W. 7th Street
PO Box 748
Hopkinsville, KY 42240
270–881–1200
Fax: 270–881–1201
William Scheid, Pres/CEO
Robert Reid, VP Mktg
Regina Bibbs, Dir Personnel
Major Brands: Ebonite
www.ebonite.com
Bowling

ELAN USA CORPORATION
5 Commerce Avenue
West Lebanon, NH 03784–1878
603–298–9017
Fax: 603–298–9018
Dan McKenna, VP Sls/Mktg
Ona Pecor, Dir Human Resources
Major Brands: Dolomite, Elan
www.elanskis.com
Skiing

ESCALADE SPORTS
817 Maxwell Avenue
PO Box 889
Evansville, IN 47706
812–467–1200
Fax: 812–425–1425
Robert E. Griffin, COB
Jim Allshouse, Pres
Gary Allan, Dir Employment Services
Major Brands: Accudart, Goalrilla, Harvard, Indian Archery, Murrey, Silverback
www.escaladesports.com
Fitness, Indoor Games

EVERLAST WORLDWIDE, INC.
1350 Broadway, Ste 2300
New York, NY 10018
212–239–0990
Fax: 212–239–4261
George Horowitz, Pres/CEO
John Toms, VP Sls/Mktg
Joanne Ruben, Dir Pub Rel
Ronni Kornblum, Mgr Human Resources
Major Brands: Everlast
www.everlast.com
Boxing

FILA U.S.A., INC.
(Sports Brands International)
1 Fila Way
Sparks, MD 21152
410–773–3000
Fax: 410–773–4979
Paul Clark, Pres/CEO
Mark Westerman, Sr VP Global
Comm/Sports Mktg
Tammy Jones, VP Human Resources
Major Brands: Fila
www.fila.com
Apparel, Footwear

FISHER ATHLETIC EQUIPMENT, INC.
PO Box 1985
Salisbury, NC 28145–1985
704–636–5713
Fax: 704–637–7941
Bob Pritchard, Pres/CEO
Brian Pritchard, Mktg
Kay Earnhardt, Dir Human Resources
Major Brands: Fisher
www.fisherathletic.com
Team Sports

FRANKLIN SPORTS, INC.
17 Campanelli Parkway
PO Box 508
Stoughton, MA 02072–3703
781–344–1111
Fax: 781–341–3220
Larry J. Franklin, Pres/CEO
Charles Quinn, VP Mktg
Beverly O'Donnell, Dir Human
Resources
Major Brands: Franklin, MLB (Lic.),

MLS (Lic.), NASCAR (Lic.), NBA (Lic.), NFL (Lic.), NHL (Lic.), NCAA (Lic.)
www.franklinsports.com
Team Sports

FUBU
350 Fifth Avenue, Ste 6617
New York, NY 10018–0110
212–273–3300 or 888–438–3828
Fax: 212–273–3333
Damond John, Pres/CEO
Joe Levin, Pres Sls
Leslie Short, Dir Mktg/Pub Rel
Major Brands: FUBU
www1.fubu.com
Apparel

GARED SPORTS
707 N. Second Street, Ste 220
St. Louis, MO 63102
314–421–0044
Fax: 314–421–6014
Dean Baker, Dir Natl Sls
Major Brands: Gared, NBA (Lic.)
www.garedsports.com
Basketball, Field Equipment

GARMONT U.S.A.
170 Boyer Circle, Ste 20
Williston, VT 05495
802–658–8426
Fax: 802–658–0431
John Schweizer, Pres
Karen Malley, Mgr Human Resources
Major Brands: Exel, Garmont, Rottefella
http://gusa.site.yahoo.net
Skiing

G-III APPAREL
512 Seventh Avenue
New York, NY 10018
212–403–0500
Fax: 212–403–0551
Morris Goldfarb, CEO
Stephanie Bidlake, VP Sls
Major Brands: MLB (Lic.), NASCAR (Lic.), NFL (Lic.), NHL (Lic.), NCAA (Lic.)
www.g-iii.com
Apparel

HEAD PENN RACQUET SPORTS
(Head USA/Head NV)
306 S. 45th Avenue
Phoenix, AZ 85043–3913
602–269–1492
Fax: 800–329–7366
Dave Haggerty, Pres
Kevin Kempin, VP Sls/Mktg
Tom Daoust, Dir Human Resources
Major Brands: Head, Penn
www.head.com
Racquetball, Tennis

HEAD TYROLIA WINTER SPORTS
(Head USA/Head NV)
Shore Pointe, 1 Sellect Street
Norwalk, CT 906855–1120
203–855–8666
Fax: 203–855–5719
Dave Haggerty, Pres/CEO Head U.S.A.
Robert Langlois, VP Sls/Mktg
Susan Ariano, Human Resource Adm
Major Brands: Head, Tyrolia
www.head.com
Skiing

HELLY HANSEN US, INC.
3326 160th Avenue S.E., Ste 200
Bellevue, WA 98008–5463
425–378–8700
Fax: 425–649–3740
Rick Long, Pres/CEO
Shelley Becker, Dir Mktg
Major Brands: Helly Hansen
www.hellyhansen.com
Outdoor Apparel

HILLERICH & BRADSBY CO., INC.
800 West Main Street
PO Box 35700
Louisville, KY 40232–5700
502–585–5226
Fax: 502–585–1179
John A. Hillerich IV, Pres
Marty Archer, Pres Louisville Slugger
Ron Santella, Dir Human Resources
Major Brands: Grand Slam, Louisville, Louisville Slugger, Powerbilt
www.slugger.com
Baseball, Golf, Ice Hockey

HOLLOWAY SPORTSWEAR, INC.
2633 Campbell Road
PO Box 4489
Sidney, OH 45365
937–497–7575
Fax: 937–497–7337
Mark Vondenhuevel, Pres
Mike Platt, Dir Sls/Mktg
Julie Manning, Mgr Human Resources
www.hollowayusa.com
Team Sports Apparel

HUFFY BICYCLE COMPANY
225 Byers Road
Miamisburg, OH 45342
937–743–5011
Fax: 937–704–3025
Paul D'Aloia, CEO
Bill Smith, Pres/Gen Mgr
Robert Stead, VP Human Resources
Major Brands: Huffy, Ram (Golf), Tommy
   Armour (Golf)
www.huffybikes.com
Cycling, Golf

HUFFY SPORTS CO.
N 53 W 24700 South Corp Circle
Sussex, WI 53089
262–820–3440
Fax: 262–820–3195
Randy Schieckert, Pres/Gen Mgr
Robert Diekman, VP Global Opns/Huffy
Corp.
Patrick Ehren, VP Sls/Mktg
Ted Masters, Dir Personnel
Major Brands: Huffy, NBA (Lic.), NCAA
   (Lic.)
www.huffysports.com
Basketball

ICON HEALTH & FITNESS, INC.
1500 S 1000 W
Logan, UT 84321–8206
435–750–5000
Fax: 435–750–5238
Matt Allen, Pres
Mark Thatcher, Dir Mktg
Douglas Yonker, Human Resource
Dept/(435–786–5560)
Major Brands: Gold's Gym, Healthrider,

Icon, Image, Jump King, Nordic Track,
   Proform, Reebok (Lic.), Weider, Weslo
www.iconfitness.com
Fitness

IGLOO PRODUCTS CORP.
(Westar Capital)
777 Igloo Road
Katy, TX 77494
713–584–6900
Fax: 713–465–2009
James Morley, Pres/CEO
Larry Blab, VP Mktg
Jim House, Dir Human Resources
Major Brands: Igloo, Koolmate, Playmate
www.igloocoolers.com
Outdoor Products

IMPLUS FOOTCARE, LLC/SOF SOLE
9221 Globe Center Drive, Ste 120
Morrisville, NC 27560
919–544–7900
Fax: 919–544–0975
Seth Richards, CEO
Todd Vore, Pres
Bill Alfano, Mgr Human Resources
Major Brands: Airplus, Sof Sole
www.sofsole.com
Footcare Products

IZOD/PHILLIPS VAN HEUSEN
(VF Corp.)
1001 Frontier Road, Ste 100
Bridgewater, NJ 08807
908–685–0050
Fax: 908–253–6833
Major Brands: Izod
www.izod.com
Apparel

JANSPORT, INC.
(VF Corp.)
2011 Farallon Drive
San Leandro, CA 94577
310–614–4000
Fax: 310–614–4021
Mike Corvino, Pres
Todd Yates, VP Mktg
Karen Apitz, VP Human Resources
Major Brands: JanSport

www.jansport.com
Outdoor

JAYPRO SPORTS, INC.
976 Hartford Turnpike
Waterford, CT 06385–4002
860–447–3001
Fax: 860–444–1779
Robert Ferrara, Pres/CEO
Bill Wild, Mgr Sls/Mktg
Major Brands: Jaypro
www.jaypro.com
Team Sports Field Equipment

JOHNSON OUTDOORS, INC.
555 Main Street
Racine, WI 53403
262–631–6600
Fax: 262–631–6601
Helen Johnson-Leipold, CEO/COB
Jerry Perkins, Pres/COO
Floyd Wilkinson, Dir Human Resources
Major Brands: Johnson, Camp Trails (Lic.),
    Eureka (Lic.), MinnKota (Lic.), Ocean
    Kayak (Lic.), Scubapro (Lic.), Silva (Lic.)
www.johnsonoutdoors.com
Outdoor Products

K2, INC.
19215 Vashon Highway SW
Vashon, WA 98070–5236
206–463–3631
Fax: 206–463–5463
Richard Heckmann, CEO/COB
J. Wayne Merck, Pres/COO
Sean Andrews, Mgr Human Resources
Major Brands: Adio, Brass Eagle, Dana
    Design, DeBeer Lacrosse, Hilton, K2,
    Marker, Marmot, Morrow, Pflueger,
    Rawlings, Ride, Shakespeare, Stearns,
    Volkl, Worth
www.k2sports.com
Apparel, Fishing, Inline Skating, Skiing,
    Snowboarding, Team Sports, Water
    Sports

K2 LICENSING & PROMOTIONS
5818 El Camino Real
Carlsbad, CA 92008
760–494–1000

Scott Dickey, Pres/CEO
Steven Katzke, VP Sls/Mktg
Lisa Hendrickson, Dir Human Resources
Major Brands: MLB (Lic.), NFL (Lic.),
    NBA (Lic.), NFL (Lic.), NHL (Lic.),
    NCAA (Lic.)
www.k2lp.com
Licensed Products, Team Sports

KEEN FOOTWEAR
1201 Marina Village Parkway, Ste 301
Alameda, CA 94501
510–337–3033
Fax: 510–52208255
James Van Dine, Pres
Zoe Ryan, Dir Human Resources
Major Brands: Keen
www.keenfootwear.com
Footwear

KING LOUIE INTERNATIONAL
13500 15th Street
Grandview, MO 64030
816–765–5212
Fax: 816–765–3228
Robert Palan, Pres
Roger Carroll, Dir Mktg
Major Brands: King Louie
www.kinglouie.com
Team Sports Apparel

K-SWISS
31248 Oak Crest Drive
Westlake Village, CA 91361
818–706–5100
Fax: 818–706–5390
Steven Nichols, Pres/CEO
Debbie Mitchell, VP Mktg
Teresa Boyd, Mgr Personnel
Major Brands: K-Swiss
www.kswiss.com
Footwear

LACROSSE FOOTWEAR, INC.
18550 NE Riverside Parkway
Portland, OR 97230
503–766–1010
Fax: 503–766–1015
Joe Schneider, Pres/CEO
Darren McClintok, Dir Sls/Mktg

Gary Rebello, VP Human Resources
Major Brands: Danner, Lacrosse
www.lacrosse-outdoors.com
Outdoor Footwear

LIFE FITNESS
(Brunswick Corp.)
5100 North River Road
Schiller Park, IL 60176
847–288–3300
Fax: 847–288–3693
Peter Hamilton, Pres
Adam Horwitz, VP Consumer Prod
Judy Gustafson, VP Human Resources
Major Brands: Life Fitness, Lifecycle, Life-
  gym, Parabody
www.lifefitness.com

LIFETIME PRODUCTS, INC.
Bldg D-11, Freeport Circle
PO Box 160010
Clearfield, UT 84016–0010
801–776–1532
Fax: 801–776–4397
Kathy Mower, Co-Pres
Barry O. Mower, Co-Pres
Sandy Hatch, Mgr Personnel
Major Brands: Slam-Dunk
www.lifetime.com
Basketball, Outdoor Products

LOWRANCE ELECTRONICS, INC.
12000 E. Skelly Drive
Tulsa, OK 74128
918–437–6881
Fax: 918–438–3277
Darrel Lowrance, Pres
Tracy Smith, Mgr Human Resources
Major Brands: Eagle, Lowrance
www.lowrance.com
Fishing

MACGREGOR GOLF CO.
1000 Pecan Grove Drive
Albany, GA 31701
229–420–7000
Fax: 800–455–1220
Barry Schneider, CEO/COB
Dana Shertz, Pres/COO
Barbara Birdzell, Mgr Human Resources

Major Brands: MacGregor
www.macgregorgolf.com
Golf

MAJESTIC ATHLETIC
100 Majestic Way
Bangor, PA 18013–2860
610–588–0100
Fax: 610–588–3800
Faust Capobianco III, COB
Faust Capobianco IV, Pres/CEO
George Goodwin, VP Adm/Mgr Human
Resources
Major Brands: Majestic, MLB (Lic.), NBA
  (Lic.), NFL (Lic.), NHL (Lic.), NCAA
  (Lic.)
www.majesticathletic.com
Team Sports Apparel

MARES AMERICA
(Head USA/Head NV)
Shore Point, One Selleck Street
Norwalk, CT 06855
203–855–0631
Fax: 203–855–5719
Carlo Bertodezz, Pres
Betsy Royal, VP Sls/Mktg
Susan Ariana, Mgr Human Resources
Major Brands: Dacor, Dacor Sport
www.mares.com
Water Sports

MARKER U.S.A.
(K2, Inc.)
1070 W 2300 S, Ste A
Salt Lake City, UT 84119
801–972–0404
Fax: 801–972–3938
Kirk Langford, Pres
Major Brands: Marker
www.markerusa.com
Skiing Apparel, Bindings

MARKWORT SPORTING GOODS
1101 Research Blvd.
St. Louis, MO 63132
314–652–8935
Fax: 314–652–6241
Glenn Markwort, CEO
Herb Markwort, Jr., Pres

Robert Herman, Gen Mgr/Human
Resources
Distributor
www.markwort.com
Team Sports

MARLIN FIREARMS
100 Kenna Drive
North Haven, CT 06473
203–239–5621
Fax: 203–234–7991
Frank Kenna, CEO
William Shermerer, VP Sls/Mktg
Kevin O'Brien, Mgr Human Resources
Dir Human Resources
www.marlinfirearms.com
Firearms

**MCDAVID SPORTS MEDICAL
    PRODUCTS**
10305 Argonne Drive
Woodridge, IL 60517
630–783–0600
Fax: 630–783–1270
Robert F. McDavid, Pres
Grisel Correa, Mgr Human Resources
Major Brands: McDavid, MKG
www.mcdavidinc.com
Sports Medicine

MERCURY MARINE
(Brunswick Corp.)
W6250 W. Pioneer Road
PO Box 1939
Fond du Lac, WI 54936
920–929–5040
Fax: 920–929–5893
Major Brands: Mercury www.mercuryma-
    rine.com
Outboard Motors

M-F ATHLETIC COMPANY
11 Amflex Drive
PO Box 8090
Cranston, RI 02920–0090
401–942–9363
Fax: 401–942–7645
William Falk, Pres
Major Brands: M-F
www.everythingtrackandfield.com
Track and Field

MISSION-ITECH HOCKEY
1801 S. Standard Avenue
Santa Ana, CA 92707
714–556–8856
Fax: 714–556–8858
Bob Naegele, Jr., COB
Wendy Cadacio, Dir Human Resources
Major Brands: Mission
www.missionhockey.com
Inline Skating, Roller Hockey

MIZUNO U.S.A.
4925 Avalon Ridge Parkway
Norcross, GA 30071
770–441–5553
Fax: 770–448–3234
Bob Puccini, Pres
Patricia Douglas, Sr Dir Human
    Resources
Major Brands: Mizuno
www.mizunousa.com
Baseball, Golf, Softball

M.J. SOFFE CO.
(Delta Apparel)
1 Soffe Drive
PO Box 2507
Fayetteville, NC 28312
910–483–2500
Fax: 910–486–9030
Jim Soffe, Pres/CEO
Steve Wheeler, VP Mktg
David Williford, Dir Human Resources
Major Brands: Soffe
www.mjsoffe.com
Team Sports Apparel

MOLTEN U.S.A. INC.
(Molten Japan)
1170 Trademark Drive
Suite 109
Reno, NV 89521
775-353-4000
Fax: 775-358-9407
Melissa Dawson, Pres
Michael Davis, VP Sales
Major Brands: Molten
www.moltenusa.com
Inflated Balls, Uniforms

MOUNTAIN HARDWARE
(Columbia Sportswear Company)
4911 Central Avenue
Richmond, CA 94804–5803
510–559–6700
Fax: 510–559–6709
Mike Wallenfels, Pres
Roberta Hernandez, Dir Human Resources
Major Brands: Mountain Hardware
www.mountainhardwear.com
Outdoor Apparel, Equipment

MUELLER SPORTS MEDICINE, INC.
1 Quench Drive
Prairie du Sac, WI 53578
608–643–8530
Fax: 608–643–2568
Curt Mueller, CEO
Herb Raschka, VP Sls/Mktg
Carol Wilcenski, Dir Human Resources
Major Brands: Mueller
www.muellersportsmed.com
Sports Medicine

NATIONAL SPORTING GOODS
376 Hollywood Avenue
Fairfield, NJ 07004
973–779–2323
Fax: 973–779–0084
Joel C. Aranson, Pres
David Aranson, Dir Mktg
Major Brands: Chicago Roller Skates (Lic.),
  Riedell (Lic.)
www.chicagoskates.com
Inline Skating, Roller Skating, Scooters

THE NAUTILUS GROUP, INC.
16400 SE Nautilus Drive
Vancouver, WA 98683
360–859–2900
Gregg Hammann, Pres/CEO
Tim Hawkins, Chief Mktg Officer
Major Brands: Bowflex, Nautilus, Schwinn,
  StairMaster, Trimline
www.nautilusinc.com
Fitness

NEW BALANCE ATHLETIC SHOE, INC.
Brighton Landing, 20 Guest Street
Boston, MA 02135

617–783–4000
Fax: 617–787–9355
James Davis, COB
James E. Thompkins, Pres/COO
Carol O'Donnell, VP Corp Human
  Resources
Major Brands: Dunham, New Balance, P.F.
  Flyer
www.newbalance.com
Footwear

NEW ERA CAP COMPANY, INC.
PO Box 208
8061 Erie Road
Derby, NY 14047–0208
716–549–0445
Fax: 718–549–5424
Christopher Koch, CEO
John DeWaal, VP Global Mktg
Timothy Freer, Dir Human Resources
Major Brands: New Era, MLB (Lic.),
  NASCAR (Lic.), NBA (Lic.), NHL (Lic.),
  NCAA (Lic.)
www.neweracap.com
Headwear

NIKE, INC.
One Bowerman Drive
Beaverton, OR 97005
503–641–6453
Fax: 503–641–4195
Philip H. Knight, Pres/CEO/COB
Charlie Denson, Co-Pres Nike Brand
Mark G. Parker, Co-Pres Nike Brand
Bob Wood, VP/Pres Nike Golf
Wesley Coleman, VP Global Human
  Resources
Major Brands: Bauer, Converse, Jordan,
  Nike, Shaq, Starter
www.nike.com
Apparel, Baseball, Footwear, Ice Hockey,
  Outdoor

NOKONA ATHLETIC GOODS CO.
208 W. Walnut Street
PO Box 329
Nocona, TX 76255–0329
940–825–3326
Fax: 940–825–4994
Robert Storey, Sr., CEO

Robert M. Storey, Jr., Pres
Major Brands: Nokona
www.nokona.com
Team Sports

NORDICA USA CORP.
12 Commerce Avenue
West Lebanon, NH 03784
603–298–6900
Fax: 603–298–7152
Andy Knittle, Pres/CEO
Sue Shaw, Mgr Human Resources
Major Brands: Lowa, Marker, Nordica, Tecnica
www.nordicausa.com
Skiing, Outdoor

THE NORTH FACE
(VF Corp.)
2013 Farallon Drive
San Leandro, CA 94577–6601
510–618–3500
Fax: 510–618–3571
Mike Egeck, Pres Outdoor/North America
Steve Rendle, Pres North Face America
Joe Flannery, VP Mktg
Patty Pierce, Dir Human Resources
Major Brands: North Face
www.thenorthface.com
Outdoor Apparel

OAKLEY
1 Icon
Foothill Ranch, CA 92610–3000
949–951–0991
Fax: 949–699–3500
Jim Jannard, COB
Colin Baden, Pres
Darlene Kennedy, Dir Human Resources
Major Brands: Oakley
www.oakley.com
Eyewear

O'BRIEN INTERNATIONAL, INC.
14615 N.E. 91st Street
PO Box 97087
Redmond, WA 98073
425–881–5900
Fax: 425–202–2199
Jeff Bannister, Pres

Paul Kennedy, Dir Mktg
Major Brands: O'Brien
www.obrien.com
Water Sports

O'NEILL, INC.
1071 41st Avenue
PO Box 6300
Santa Cruz, CA 95063–6300
831–475–7500
Fax: 831–475–5133
Pat O'Neill, Pres
Mark Tinkiss, VP Sls/Mktg
Major Brands: O'Neill
www.oneill.com
Water Sports

PACIFIC TRAIL, INC.
1700 Westlake Avenue N., Ste 200
Seattle, WA 98109
206–270–5300
Fax: 206–270–5301
David Greenstein, CEO
Todd Gilmer, Mgr Mktg
Major Brands: Pacific Trail, Roffe
www.pacifictrail.com
Outdoor Apparel

PATAGONIA, INC.
259 W. Santa Clara Street
PO Box 150
Ventura, CA 93002–0150
805–643–8616
Fax: 805–643–2367
Casey Sheahan, CEO
Rick Riddway, Exec VP Sls/Mktg
Huntley Dornan, Exec VP Human Resources
Major Brands: Patagonia
www.patagonia.com
Outdoor Apparel

PENN FISHING TACKLE
3028 W. Hunting Park Avenue
Philadelphia, PA 19132–1121
215–229–9415
Fax: 215–223–3017
David Martin, Pres/CEO
Brian Melfin, VP Sls
Dawn Thompson, Mgr Human Resources

Major Brands: Penn
www.pennreels.com
Fishing

PING, INC.
(Karsten Manufacturing Corp.)
2201 W. Desert Cove
PO Box 82000
Phoenix, AZ 85029
602–687–5000
Fax: 602–687–4482
John Solheim, Pres
Pat Loftus, VP Sls/Mktg
Dorothy Glueck, Dir Human Resources
Major Brands: Ping
www.pinggolf.com
Golf

POLAR ELECTRO, INC.
1111 Marcus Avenue, Ste M15
Lake Success, NY 11042–1034
516–364–0400
Fax: 516–364–5454
Corey Comacchio, Dir Mktg
Jo Ann Harrington, Mgr Human Resource
Major Brands: Polar Electro
www.polar.fi
Fitness

PORTER ATHLETIC EQUIPMENT CO.
2500 S. 25th Avenue
Broadview, IL 60155
708–338–2000
Fax: 708–338–2060
John McGinnis, Pres/CEO
Dan Morgan, VP Sls/Mktg
Dennis Cech, Dir Human Resources
Major Brands: Porter
www.porter-ath.com
Basketball

PRECOR, INC.
(Amer Sports Corporation)
20031 142nd Avenue N.E.
PO Box 7202
Woodinville, WA 98072–4002
425–486–9292
Fax: 425–486–3856
Paul Byrne, Pres
Elisa Humphrey, VP Mktg

Lynn Takaki, VP Human Resources
Major Brands: Precor
www.precor.com
Fitness

PRINCE SPORTS, INC.
One Advantage Court
Bordentown, NJ 08505–9630
609–291–5800
Fax: 609–291–5900
George Napier, CEO
Doug Fonte, Pres Prince USA
Deborah Edwards, Dir Human
   Resources
Major Brands: Ektelon, Prince
www.princetennis.com
Racquetball, Squash, Tennis

PROKENNEX
2335 Camino Vida Roble, Ste A
Carlsbad, CA 92009
760–804–8322
Fax: 760–804–8326
Kevin Gilbert, Pres
Lori Monroe, Mgr Human Resources
www.prokennex.com
Golf, Racquetball, Squash, Tennis

PUMA NORTH AMERICA
5 Lyberty Way
Westford, MA 01886
978–698–1000
Fax: 978–698–1174
Jay Picolla, Pres/Gen Mgr Puma USA
Tom Morgan, VP Sls/Mdsng
Mike Metivier, Mgr Human Resources
Major Brands: Puma, Nuala
www.puma.com
Footwear

PURE FISHING
1900 18th Street
Spirit Lake, IA 51360–1099
712–336–1520
Fax: 712–336–5183
Tom Bedell, Pres/CEO
Ron Kliegl, VP Mktg
Mike Brenney, Dir Human Resources
Major Brands: Abu Garcia, Berkley, Fen-
   wick, Johnson, Mitchell, Spider, Stren

www.purefishing.com
Fishing

QUIKSILVER, INC.
15202 Graham Street
Huntington Beach, CA 92649
714–889–2200
Fax: 714–889–3700
Robert B. McKnight, Jr., CEO
DeAnna Holloway, Mgr Human Resources
Major Brands: Quiksilver, Rossignol
www.quiksilver.com
Apparel

**RAWLINGS SPORTING GOODS
  COMPANY**
(K2, Inc.)
1859 Bowles Avenue
Fenton, MO 63026
636–349–3500
Fax: 636–349–3588
Robert Parish, Pres
David Zumbach, VP Mktg
Rita Carel, Mgr Human Resources
Major Brands: Hilton, Rawlings, Worth
www.rawlings.com
Team Sports Equipment, Apparel

REDFEATHER SNOWSHOES, INC.
4705-A Oakland Street
Denver, CO 80239
303–375–0410
Fax: 303–375–0357
Allan Kettlehut, Pres
Lynn Cariffe, Dir Sls/Mktg
Major Brands: Redfeather
www.redfeather.com
Snowshoes

REEBOK INTERNATIONAL LTD.
(Note: At press time, in the process of
  being acquired by Adidas.)
1895 J.W. Foster Blvd.
Stoughton, MA 02020
781–401–5000
Fax: 781–401–4702
Paul B. Fireman, CEO/COB
Bob Myers, Sr VP Human Resources
Major Brands: CCM, Greg Norman (Lic.),
  RBK, Reebok, Rockport

www.rbk.com
Apparel, Fitness, Footwear

REGENT SPORTS CORP.
PO Box 11357, 45 Ranick Road
Hauppauge, NY 11788
631–234–2800
Fax: 631–234–2948
Jay Lipman, CEO/COB
Major Brands: Halex, MacGregor, Mitre,
  Spalding (Lic.)
www.regent-halex.com
Sports Games, Team Sports

REMINGTON ARMS CO.
870 Remington Drive
PO Box 700
Madison, NC 27025
336–548–8700
Fax: 336–548–7801
Thomas C. Millner, Pres/CEO
Mark Little, CFO
Celeste Graves, Mgr Human Resources
Major Brands: Remington
www.remington.com
Firearms

RIDDELL SPORTS
9801 W. Higgins Road
Rosemont, IL 60018
773–794–1994
Fax: 773–794–6155
Bill Sherman, Pres/CEO
Bob Brasser, VP Sls/Mktg
Rudy VanCamper, Mgr Human Resources
Major Brands: MLB (Lic.), NFL (Lic.), Rid-
  dell
www.riddell.com
Team Sports

ROCKY SHOES & BOOTS
39 E. Canal Street
Nelsonville, OH 45764
740–753–1951
Fax: 740–753–4024
Mike Brooks, CEO/COB
David Sharp, Pres
Terese Ragosta, Mgr Human
Resources
Major Brands: Rocky

www.rockyboots.com
Outdoor Footwear

ROLLERBLADE USA
(Nordica S.p.A.)
3705 Quakerbridge Road
Hamilton, NJ 08619
609–249–1700
Fax: 609–249–1790
Nick Skally, Dir Mktg
Ona Pecor, Dir Human Resources
(603–298–6348)
Major Brands: Rollerblade
www.rollerblade.com
Inline Skating

ROSSIGNOL SKI CO., INC.
(Quiksilver, Inc.)
426 Industrial Avenue
PO Box 298
Williston, VT 05495
802–863–2511
Fax: 802–764–2520
Francois Goulet, Pres USA
Steve Dudley, VP Mktg
Beth Gilpin, Mgr Human Resource
Major Brands: Cleveland (Golf), Rossignol,
    R-Gear
www.rossignol.com
Skiing, Golf

RUSSELL ATHLETIC
(Russell Corp.)
3330 Cumberland Blvd., Ste 700
Atlanta, GA 30339
678–742–8000
Fax: 678–742–8300
Calvin Johnston, CEO
Gary Barfield, VP Team Sports Sls
Ed Flowers, Sr VP Human Resources
Major Brands: Bike, Cross Creek, Jerzees,
    Moving Comfort, Nutmeg, Russell,
    Spalding
www.russellathletic.com
Team Sports Apparel/Equipment

SARANAC GLOVE CO.
999 Lombardi Avenue
Green Bay, WI 54304
920–435–3737

Fax: 920–435–7618
John Fabry, Pres/CEO
Tina Rooks, CFO/Mgr Human Resources
Major Brands: Saranac
www.saranacglove.com
Sports Gloves

SCHUTT SPORTS
1200 E. Union
PO Box 426
Litchfield, IL 62056–0426
217–324–2712
Fax: 217–324–2855
Julie Nimmons, Pres/CEO
Peter Donahoe, Dir Human Resources
Major Brands: Air, Hollywood
www.schuttsports.com
Team Sports

SCOTT U.S.A.
101 Lewis Street
PO Box 2030
Sun Valley, ID 83353–2030
208–622–1000
Fax: 208–622–1005
Scott Morton, VP/Gen Mgr
Larry Morton, VP Optics
Brian Marcouiller, Mgr Human Resources
Major Brands: Scott
www.scottusa.com
Eyewear

SEVYLOR U.S.A., INC.
6651 E. 26th Street
Los Angeles, CA 90040–3215
323–727–6013
Fax: 323–726–0481
Konstantin Klimenko, Pres/CEO
Beth Sugapong, Mgr Personnel
Major Brands: Sevylor
www.sevylor.com
Inflatable Boats

SHAKESPEARE FISHING TACKLE
(K2, Inc.)
3801 Westmore Drive
Columbia, SC 29223
803–754–7000
Fax: 803–754–7342
Scott Hogsett, Pres

Randy Spatharose, Dir Mktg
Chris Rankin, Mgr Human Resources
Major Brands: Shakespeare
www.shakespeare-fishing.com
Fishing

SHIMANO AMERICAN CORP.
One Holland
Irvine, CA 92618
949–951–5003
Fax: 949–768–0920
Dave Pfeiffer, Exec VP
Susan Tarney, Mgr Human Resources
Major Brands: Shimano
www.shimano.com
Cycling, Fishing

SKECHERS U.S.A., INC.
228 Manhattan Beach Blvd, Ste 200
Manhattan Beach, CA 90266
310–318–3100
Fax: 310–318–5019
Bob Greenberg, COB/CEO
Michael Greenberg, Pres
Marcee Mackey, Dir Human Resources
Major Brands: Skechers
www.skechers.com
Footwear

SPEEDLINE ATHLETIC WEAR
1804 N. Habana
Tampa, FL 33607–3353
813–876–1375
Fax: 813–873–8714
Steven J. Malzone, Pres/CEO
David Aubuchon, VP Mktg
Major Brands: Speedline
www.propakspeedline.com
Team Sports Uniforms

SPEEDO AMERICA
(Warnaco Swimwear)
6040 Bandini Blvd
City of Commerce, CA 90040
323–837–6000
Fax: 323–721–3613
Sheree Waterson, Pres Speedo North Amer
Craig Brummel, VP Mktg
Marti Meyers, Dir Human Resources
Major Brands: Speedo

www.speedo.com
Swimwear Apparel

SPENCO MEDICAL CORP.
6301 Imperial Drive
PO Box 2501
Waco, TX 76712
254–772–6000
Fax: 254–751–5783
Steve Smith, Pres/CEO
Blake Boulden, Dir Mktg/Opns
Euneta Jones, Mgr Personnel
Major Brands: Spenco
www.spenco.com
Sports Medicine

SPORT SUPPLY GROUP, INC.
(Collegiate Pacific)
1901 Diplomat Drive
Dallas, TX 75234
972–484–9484
Fax: 972–884–7465
Jeff Jurick, Pres
Mechell Gotelli, Dir Human Resources
www.sportssupplygroup.com
Team Sports

SPORTCRAFT, LTD.
313 Waterloo Valley Road
Mt. Olive, NJ 07828
973–347–3800
Fax: 973–347–8282
Mike Nally, Pres
Laura Moreno, Mgr Human Resources
Major Brands: Sportcraft
www.sportcraft.com
Fitness, Indoor/Outdoor Games

SPORT-HALEY
4600 E. 48th Avenue
Denver, CO 80216
303–320–8800
Fax: 303–320–8822
Tom Tomlinson, Pres
Mark Maley, VP Sls
Gail Moul, Mgr Human Resources
Major Brands: Ben Hogan (Lic.), Sport-
Haley
www.sporthaley.com
Apparel

STAHLS,' INC.
20600 Stephens Street
St. Clair Shores, MI 48080
586–772–6161
Fax: 800–346–2216
Ted Stahl, Pres
Marilyn Elliott, Mgr Human Resources
www.stahls.com
Team Sports Apparel-Heat Transfers

STEARNS MFG. CORP.
(K2, Inc.)
1100 Stearns Drive
Sauk Rapids, MN 56379
PO Box 1498
St. Cloud, MN 58302–1496
320–252–1642
Fax: 320–252–4425
Paul Ebnet, Pres
Steve Saxton, Dir Mktg
Loretta Trulson, Dir Human Resources
Major Brands: Stearns, Windjammer
www.stearnsinc.com
Water Sports

STRIDE-RITE CORP.
191 Spring Street
Lexington, MA 02421
617–824–6000
David Chamberlain, CEO/COB
Shawn Neville, Pres Keds
Janet DePiro, Sr VP Human Resources
Major Brands: Grasshoppers, Hind, Keds,
    Pro Keds, Saucony, Sperry Top-Sider,
    Spot-Bilt, Tommy Hilfiger (Lic.)
www.strideritecorp.com
Footwear

STURM RUGER & COMPANY, INC.
1 Lacey Place
Southport, CT 06890
203–259–7843
Fax: 203–256–3367
Steven L. Sanetti, Pres
Randall Pence, Dir Sls/Mktg
Carole Markland, Dir Human Resources
Major Brands: Ruger
www.ruger-firearms.com
Firearms

STX
1500 Bush Street
Baltimore, MD 21230
410–837–2022
Fax: 410–539–3908
Richard Tucker, Sr., Pres/CEO
Krissy Testen, Mgr Mktg
Jim Rogers, Mgr Human Resources
Major Brands: STX
www.stxputters.com
www.stxlacrosse.com
Field Hockey, Golf, Lacrosse

TACHIKARA USA, INC.
8000 W. 110th Street, Ste 150
Overland Park, KS 66210
913–498–1881
Fax: 913–498–1882
Dan Burke, Pres/CEO
Roger Revelle, VP Sls/Mktg
Major Brands: Tachikara
www.tachikara.com
Team Sports

TAYLORMADE-ADIDAS GOLF
5545 Fermi Court
Carlsbad, CA 92008–7324
760–918–6000
Fax: 760–918–6014
Mark King, Pres/CEO
Sean Toulon, Exec VP TaylorMade
John Kawaja, Exec VP Adidas Golf
Blake McHenry, VP Global Human
Resources
Major Brands: Adidas, Maxfli, TaylorMade
www.tmag.com
Golf

TECNICA U.S.A. CORP.
19 Technology Drive
West Lebanon, NH 03784–1673
603–298–8032
Fax: 603–298–5790
John C. Stahler, CEO
Mike Noonan, Pres
Marjorie Tibbetts, Mgr Human Resources
Major Brands: Tecnica, Volkl
www.tecnicausa.com
Footwear

TIMBERLAND
200 Domain Drive
Stratham, NH 03885
603–772–9500
Fax: 603–773–1640
Jeffrey Swartz, Pres/CEO
Bruce Johnson, VP Human Resources
Major Brands: Timberland
www.timberland.com
Footwear

TRENWAY TEXTILES, INC.
609 Wesinpar Street
Westside Industry Park
PO Box 2180
Johnson City, TN 37605
423–928–8196
Fax: 800–441–8138
Harlen Booth, Pres
Roger Cox, VP Mktg
Major Brands: Trenway
www.trenwaytextiles.com
Socks

TRUE FITNESS TECHNOLOGY, INC.
865 Hoff Road
O'Fallon, MO 63366
636–272–7100
Fax: 636–272–7148
Frank Trulaske, Pres
Paul Gillstrom, VP Mktg
Deb Cobb, Mgr Human Resources
www.truefitness.com
Fitness

TRUE TEMPER SPORTS
8275 Tournament Drive, Ste 200
Memphis, TN 38125
901–746–2000
Fax: 901–746–2160
Scott Hennessy, Pres/CEO
Adrian McCall, Sr VP Global Sls/Distr
Stephen Brown, VP Human Resources
Major Brands: Dynamic Gold, True Temper
www.truetemper.com
Golf, Ice Hockey, Lacrosse

TWIN CITY KNITTING COMPANY, INC.
710 1st Street, East
PO Box 1179

Conover, NC 28613
828–464–4830
Fax: 828–465–3209
Francis B. Davis, Pres
Major Brands: Twin City
www.twincityknitting.com
Headwear, Hosiery

TWINS ENTERPRISE, INC.
82 Brookline Avenue
Boston, MA 02215
617–437–1384
Fax: 617–437–7581
Robert D'Angelo, Pres
David D'Angelo, VP Mktg
Anita D'Angelo, Mgr Human Resources
MLB (Lic.), NBA (Lic.), NHL (Lic.), NCAA
   (Lic.)
www.twinsenterprise.com
Headwear

UNDER ARMOUR ATHLETIC APPAREL
1020 Hull Street
Baltimore, MD 21230–5358
410–468–2512
Fax: 410–468–2516
Kevin Plank, Pres
Steve Battista, VP Mktg
Jim Fulks, Corp Dir Human Resources
www.underarmour.com
Team Sports Apparel

U.S. REPEATING ARMS/WINCHESTER
344 Winchester Avenue
New Haven, CT 06511
203–789–5000
Dolores Bystrack, Mgr Human Resources
Major Brands: Winchester
www.usracmfg.com
Firearms

VANS, INC.
(VF Corp.)
15700 Shoemaker Avenue
Santa Fe Springs, CA 90670
562–565–8267
Fax: 562–565–8406
Steve Murray, Pres
Cheryl Van Doren, VP Human Resources
Major Brands: Vans

www.vans.com
Footwear, Skateboarding

VARIFLEX, INC.
5152 N. Commerce Avenue
Moorpark, CA 93021
805–523–1590
Fax: 805–523–8497
Raymond H. "Jay" Losi, CEO/COO
Steven L. Muellner, Pres
Elizabeth Ashwell, Mgr Human
    Resources
www.variflex.com
Inline Skating, Scooters, Skateboarding,
    other sports products

VARSITY BRANDS
6745 Lenox Center Court, Ste 300
Memphis, TN 38115–4300
901–387–4300
Fax: 800–792–4337
Jeffrey Webb, Pres/CEO
Robert Tisdale, Dir Human Resources
Major Brands: Varsity Brands
www.varsity.com
Cheerleading

WIGWAM MILLS, INC.
3402 Crocker Avenue
PO Box 818
Sheboygan, WI 53081–6426
920–457–5551
Fax: 920–457–0311
Robert E. Chesebro, Jr., Pres/CEO
Jim Einhauser, Exec VP Sls/Mktg
Vi Miller, Human Resource Facilitator
Major Brands: Wigwam
www.wigwam.com
Headwear, Socks

WILSON SPORTING GOODS COMPANY
(Amer Sports Corporation)
8700 W. Bryn Mawr Avenue
Chicago, IL 60631–3507
773–714–6400
Fax: 773–714–4598
Chris Considine, Pres
Mary Lally, Dir Human Resources
Major Brands: DeMarini, Fruit of the Loom
    (Lic.), Hammer, Pro Staff, Staff, Wilson

www.wilson.com
Golf, Racquetball, Team Sports, Tennis

**WINCHESTER AMMUNITION/OLIN
    CORPORATION**
427 N. Shamrock Street
East Alton, IL 62024
618–258–2000
Fax: 618–258–2000,
Gregg Kofteck, Dir Mktg
Val Peters, Dir Human Resources
Major Brands: Winchester
www.winchester.com
Ammunition

W.L. GORE & ASSOCIATES, INC.
555 Paper Mill Road
Newark, DE 19714
410–392–3600
410–506–2644
Chuck Carroll, Pres
Jackie Boatwright, Dir Sls/Mktg
Major Brands: Gore-Tex
www.gorefabrics.com
Outdoor Apparel

WOLVERINE WORLD WIDE, INC.
9341 Courtland Drive
Rockford, MI 49351
616–866–5500
Fax: 616–866–0257
Tim O'Donovan, Pres/CEO/COB
Mike Donabauer, VP Mktg Footwear
Major Brands: Hush Puppies, Merrell,
    Wolverine
www.wolverineworldwide.com
Footwear

WOOLRICH, INC.
2 Mill Street
Woolrich, PA 17779
570–769–6464
Fax: 570–769–7662
Roswell Brayton, Jr., Pres/CEO
Jerry Rinder, VP Sls/Mktg
Roger Sheets, VP Human Resources
Major Brands: Woolrich
www.woolrich.com
Outdoor Apparel

WORTH, INC.
(K2, Inc.)
2100 N. Jackson Street
PO Box 88104
Tullahoma, TN 37388–8104
931–455–0691
Fax: 931–454–9164
Robert Parish, Pres/CEO
David Zumbach, VP Mktg
Sherri Willis, Dir Human Resource
Major Brands: Worth, Blue Dot, Red Dot
www.worthsports.com
Baseball, Softball

YORK BARBELL
3300 Board Road
York, PA 17402–9409
717–767–6481
Fax: 717–764–0044

William Thierfelder, Pres
Cisco Adler, Dir Mktg
Dana Grim, Dir Personnel
Major Brands: York
www.yorkbarbell.com
Fitness

ZEBCO CORP.
(W.C. Bradley Co.)
6505 Tower Lane
Claremore, OK 74017
918–836–5581
Fax: 918–836–0154
Jeff Pontius, Pres/CEO
Bob Bagby, Dir Mktg
Tammy Bailey, Dir Human Resources
Major Brands: Martin, Quantum, Zebco
www.zebco.com
Fishing

SPORTING GOODS RETAILER DIRECTORY

This directory contains listings for leading sporting goods retailers in the U.S. and Canada. The combined storefronts of listed retailers comprise over 80 percent of sales volume for all retailers who specialize in one or more sporting goods categories. It does not include retailers such as Wal-Mart, Sears, Target or other mass merchants who sell sporting goods as well as many other merchandise categories.

ACADEMY SPORTS & OUTDOORS
1800 N. Mason Road
Katy, TX 77449
281–646–5200
Fax: 281–646–5204
David Gochman, Pres/CEO/COB
Christine Brinkley, Mgr Human Resources
Full-line Retailer
www.academy.com

ANACONDA SPORTS
85 Katrine Lane
Lake Katrine, NY 12449
845–336–4550
Fax: 845–336–4593
John Stote, III, Pres
Fullline Retailer
www.anacondasports.com

THE ATHLETE'S FOOT
1412 Oakbrook Drive, Ste 100

Norcross, GA 30144
770–514–4500
Fax: 770–514–4903
Paul Schaefer, Dir Human Resources
Footwear Retailer
www.theathletesfoot.com

AUSTAD'S GOLF
2801 E. 10th Street
Sioux Falls, SD 57103
605–336–3135
Fax: 605–336–7221
Dave Austad, Owner/Pres
Golf Retailer
www.austads.com

BASS PRO SHOPS
2500 E. Kearney Street
Springfield, MO 65898
417–873–5000
Fax: 417–831–2802

Jim Hagale, Pres Retail Stores
Mike Rowland, VP Human Resources
Outdoor Retailer
www.basspro.com

BIG 5 SPORTING GOODS
2525 East El Segundo Blvd.
El Segundo, CA 90245
310–536–0611
Fax: 310–287–7575
Robert Miller, CEO/COB
Jeff Fraley, Sr VP Human Resources
Full-line Retailer
www.big5sportinggoods.com

BOB'S STORES
160 Corporate Court
Meriden, CT 06450
203–235–5775
Fax: 203–634–0129
David Farrell, Pres/CEO
Allison Baldwin, Mgr Human Resources
Full-line Retailer
www.bobstores.com

BUSY BODY
(Fitness Holdings International, Inc.)
1000 N. Studebaker, Ste 1
Long Beach, CA 90815
562–296–1095
Fax: 562–493–3798
Brian McDermott, COB
Anna Kyritsis, Mgr Human Resources
Fitness Retailer
www.busybody.com

CABELA'S
One Cabela Drive
Sidney, NE 69160
308–254–5505
Fax: 308–254–8490
James W. Cabela, Pres
Larry Hiers, Dir Human Resources
Outdoor Retailer
www.cabelas.com

CAMPMOR
400 Corporate Drive
Mahwah, NJ 07430
201–335–9064

Fax: 201–236–3601
Mort Jarashow, CEO/COB
William O'Donnell, Mgr Human Resources
Outdoor Retailer
www.campmor.com

CAROLINA CUSTOM GOLF
1319 Capital Blvd.
Raleigh, NC 27603
919–833–2128
Fax: 919–831–2895
Julian Bunn, Pres
Golf Retailer
www.carolinagolf.com

CHAMP'S SPORTS
311 Manatee Avenue W.
Bradenton, FL 34205
941–748–0577
Fax: 941–741–7524
Ron Halls, Pres/CEO
Full-line Retailer
www.champssports.com

CHICK'S SPORTING GOODS
979 S. Village Oaks Drive
Covina, CA 91724
626–915–1685
Fax: 626–339–1713
James Chick, Pres/CEO
LeeAnn Baker, Dir Human Resources
Full-line Retailer
www.chickssportinggoods.com

CHRISTY SPORTS, LLC
875 Parfet Street
Lakewood, CO 80215
303–237–6321
Fax: 303–233–5946
Keith Van Velkinburg, COB
Nancy Ross, Mgr Human Resources
Skiing, Outdoor Retailer
www.christysports.com

CITY SPORTS
64 Industrial Way
Wilmington, MA 01887
978–988–5100
Fax: 978–664–8048
Michael R. Kennedy, CEO

Brendan Burke, Gen Mgr
Full-line Retailer
www.citysports.com

COPELAND SPORTS
775 Fiero Lane, Ste 200
San Luis Obispo, CA 93401
805–543–0660
Fax: 805–541–3642
Joe Fernandez, Pres/CEO
Maryellen Metcalf, Mgr Human Resources
Full-line Retailer
www.copelandsports.com

DICK'S SPORTING GOODS
300 Industry Drive
Pittsburgh, PA 15275
412–809–0100
Fax: 412–227–1214
Edward W. Stack, CEO/COB
Jay Crosson, VP Human Resources
Full-line Retailer
www.dickssportinggoods.com

DOWNTOWN ATHLETIC STORE, INC.
PO Box 6247
Charlottesville, VA 22906
434–975–0750
Fax: 434–975–0754
David Deane, Owner
Jason Agee, Mgr Human Resources
Full-line Retailer
www.downtownathletic.com

DUNHAM'S
5000 Dixie Highway
Waterford, MI 48239
248–674–4991
Fax: 248–674–4980
Jeffrey G. Lynn, CEO/COB
Dan Cleslak, Sr VP Human Resources
Outdoor Retailer
www.dunhamssports.com

EASTBAY
111 S. 1st Avenue
Wausau, WI 54401
715–845–5538
Fax: 715–845–2031
Richard Johnson, Pres

Carrie Madson, Dir Human Relations
Catalog, Online
Footwear Retailer
www.eastbay.com

EASTERN MOUNTAIN SPORTS
One Vose Farm Road
Peterborough, NH 03458
603–924–9571
Fax: 603–924–9138
William Manzer, CEO
Tom Connolly, Dir Human Resources
Outdoor Retailer
www.ems.com

EDWIN WATTS GOLF SHOPS
20 Hill Avenue
Fort Walton Beach, FL 32548
850–244–2066
Fax: 850–244–5217
Ron Watts, Pres/CEO
Mrs. Chris Long, Mgr Human Resources
Golf Retailer
www.edwinwatts.com

EFINGER SPORTING GOODS
513 W. Union Avenue
Bound Brook, NJ 08805
732–356–0604
Fax: 732–805–9860
Thomas Hoey, Pres
Full-line Retailer, Team Dealer
www.efingersports.com

EUROSPORT
(see Sports Endeavors/Eurosport)

THE FINISH LINE
3308 N. Millhoeffer Road
Indianapolis, IN 46235
317–899–1022
Fax: 317–895–2884
Alan Cohen, Pres/CEO
Cindy L. Cook, VP Human Resources
Footwear Retailer
www.finishline.com

FLEET FEET
110 E. Main Street, Ste 200
Carrboro, NC 27510

919–942–3102
Fax: 919–932–6176
Tom Raynor, CEO/COB
Footwear Retailer
www.fleetfeet.com

FOOT LOCKER, INC.
112 W. 34th Street
New York, NY 10120
212–720–3700
Fax: 212–720–3831
Matt Serra, Pres/CEO
Laurie Petrucci, Sr VP Human
    Resources
Footwear Retailer
www.footlocker.com

THE FORZANI GROUP, LTD.
824 41st Avenue NE
Calgary, Alberta CA T2E 3R3
403–717–1400
Fax: 403–717–1490
Bob Sartor, CEO
Leslie Shikaze, VP Human Resources
Full-line Retailer
www.forzanigroup.com

GANDER MOUNTAIN
(Holiday Companies)
180 Fifth Street, Ste 1300
St. Paul, MN 55101
651–325–4300
Fax: 651–325–2005
Mark Baker, Pres/CEO
Joann Boldt, Mgr Human Resources
Outdoor Retailer
www.gandermountain.com

GART SPORTS
(See The Sports Authority)

GERRY COSBY & CO., INC.
3 Penn Plaza
New York, NY 10001
212–563–6464
Fax: 212–967–0876
Michael Cosby, Pres/CEO
Full-line Retailer
www.cosbysports.com

G.I. JOE'S
9805 S.W. Boeckman Road
Wilsonville, OR 97070
503–682–2242
Fax: 503–682–7200
Norman Daniels, Pres/CEO/COB
Robb Simmons, Mgr Human Resources
Full-line Retailer
www.gijoes.com

**GOLFER'S WAREHOUSE & TENNIS
    CENTER**
81 Brainard Road
Hartford, CT 06114
860–246–6746
Fax: 860–522–5309
Mark Dube, Pres
Jody Gallagher, Dir Human Resources
Golf Retailer
www.golferswarehouse.com

GOLF USA
3705 W. Memorial, Suite 801
Oklahoma City, OK 73134
405–751–0015
Fax: 405–755–0065
Tom Anthony, Pres/CEO
Donna Murrah, Dir Human Resources
Golf Retailer
www.golfusainc.com

GSI COMMERCE
935 First Avenue
King of Prussia, PA 19406
610–491–7000
Fax: 610–491–8004
Michael G. Rubin, CEO/COB
James Flanagan, Sr VP Human
    Resources
Internet Provider for Selected Retailers
Online Only
www.gsicommerce.com

THE GYM SOURCE
40 East 52nd Street
New York, NY 10022
212–688–4222
Fax: 212–750–2886
Richard Miller, Pres/CEO
Tom Lourenso, Dir Human Resources

Fitness Retailer
www.gymsource.com

HIBBETT SPORTING GOODS
451 Industrial Lane
Birmingham, AL 35211
205–942–4292
Fax: 205–912–7290
Mickey Newsome, Pres/CEO
Harvey Knighten, Dir Human Resources
Full-line Retailer
www.hibbett.com

MARK'S OUTDOOR SPORTS
1400-B Montgomery Hwy, Ste B
Birmingham, AL 35216
205–822–2010
Fax: 205–822–2984
Mark Whitlock, Pres
Outdoor Retailer
www.marksoutdoorsports.com

MARTIN'S PGA TOUR SUPERSTORE
2310 Highway 17 South
North Myrtle Beach, SC 29582
843–272–6030
Fax: 843–272–4772
Paul Rodriguez, Gen Mgr
Golf, Tennis Retailer
www.pgatoursuperstore.com

MC SPORTS
3070 Shaffer Avenue S.E.
Grand Rapids, MI 49512
616–942–2600
Fax: 616–942–2312
Bruce Ullery, Pres/CEO
Connie Rush, Dir Human Resources
Full-line Retailer
www.mcsports.com

MODELL'S SPORTING GOODS
498 Fashion Avenue, 20th Floor
New York, NY 10018
212–822–1000
Fax: 212–822–1025
Mitchell Modell, Pres
Phyllis Siegel, Mgr Human Resources
Full-line Retailer
www.modells.com

OLYMPIA SPORTS
5 Bradley Drive
Westbrook, ME 04092
207–854–2794
Fax: 207–854–4168
Richard Coffey, Pres
Thom Meschinelli, Mgr Human Resources
Full-line Retailer
www.olympiasports.net

OMNI FITNESS EQUIPMENT, INC.
60 Oxford Drive
Moonachie, NJ 07074
201–334–1100
Fax: 201–807–0185
Bob Prosse, VP Sls
Fitness Retailer
www.omnifitness.com

THE ORVIS CO., INC.
P.O. Box 798
Manchester, VT 05254
802–362–3622
Fax: 802–362–3525
Leigh Perkins, Jr., Pres/CEO
Lynne Gawtry, Dir Human Resources
Outdoor Catalog, Retailer
www.orvis.com

OSHMAN'S
(See The Sports Authority, Inc.)

OUTDOOR WORLD SPORTING GOODS
2720 S. Rodeo Gulch Road
Soquel, CA 95073
831–476–0233
Fax: 831–476–8597
Bob Thomas, Pres/CEO
Outdoor Products Retailer
www.theoutdoorworld.com

OVERTON'S
111 Red Banks Road
Greenville, NC 27858
252–355–7600
Fax: 252–355–2923
Mark Metcalfe, Pres
Greg Britt, Mgr Human Resources
Full-line Retailer
www.overtons.com

PACIFIC SUNWEAR
3450 E. Mira Loma Avenue
Anaheim, CA 92806
714–414–4000
Fax: 714–414–4260
Greg Weaver, CEO/COB
Action Sports Retailer
www.pacificsunwear.com

PARAGON SPORTS
867 Broadway
New York, NY 10003
212–255–8036
Fax: 212–929–1831
Bruce Blank, CEO
Andrea Ross, Mgr Human Resources
Full-line Retailer
www.paragonsports.com

PERFORMANCE, INC.
1 Performance Way
Chapel Hill, NC 27514
919–933–9113
Fax: 919–942–4531
Bob Martin, Pres
Mike Hydrick, Mgr Human Resources
Cycling Catalog, Retailer
www.performancebike.com

PLAY IT AGAIN SPORTS
(Winmark Corporation)
4200 Dahlberg Drive
Minneapolis, MN 55422
763–520–8500
Fax: 763–520–8470
John Morgan, Pres/CEO
Leah Goff, Mgr Human Resources
Full-line Retailer
www.playitagainsport.com

PRO GOLF OF AMERICA
37735 Enterprise Court, Ste 600
Farmington Hills, MI 48331
248–994–0553
Fax: 248–994–9077
Brian Donnelly, Pres
Golf Retailer
www.progolfamerica.com
Online store: www.progolf.com

PRO IMAGE
233 North 1250 West, Ste 200
Centerville, UT 84014
801–296–9999
Fax: 801–296–1319
David Riley, Pres/CEO
Licensed Products Retailer
www.proimage.net

PUSH PEDAL PULL FITNESS GROUP
3110 W 12th Street
Sioux Falls, SD 57104
605–334–7740
Fax: 605–336–3328
Roger D. Stewart, Pres/CEO/COB
Kay Bahnson, Mgr Human Resources
Fitness Retailer
www.pushpedalpull.com

REI/RECREATIONAL EQUIPMENT, INC.
6750 S. 228th Street
Kent, WA 98032
253–395–3780
Fax: 253–395–4352
Sally Jewell, CEO
Michelle Clements, VP Human Resources
Outdoor Retailer
www.rei.com

ROAD RUNNER SPORTS
5549 Copley Drive
San Diego, CA 92111
858–974–4200
Fax: 800–453–5433
Michael Gotfredson, CEO
Patty Ewing, Dir Human Resources
Footwear Retailer
www.roadrunnersports.com

RON JON SURF SHOP
3850 South Banana River Blvd.
Cocoa Beach, FL 32931
321–799–8880
Fax: 321–799–8805
Edward Moriarty, Pres
Action Sports Retailer
www.ronjons.com

SAGESPORT
815 Floyd Street

PO Box 1129
Kings Mountain, NC 28086
704–739–2366
Fax: 704–739–7059
William S. Fulton, Jr., Pres
Crystal Arthurs, Mgr Human Resources
Full-line Retailer
www.sagesport.com

SCHEEL'S ALL SPORTS, INC.
3218 13th Avenue South
Fargo, ND 58103
701–232–3665
Fax: 701–232–3735
Steve Hulbert, Pres
Jane McGoldrick, Mgr Human Resources
Full-line Retailer
www.scheelssports.com

SCHUYLKILL VALLEY SPORTING

GOODS
118 Industrial Drive
Pottstown, PA 19464
610–495–8813
Fax: 610–495–8814
Randall R. Ruch, CEO
Rose Baumgardner, Mgr Human Resources
Full-line Retailer
www.svsports.com

THE SKI MARKET
265 Winter Street, Ste 2
Waltham, MA 02451
781–890–1212
Fax: 781–890–1811
Andrew Ferguson, Pres/CEO
Chuck Russum, Dir Store Opns
Skiing Retailer
www.skimarket.com

SPECIAL TEE GOLF
620 E. Altamont Drive
Altamont Springs, FL 32701
407–834–1000
Fax: 407–834–1689
Jack Hazen, Partner
Golf Retailer
www.specialteegolf.com

SPORT CHALET
One Sport Chalet Drive
La Canada, CA 91011
818–949–5300
Fax: 818–949–5301
Craig Levra, Pres/CEO
Cynthia Stein, Mgr Human Resources
Full-line Retailer
www.sportchalet.com

SPORTMART
(See The Sports Authority, Inc.)

THE SPORTS AUTHORITY, INC.
(The Sports Authority, Inc. operates stores
   under The Sports Authority, Gart Sports,
   Sportmart, and Oshman's names.)
1050 West Hampden Avenue
Englewood, CO 80110
303–200–5050
Fax: 303–864–2967
Doug Morton, CEO/COB
Kerry Sims, EVP Human Resources
Full-line Retailer
www.sportsauthority.com

SPORTS ENDEAVORS/EUROSPORT
431 U.S. Highway 70A East
Hillsborough, NC 27278
919–644–6800
Fax: 800–950–1994
Mike Moylan, CEO
Mail Order, Internet
Soccer, Lacrosse Retailer
www.soccer.com

SPORTSHOE CENTER
10 Main Street
PO Box 208
Kennebunk, ME 04043
207–985–4966
Fax: 207–985–4965
Marc Brunelle, Pres/COB
Pam Salvas, Mgr Human Resources
Footwear Retailer
www.sportshoecenter.com

THE SPORTSMAN'S GUIDE
411 Farwell Avenue
South St. Paul, MN 55075

651–451–3030
Fax: 651–451–5367
Greg Binkley, Pres/CEO
Mail Order, Internet
Outdoor Retailer
www.sportsmansguide.com

SPORTSMAN'S WAREHOUSE
7035 High Tech Drive
Midvale, UT 84047
801–566–6681
Fax: 801–304–4343
Stuart Utgaard, CEO
Robin Smith, Mgr Human Resources
Outdoor Retailer
www.sportsmanswarehouse.com

SUN AND SKI SPORTS
(Retail Concepts)
4001 Greenbriar, Ste 100
Stafford, TX 77477
281–340–5000
Fax: 281–340–5020
Barry Goldware, Pres/CEO
Karen Gibson, Mgr Human Resources
Outdoor Retailer
http://sunandski.com

TRI-CITY SPORTING GOODS
40900 Grimmer Blvd.
Fremont, CA 94538
510–651–9600
Fax: 510–651–2959

Joseph L. Harrosh, COB
Full-line Retailer
http://tricitypatio.com

TURNER'S OUTDOORSMAN
12615 Colony
Chino, CA 91710
909–590–7425
Fax: 909–590–1533
Don Small, Pres
Karla Fergonise, Mgr Human Resources
Outdoor Retailer
www.turners.com

UNIVERSAL ATHLETIC
25 W. Main Street
Bozeman, MT 59715
406–587–4415
Fax: 406–587–0228
Larry Aasheim, Pres/CEO
Lorri Olson, Mgr Human Resources
Full-line Retailer
www.universalathletic.com

ZUMIEZ, INC.
6300 Merrill Creek Parkway, Ste B
Everett, WA 98203
425–551–1500
Fax: 425–551–1555
Tom Campion, Pres
Action Sports Retailer
www.zumiez.com

SPORTING GOODS SELECTED TRADE MEDIA / TRADE ASSOCIATIONS

This directory includes website links for leading multisport sporting goods media and trade associations.

Publications:

FOOTWEAR BUSINESS (magazine)
770 Broadway, 5th Floor
New York, NY 10003
646–654–4500
www.sgbmag.com

HUNTING BUSINESS (magazine)
770 Broadway, 5th Floor
New York, NY 10003
646–654–4500
www.sgbmag.com

MEDICINE & SCIENCE IN SPORTS &
EXERCISE (journal)
401 West Michigan Street
Indianapolis, IN 46202–3233
www.acsm.org/publications/MSSE.htm

OUTDOOR BUSINESS (magazine)
770 Broadway, 5th Floor
New York, NY 10003
646–654–4500
www.sgbmag.com

SPORTING GOODS BUSINESS DAILY
DISPATCH (newsletter)
770 Broadway, 5th Floor
New York, NY 10003
646–654–4500
www.sgbmag.com

SPORTBUSINESS INTERNATIONAL
(magazine)
6th Floor
Elizabeth House
39 York Road
London
SE1 7NQ, UK
+44 (0)20 7934 9000
www.sportbusiness.com

SPORTING GOODS BUSINESS
(magazine)
770 Broadway, 5th Floor
New York, NY 10003
646–654–4500
www.sgbmag.com

SPORTING GOODS DEALER
(magazine)
770 Broadway, 5th Floor
New York, NY 10003
646–654–4500
www.sgdealer.com

SPORTING GOODS INTELLIGENCE
(newsletter)
442 Featherbed Lane

Glen Mills, PA 19342
610–459–4040
www.sginews.com

Multisport Trade Associations:

NATIONAL SPORTING GOODS
ASSOCIATION (NSGA)
1699 Feehanville Drive, Suite 300
Mt. Prospect, IL 60056
(847) 296–6742
www.nsga.org

SNOWSPORTS INDUSTRIES AMERICA
(SIA)
8377-B Greensboro Drive
McLean, Virginia 22102–3587
703–556–9020
www.thesnowtrade.org

SPORTING GOODS MANUFACTURERS
ASSOCIATION INTERNATIONAL
(SGMA)
1150 17th St NW #850
Washington, DC 20036
202–775–1762
www.sgma.com

WORLD FEDERATION OF THE
SPORTING GOODS INDUSTRY
(WFSGI)
La Maison du Sport
Chemin des Marais Verts
CH-1936 Verbier
+41–27 775 35 70
www.wfsgi.org

Database Websites:

SPORTS BUSINESS RESEARCH
NETWORK (SBRnet)
PO Box 2378
Princeton, NJ 08543
609–896–1996

Bibliography

BOOKS

Bicycling Magazine. *An Illustrated History of the Bicycle*. Emmaus PA: Rodale, 2003.

Bogert, Jon, ed. *The 2006 SGI Directory*. Glen Mills PA: Sporting Goods Intelligence, 2005.

Brunner, Conrad. *All Day I Dream About Sport: The Story of the Adidas Brand*. London: Cyan Communications, 2005.

Carter, David M., and Darren Rovell. *On the Ball: What You Can Learn about Business from America's Sports Leaders*. Englewood Cliffs NJ: Prentice Hall, 2003.

Ellis, Jeffery B. *The Golf Club: 400 Years of the Good, the Beautiful, and the Creative*. Oak Harbor WA: Zephyr, 2002.

Fields, Shelly. *Career Opportunities in the Sports Industry*. 3rd ed. New York: Checkmark, 2004.

Goodstein, Madeline. *Sports Science Projects: The Physics of Balls in Motion*. Berkeley Heights NJ: Enslow, 1999.

Graham, Stedman, Lisa Delpy Neirotti, and Joe Jeff Goldblatt. *The Ultimate Guide to Sports Marketing*. New York: McGraw-Hill, 2001.

Herlihy, David V. *Bicycle: The History*. New Haven CT: Yale University Press, 2004.

Levine, Peter. *A. G. Spalding and the Rise of Baseball*. New York: Oxford University Press, 1985.

Li, Ming, Susan Hofacre, and Dan Mahony. *Economics of Sport*. Morgantown WV: Fitness Information Technology, 2001.

Mechikoff, Robert A., and Steven G. Estes. *A History and Philosophy of Sport and Physical Education: From Ancient Civilizations to the Modern World*. 4th ed. New York: McGraw-Hill, 2005.

Mullin, Bernard J., Stephen Hardy, and William A. Sutton. *Sport Marketing*. 2nd ed. Champaign IL: Human Kinetics, 2000.

Parks, Janet B., and Jerome Quarterman, eds. *Contemporary Sport Management*. 2nd ed. Champaign IL: Human Kinetics, 2003.

Pitts, Brenda G. *Case Studies in Sports Marketing*. Morgantown WV: Fitness Information Technology; 1998.

Robinson, Matthew, et al. *Profiles of Sport Industry Professionals: The People Who Make the Game Happen*. Sudbury MA: Jones & Bartlett, 2001.

Rosner, Scott. *The Business of Sports*. Sudbury MA: Jones & Bartlett, 2004.

Sneakers: The Complete Collectors' Guide. London: Thames & Hudson, 2005.

Stotlar, David K., and Brenda G. Pitts. *Fundamentals of Sport Marketing*. 2nd ed. Morgantown WV: Fitness Information Technology, 2002.

Sumner, Tracy M. *Karsten's Way: The Life-Changing Story of Karsten Solheim — Pioneer in Golf Club Design and the Founder of Ping*. Chicago: Northfield, September 2000.

Vanderbilt, Tom. *The Sneaker Book: Anatomy of an Industry and an Icon*. New York: The New Press, 1998.

Westerbeek, Hans, and Aaron Smith. *Sport Business in the Global Marketplace*. Basingstoke, Hampshire: Palgrave Macmillan, 2003.

Wilson, R.L., and G. Allan Brown. *Winchester: An American Legend: The Official History of Winchester Firearms and Ammunition from 1849 to the Present*. Secaucus NJ: Chartwell, 2005.

ARTICLES

"Adding It Up: A By-the-Numbers Look at How the Sporting Goods Industry Continues to Evolve." *Sporting Goods Business*, May 2004.

"Body Glove Signs New Sportswear Licensee." *Sporting Goods Business*, April 2005.

"Brand Perceptions." *Sporting Goods Business*, July 2005.

"Breaking New Trail: Top 25 Retail Report." *Outdoor Business*, July 2005.

"Bret Favre to Endorse Starter." *Sporting Goods Business Daily Dispatch*, March 15, 2005.

"Easton Sports Launches New TV Ad Campaign." *Sporting Goods Business Daily Dispatch*, May 23, 2005.

"89% of Core Golfers Have Internet Access: NGF." *Sporting Goods Business Daily Dispatch*, April 29, 2005.

Fielding, L.W., and L.K. Miller. "The ABC Trust: A Chapter in the History of Capitalism in the Sporting Goods Industry." *Sport History Review* 29, no. 1 (1998): 44–58.

_____, and _____. "Advertising and the Development of Consumer Purchasing Criteria: The Sporting Goods Industry, 1900–1930." *Sport Marketing Quarterly* 5, no. 4 (1996): 37–50.

_____, and _____. "The Foreign Invasion of the American Sporting Goods Market." *Sport Marketing Quarterly* 7, no. 3 (1998): 19–29.

"From the Archives of *Sporting Goods Dealer*—August 1980." *Sporting Goods Dealer*, August 1980.

"How America Shops." *Sporting Goods Business*, November 2003.

"How to Sell a $20 Mouthguard." *Sporting Goods Dealer*, May/June 2004.

Jacobsen, Michael. "Acquisition Fever." *Sporting Goods Dealer*, November/December 2003.

"Looking Back at 2004." *Sporting Goods Business*, December 2004.

Margulis, Ronald. "The Store of the Future." *SGB's Inside Sporting Goods*, January 21, 2003.

"News & Observations." *Sporting Goods Business*, January 2004.

"Reebok Launches 'I Am What I Am' Campaign." *Sporting Goods Business Daily Dispatch*, February 10, 2005.

"Research: Fan Fare." *Sporting Goods Business*, March 2005.

Roberts, Kevin. "TV Exposure Isn't Everything." *SportBusiness International*, May 2005.

Ryan, Thomas J. "Selling It." *Sporting Goods Business*, October 2004.

"Team Dealer POP Quiz." *Sporting Goods Dealer*, January/February 2005.

Index